JUSTICE AND THE

YOUNG OFFENDER IN CANADA

**Joe Hudson, Joseph P. Hornick,
Barbara A. Burrows, Editors**

*Canadian Research Institute for Law and the Family,
Calgary, Alberta*

*With a Foreword by
Judge Herman Litsky (retired)*

WALL & THOMPSON
TORONTO

Canadian Cataloguing in Publication Data

Main entry under title:
Justice and the young offender in Canada
Bibliography: p.
Includes index.
ISBN 0–921332–07–6

1. Canada. Young Offenders Act. 2. Juvenile justice, Administration of - Canada. 3. Youth - Legal status, laws, etc. - Canada. 4. Juvenile delinquents - Canada.
I. Hudson, Joe, 1940- .
II. Hornick, Joseph P. (Joseph Phillip), 1946- .
III. Burrows, Barbara A., 1956- .

KE9445.J88 1988   345.71'08   C88-094377-7
KF9779.J88 1988

ISBN 0–921332–07–6

Printed in Canada by John Deyell Company
1 2 3 4 5 92 91 90 89 88

FOREWORD

After nearly 25 years of judicial experience, it is most gratifying to acknowledge a comprehensive Canadian text in the field of juvenile justice. *Justice and the Young Offender in Canada* represents the genesis of a body of knowledge that lays the foundation for continued study and application by scholar and practitioner alike.

The *Young Offenders Act* (*YOA*) made its dramatic debut in the juvenile courts in 1984. After many years of political and legal histrionics, the *YOA* was finally enacted; it seemingly enshrined all that was expeditious in philosophy and due process when dealing with the young offender. Enthusiasm for the former *Juvenile Delinquents Act* (enacted in 1908) dampened with the passing of time. The sociological inclinations and "best interest of the delinquent" approach of the *Juvenile Delinquents Act* (*JDA*) began to wear thin in its latter legislative years, mainly because the promise of these principles was largely unfulfilled. In addition, the *JDA* became increasingly controversial because it essentially lacked due process provisions. The development and attendant principles of the new legislation for dealing with young offenders are aptly described in the text.

At this point in the evolution of this legislative enactment, the most difficult and necessary task lies ahead. The challenge is to provide the human element for this somewhat skeletal statute. We cannot deal with the young offender merely by procedural technocracy or mechanistic jurisprudence alone. We need to blend and balance the rule of law with the social sciences; a legal right without a rehabilitative remedy is no better than a rehabilitative remedy without a legal right. To this extent the text begins to deal with the important aspect of policy implementation, distinguishing between the child welfare and juvenile justice systems. This is essential in order to provide a rehabilitative and legal balance for young persons within the spectrum of services.

It seems that the juvenile justice system is focusing too much on developing legal procedure for dealing with young offenders; the administration of justice struggles to set standards of due process practice in such areas as right to counsel and in prosecutorial and defense expertise. This has resulted in an implosion of paperwork and an expansion of precedential rules of criminal law for individual justice, leaving rehabilitative rights and services badly underdeveloped. Federal and provincial cooperation in developing fiscal, legal and social policy is required if rehabilitative rights and services are to attain their desired level.

Another important issue dealt with in the text is custody for the young offender. Quality classification of the young offender into remedial programs, particularly in the initial stages of custody, is essential. Without it, we will invariably develop custodial warehouses and sterile programs, with the potential for rehabilitation to give way to insular control by zealous correctional authorities. Presently, the reliance on custody programs is accelerating, particularly for 14- to 17-year-olds, because of over-identification with the adult system. In the kaleidoscope of change evidenced under this new legislation, it is imperative to build a malleable mosaic of services for young persons whose needs vary greatly.

In essence the helping professionals, both in the child welfare and correctional fields, must exert their efforts and apply their expertise towards fashioning the legal framework of justice. If they do not, it is possible that in a few years the disciples of deterrence, retribution and incarceration will become the common denominator. Let us not be mesmerized by the mechanics of justice to the detriment of the young offender. Surely it is time to progress from the twilight concept of punishment *per se* to a more enlightened era of legal compassion.

What will the future be like for justice and the young offender in Canada? Here again the book addresses the key area of probable future directions for research into and program development under the Act. The book also provides a universal overview of the principles and policies of the Act. From my personal perspective as a judge and researcher on juvenile justice systems in many countries, one truth is apparent. Justice systems are cyclical and evolutionary; they grow, die and then reincarnate themselves from old forms to a so-called modern metamorphosis. History repeats itself. The elements of legal justice cannot be created in perpetuity. At best, we could ultimately devise an equitable balance between the law and rehabilitative services. Former Chief Justice Bora Laskin said it best:

> The Law is not a still pool merely to be tended and occasionally skimmed of accumulative debris, rather it should be looked upon as a running stream, carrying society's hopes, and reflecting all its values, and hence requiring a constant attention to its tributaries, the social and other sciences, to see that they feed in sustaining elements.

Justice and the Young Offender in Canada makes a relevant contribution to the field of juvenile justice in a period when critical evaluation is essential to fulfilling the principle of a balanced approach to the young offender.

Judge Herman Litsky (retired)
Vancouver, British Columbia

ACKNOWLEDGEMENTS

Completion of *Justice and the Young Offender in Canada* would not have been possible without the support of numerous organizations and individuals. In particular, support provided by the Alberta Law Foundation, in the form of funding to the Canadian Research Institute for Law and the Family (CRILF), is gratefully acknowledged. Thanks are also extended to the Faculties of Law and Social Welfare, The University of Calgary, for their roles in establishing CRILF.

In addition, the production of this text was made possible by the direct involvement of the contributing authors. We were fortunate to secure the expertise of numerous individuals whose knowledge of Canadian juvenile justice is widely recognized.

We would also like to thank Joanne Paetsch and Candy Tedford for meticulously typing and revising the manuscript. Finally, thanks are due to Donna Phillips for her assistance in researching and indexing the manuscript.

Joe Hudson
Joseph P. Hornick
Barbara A. Burrows

June 30, 1988
Calgary, Alberta

LIST OF CONTRIBUTORS

Nicholas Bala, Associate Professor, Faculty of Law, Queen's University, Kingston, Ontario

Hélene Beaumont, Researcher, International Centre for Comparative Criminology, Université de Montréal, Montréal, Québec

Denis C. Bracken, Associate Professor, School of Social Work, University of Manitoba, Winnipeg, Manitoba

Barbara A. Burrows, Research Associate, Canadian Research Institute for Law and the Family, Calgary, Alberta

Tullio Caputo, Assistant Professor, Department of Sociology, Carleton University, Ottawa, Ontario

Jim Coflin, Director, Policy Development Section, Programs and Policy Directorate, Department of Justice, Ottawa, Ontario

Catherine Heinrich, Sessional Lecturer, School of Social Work, University of Manitoba, Winnipeg, Manitoba

Joseph P. Hornick, Executive Director, Canadian Research Institute for Law and the Family, Calgary, Alberta

Joe Hudson, Division Head (Edmonton), Faculty of Social Welfare, The University of Calgary, Calgary, Alberta

Peter G. Jaffe, Director, Family Court Clinic, London, Ontario; Adjunct Assistant Professor, Department of Psychiatry and Adjunct Associate Professor, Department of Psychology, University of Western Ontario, London, Ontario

Carol Pitcher LaPrairie, Senior Policy Analyst, Policy Development Section, Programs and Policy Directorate, Department of Justice, Ottawa, Ontario

Marc LeBlanc, Professor, School of Psycho-Education, Université de Montréal; Research Associate, International Centre for Comparative Criminology, Université de Montréal, Montréal, Québec

Alan W. Leschied, Assistant Director, Family Court Clinic, London, Ontario; Adjunct Assistant Professor, Department of Psychology, University of Western Ontario, London, Ontario

Brian Mason, Executive Director, Young Offender Branch, Correctional Services Division, Alberta Solicitor General, Edmonton, Alberta

Kimberly J. Pate, Executive Assistant, Calgary John Howard Society, Calgary, Alberta

Dean E. Peachey, Coordinator, Network for Community Justice and Conflict Resolution, Kitchener, Ontario

Joseph C. Ryant, Professor, School of Social Work, University of Manitoba, Winnipeg, Manitoba

Howard Sapers, Provincial Executive Director, John Howard Society of Alberta, Edmonton, Alberta

Brian Ward, Executive Director, Canadian Council on Children and Youth, Ottawa, Ontario

Richard Weiler, Senior Policy Associate, Canadian Council on Social Development, Ottawa, Ontario

TABLE OF CONTENTS

CHAPTER 1

INTRODUCTION

Barbara A. Burrows, Joe Hudson, and Joseph P. Hornick

BACKGROUND

The *Young Offenders Act* (1982) received Royal Assent in the Canadian House of Commons on July 7, 1982, and became law on April 2, 1984. This new legislation for dealing with young persons in conflict with the law replaced the *Juvenile Delinquents Act* (1970), which had remained virtually unchanged since its original passage in 1908. The Young Offenders Act (*YOA*) symbolizes and embodies a fundamental shift in the Canadian approach to juvenile justice. While the focus of the *Juvenile Delinquents Act* (*JDA*) was on the welfare of children, the central philosophy of the *YOA* is to hold young persons who break the law responsible for their actions, protect society from illegal behaviour and at the same time, protect the legal rights of young offenders (Archambault, 1983). The *YOA* tempers the principle of responsibility with the principle of "mitigated accountability," whereby "...young persons should not, generally speaking, be held accountable in the same manner as would adults" (Archambault, 1983, p. 4). Under the *YOA*, the youth court is, first and foremost, a criminal court responsible for adjudicating the guilt or innocence of a young person in respect to a particular offence.

Since its inception in 1984, the *YOA* has received mixed reviews. Civil libertarians have welcomed the extensive protection of young persons' rights. Other observers, however, contend that concern for children's *rights* has been at the expense of attention to children's *needs*. For example, some mental health practitioners contend that the *YOA* pays insufficient attention to the treatment and rehabilitation of young offenders, and that custody is used excessively. A further criticism has been the failure of some provinces to implement the Act completely, and in conformance with the underlying spirit of the legislation. The application of a uniform age jurisdiction across the country has been generally applauded, but in some quarters, raising the maximum age to 17 years inclusive has been criticized.

The remainder of this chapter provides an overview and sets the context for the more specific discussions in the individual chapters that follow. Some generic models of juvenile justice are described and the *YOA* related to them. A brief summary of significant developments in Canadian juvenile justice is then provided and highlights of the *YOA* are discussed and compared with provisions of the 1908 Juvenile Delinquents Act. The organizational framework for this book is then described and reference made to the chapters that follow.

MODELS OF JUVENILE JUSTICE

Reid and Reitsma-Street (1984) provide a useful summary of different approaches to juvenile justice. They describe four models of juvenile justice falling on a continuum from the "far right" (conservative) to the "far left" (socialist). On the conservative end is the crime control model, which gives priority to maintaining order and protecting the community from criminal activity. According to this model, offenders have little opportunity to challenge decisions made about them, and the meaning of "criminal activity" is broadly defined. A major emphasis of this model is on retribution and punishment, and the key figures are the police, courts and penal agents (Reid & Reitsma-Street, 1984).

Next on the continuum is the justice model, which is similar to the crime control model in emphasizing the protection of society as a dominant goal. The justice model, however, goes further in protecting the rights of the accused. Principles such as "innocent until proven guilty" and the right to a fair trial apply. Punishments are strictly defined in the law, and vary according to the nature of the crime. The justice model is based on the classical school of criminology, which holds that crime prevention may best be achieved by ensuring "...that the pain inflicted on criminals as punishment for their misdeeds, sufficiently outweigh[s] the pleasure they acquired through illegal activity so as to make further illegal activity unattractive" (Caputo, 1987, p. 131).

Further along the continuum is the welfare model. This model largely rejects the notion of free will, contending that antisocial behaviour reflects a person's response to external stimuli largely transcending individual control (Archambault, 1983). The welfare model is based on the positivist school of criminology, which became popular at the end of the 19th century and maintained "...that crime was the result of physiological, psychological and environmental factors over which individuals had little control" (Caputo, 1987, p. 130). Therefore, the individual should not be held completely responsible for his/her behaviour; society must be held to be at least partly responsible. As expressed by Reid and Reitsma-Street (1984), the main objective of the welfare model is to prevent and ameliorate the "anti-social syndrome." Thus, education and treatment are emphasized as ways for reducing criminal activity. The needs and welfare of delinquent children are the principal concern of proponents of the welfare model and this philosophy was most clearly expressed in the establishment of the juvenile court.

Finally, the community change model stands at the "far left" of the continuum. This model shares with the welfare model a concern for the welfare of delinquent youth and seeks to reduce youth crime by altering the fundamental environmental factors thought to promote such criminal activity. Thus, social equality and citizen involvement are emphasized and the aim of social policy, "...is to change the processes that lead to inequality, poverty and delinquency: youthful crime is prevented by promoting the welfare of all youth" (Reid & Reitsma-Street, 1984, p. 4).

The four models discussed by Reid and Reitsma-Street are general representations or idealized versions of justice, not descriptions of actual practices found in any particular jurisdiction. As ideal representations, they are useful in assessing actual practices, such as those under the JDA and the YOA. The general consensus is that juvenile justice in Canada has changed from being based on the welfare model under the JDA to incorporating elements from all four models under the YOA. That is, the YOA is made up mainly of elements from the justice and welfare models, along with elements of the crime control and community change models (Reid & Reitsma-Street, 1984).

DEVELOPMENT OF JUVENILE JUSTICE IN CANADA

Historical Basis for Differential Treatment of Children

As enunciated by Dalby (1985), the determination of criminal responsibility or liability has traditionally required the existence of two elements. The first is *actus reus*, or the physical action of committing a crime. The second requirement is *mens rea*, or the existence of conscious intention or fault in violating prescribed legal standards. These two concepts have been applied over time and in a variety of societies, in attempts to define the age at which individuals should be legally responsible for their own behaviour. For example, parents in ancient China were responsible for their children's infractions of public order. In contrast, the Hebrew Codes maintained that children themselves were responsible for their own criminal behaviour. In early Roman times, the onset of puberty was declared as the beginning of responsibility.

In the 1800s, and until the enactment of the *Young Offenders Act* in 1984, the English common law standard was applied in Canada, rendering children under seven years of age "...to be *doli incapax*, or incapable of crime" (Dalby, 1985, p. 138). Children between the ages of seven and 13 years were presumed to be incapable of crime, but could be proven otherwise, while children 14 years of age or older were considered to be fully responsible for their crimes. The *YOA* defines 12 as the minimum age of criminal responsibility, and offenders 18 years of age or older are considered as adults.

Historical Perspective on Canadian Juvenile Justice Reform

One of the earliest landmarks in the development of juvenile justice in Canada was an act passed in Upper and Lower Canada in 1857 to allow for prompt trial and punishment of young offenders (Archambault, 1983). This "...gave magistrates the power to deal summarily with children, thereby protecting them from the full rigours of the criminal law, as the sentencing powers of the lower courts were less extreme" (Archambault, 1983, p. 1). In 1892, the Criminal Code was amended to ensure that children were tried separately from adults, and without publicity. These legislative provisions for the recognition of children's needs in the criminal law setting occurred within a broader climate of concern for the welfare of children. Reform movements in the 1800s fought for "...the provision of public education and medical services, the protection of abused and abandoned children and the elimination of the exploitation of child labor, as well as the reform of criminal procedures" (Archambault, 1983, p. 1). These efforts affected the "...introduction of child protection legislation, special institutions to care for children, public education, and...at the turn of the century, the juvenile court system" (Archambault, 1983, p. 2). Although juvenile justice law contained some provisions for the separate treatment of children, it failed to distinguish between neglected and delinquent children.

The *Juvenile Delinquents Act* was passed by the federal parliament in 1908. In terms of the approaches outlined above, the *JDA* largely embodied the welfare model, based on the positivist school of criminology. The juvenile court was to serve, in whatever manner deemed necessary, the best interests of the children who came before it. The court was to act as a kind of clinic, concerned with assessing and fulfilling the needs of its clients, as opposed to a criminal court concerned with due process and the protection of society. Delinquency was viewed as a product of the social environment and susceptible to treatment (Bala, 1986). The court's role under the *JDA* was to act on behalf of parents when the best interests of children were not being met (Reid, 1986). Thus the court took on the role of a "...stern but understanding parent" (Caputo, 1987, p. 127).

The protective ideology was integral to the *JDA*. Indeed, the *JDA* is widely described as paternalistic. The *parens patriae* doctrine of the *JDA* "...emphasized treatment and minimized accountability [on the part of the young person]" (Reid, 1986, p. 3). Children were to be saved, not punished for their misdeeds. The *parens patriae* doctrine drew no distinction between criminal and noncriminal youth conduct, which supported the view that juvenile court proceedings were civil rather than criminal in nature. There was seen to be no need to differentiate between delinquent and neglected children. Rather, they were perceived by one of the original drafters of the *JDA* to be of the "same class"; the principal concern was to be on treatment (i.e. helping the child), with "minimal attention paid to accountability, or the justification for intervention" (Archambault, 1983, p. 2).

The *JDA* was revised slightly in 1929, but remained basically unchanged until it was replaced by the *Young Offenders Act* in 1984. However, the process to reform juvenile justice in Canada began in the early 1960s and, as Bala describes in Chapter 2, the *JDA* was widely criticized. One criticism was that it provided the court with too much discretionary power, with associated potential for abuse of children's rights. For example, under the *JDA* it was possible to impose indeterminate sentences that were to continue until treatment was completed; this could result in a child receiving a lengthier disposition than would an adult charged with a similar offence. Another major criticism was the perceived ineffectiveness of the *JDA* in preventing juvenile crime and promoting rehabilitation. Other common criticisms were: (a) the all-encompassing crime of "delinquency" (lack of specified offences); (b) substantial variation across the country in the maximum age of juvenile delinquents; (c) indiscriminate use of detention and indeterminate length of custodial dispositions; (d) limited due process safeguards for youth; (e) the judge's lack of legislated authority to utilize community resources for treatment; and (f) the stigma of being labelled a "juvenile delinquent."

In pursuit of juvenile justice reform, the federal government embarked on an "often tortuous process of parliamentary involvement and legislative reform" (Bala, 1986, p. 242). The process began with a 1965 study by the Department of Justice, which was critical of the existing juvenile justice system. This initiative was followed by further study and several attempts at new legislation:

- The draft *Children's and Young Persons' Act* was produced in 1967;
- Bill C-192, *An Act Respecting Young Offenders and to Repeal the Juvenile Delinquents Act*, was introduced to the House of Commons in 1970, but was not passed.
- *Young Persons in Conflict with the Law* was produced in 1975, by a committee mandated by the Solicitor General to report on, and make recommendations about, Canada's juvenile justice system.
- *Highlights of Proposed New Legislation for Young Offenders* was produced by the Solicitor General's Department in 1977.

- A preliminary draft of the *Young Offenders Act* was produced in 1979.

- Finally, the *Young Offenders Act* was put before the House of Commons in 1981, passed in July 1982 and became law in April 1984.

Thus, as many of the following chapters describe, the passage of the *YOA* in 1982 was the culmination of over 20 years of discussion and debate about the direction juvenile justice should take in Canada. Concurrent with federal reform efforts were provincial government attempts to effect changes to their juvenile justice operations (Bala, 1986). Some of these initiatives are described in chapters dealing with Ontario and Quebec. Diversion programs were implemented and deinstitutionalization increasingly emphasized: "Thus, one could argue that the major weaknesses under the *JDA* had been resolved by practices introduced in the courts" (Hackler, 1987, p. 205). The *YOA*, however, went further by providing official legislative sanction and setting the rules for the new practices.

In essence, the *YOA* is an attempt to achieve a compromise between the youth's needs for protection of rights and rehabilitation, and society's right to be protected from illegal behaviour. Since its passage in 1982, the Act has been amended three times. None of the amendments constituted a major philosophical change in the approach to juvenile justice. Rather, they were responses to difficulties that became apparent following the Act's implementation in 1984. They address such matters as records, breach of probation and publication of names of youths at large (Bala, 1986). As originally worded, the *YOA* ordered records to be destroyed upon a finding of "not guilty." This provision extended to youths who had serious psychiatric problems, and there was a concern that valuable psychological records might be destroyed. The police were also concerned about their inability to publish the names of youths at large, even if they were being sought for commission of a serious offence. Amendments in 1986 addressed both concerns, by allowing for records to be retained in some circumstances and by allowing police to publish the names of youths at large.

ORGANIZATION OF THE BOOK

The remaining 11 chapters in this book can be broadly organized into three logical sections. The development and implementation of the *YOA* is covered in the first section; the second section deals with specific programs established under the Act and the relationship between the legislation and significant interest groups; and the third section summarizes issues relevant to the *YOA* and suggests directions for future research. A brief overview of the major sections of the book and the associated chapters is provided below.

Nicholas Bala begins the first section by sketching the development of the *YOA*. He then turns to an extensive discussion of the principles and substantive provisions of the legislation, giving particular attention to matters of youth rights at the time of arrest, alternative measures, youth court proceedings, dispositions and reviews available under the Act and transfer to the adult system. Significant case law bearing on each of these matters is identified and assessed.

Following the legal framework provided by Bala, Chapters 3 through 5 describe and assess federal and provincial implementation efforts. In Chapter 3, Jim Coflin describes the role played by the federal government in developing and implementing the *YOA*. The matter of federal and provincial government jurisdiction was an important issue in the negotiations leading to passage of the legislation. Coflin describes major implementation activities carried out by the federal authorities including training and orientation, cost sharing, program development funding, information systems development and policy review. Along with the major implementation activities undertaken by the federal government, substantial amounts of financial assistance were provided to the provinces for training and orientation, program development, information system development and policy review and evaluation procedures.

The remaining chapters in the first section describe and assess provincial government implementation efforts in Alberta, Ontario and Quebec. In each of the three case studies, attention is given to changes in the relationship between child welfare and young offender systems and implementation roles and responsibilities carried out by provincial officials.

A number of substantive issues are identified in these case studies. For example, in Chapter 4 Brian Mason describes several important implementation matters in Alberta, including the time-consuming work involved in bringing cases back to court for review, the use of extended temporary release procedures, low rates of participation by native persons in alternative measures programs and the significant over-representation of native young persons handled under the Act.

In Chapter 5 Alan Leschied and Peter Jaffe describe the implementation of the Act in Ontario. They identify three contentious issues associated with Ontario implementation efforts: minimum age for accountability; maximum age for accountability; and the implementation of the alternative measures section of the legislation. Ontario has implemented the age provisions of the Act in the form of a two-tiered or split jurisdiction system. Two different government ministries administer what are in effect separate juvenile justice systems based on the age of offenders.

This chapter also points out that Ontario refused, until a recent Court of Appeal decision, to implement the alternative measures provision of the Act; this issue is described in detail by Leschied and Jaffe. Finally, these authors deal with questions about the relative severity of dispositions under the *YOA* as compared to the *JDA*, along with the consent to treatment provisions of the *YOA*.

The case study of Quebec, prepared by Marc LeBlanc and Hélene Beaumont, is presented in Chapter 6. As pointed out in this chapter, Quebec is unique by virtue of its *Youth Protection Act* (1977), which anticipated and incorporated many of the features ultimately contained in the federal *YOA*. Thus, the *YPA* led to significant changes in Quebec's juvenile justice system even before the *YOA* became law.

The second section of this book considers programs and organizations important to the Act and special interest groups affected by the Act. Three chapters describe specific types of programs established under the Act: youth court committees, victim-offender reconciliation programs and custodial programs. Two other chapters describe the role of voluntary organizations and the situation of aboriginal persons under the Act.

In Chapter 7, Joe Ryant and Catherine Heinrich describe the rationale, structure, and operations of youth court committees in Manitoba. This type of program was initiated under the *JDA* and is also provided for in the *YOA* as a means for community involvement in the justice system. The idea, however, has only infrequently been put into practice. Only a few provinces have established youth court committees and none as extensively as Manitoba. Ryant and Heinrich note that a major purpose of these committees is to help establish and monitor programs involving alternative measures for young offenders, such as requiring offenders to pay the victim financial restitution, complete a specified number of hours of service for a charitable community organization, or both. Significant issues associated with these committees are identified and some alternative directions proposed. One problem identified by Ryant and Heinrich is that highly disorganized communities with a large proportion of young offenders are also likely to have limited resources for dealing with them.

In Chapter 8, Kim Pate and Dean Peachey describe an interesting type of alternative measures, victim-offender reconciliation programs (VORPs). VORPs are based on face-to-face mediation between the victim and offender. The significant components of such programs are identified as financial restitution, community service, and victim-offender involvement. Along with the rationale for this type of program, the relative extent of its popularity across the country and the implications held for policy and programming under the Act are examined. As Pate and Peachey note, a number of significant issues must be addressed if such programs are to operate efficiently, effectively and equitably.

Chapter 9 shifts to a discussion of custodial dispositions. Tullio Caputo and Denis Bracken describe the use of custodial settings under the *JDA* and *YOA*. The two types of custodial dispositions available under the *YOA*, open and secure custody, are identified and the ways in which these dispositions have been implemented in different provincial jurisdictions are described. Caputo and Bracken conclude their chapter by identifying some significant issues associated with custodial dispositions under the Act, including concerns about variability in what constitutes open custody, the apparent increase in the number of custodial dispositions, and the variability in the criteria used in to decide which custody location is appropriate for a particular youth.

Chapter 10 by Richard Weiler and Brian Ward describes major activities carried out by voluntary organizations in respect to young offenders and the Act, such as the direct delivery of services, public education, research and advocacy. This chapter is based to a large extent on three major research studies conducted by voluntary organizations on different sets of questions about the implementation of the Act. The first research study described by Weiler and Ward is an annual survey of voluntary organizations concerned with young offenders. The second research study is a 1985 survey of 100 people working with the young offender system; respondents were asked to give their views on the implementation of the Act. The third research project was conducted by the Canadian Association of Elizabeth Fry Societies in 1987 and aimed at identifying programs and services available under the *YOA* for young women. The chapter concludes with a discussion of future challenges for voluntary organizations, with respect to the *YOA*.

In Chapter 11, Carole Pitcher LaPrairie deals with the plight of aboriginal young persons. LaPrairie identifies such features as geographic isolation, socio-economic marginality and the social disorganization of many aboriginal communities as having major implications for the manner and extent to which young aboriginal persons are handled under the *YOA*. In particular, LaPrairie notes the limited types of services likely to be available to aboriginal youth residing in isolated parts of the country, the reduced availability of sentencing options for aboriginal youth and the lack of non-custodial dispositions. LaPrairie notes the end result is that aboriginal youth may be handled more harshly than their white counterparts under the Act.

The third section of the book consists of Chapter 12, which summarizes the key issues having to do with the design, implementation and evaluation of the Act. It also contains a proposed agenda for future research.

These, then, are some of the matters dealt with in the different chapters. While there has been no shortage of heated discussion concerning the *YOA*, there has been no single volume providing a discussion of the features of this legislation and its implementation. This book seeks to redress that gap by providing a fairly comprehensive overview of the Act, its implementation and current status. We have been fortunate in recruiting the services of an outstanding group of authors, including government administrators, university researchers and justice system practitioners, who have provided a variety of perspectives on elements and issues related to the development and current operations of the Act.

REFERENCES

Archambault, O. (1983). *Young Offenders Act*: Philosophy and principles. *Provincial Judges Journal*, 7(2), 1–7, 20.

Bala, N. (1986). The *Young Offenders Act*: A new era in juvenile justice? In B. Landau (Ed.), *Children's rights in the practice of family law* (pp. 238–254). Toronto: Carswell.

Caputo, T.C. (1987). The *Young Offenders Act*: Children's rights, children's wrongs. *Canadian Public Policy*, 8, 125–143.

Dalby, J.T. (1985). Criminal liability in children. *Canadian Journal of Criminology*, 27(2), 137–145.

Hackler, J. (1987). In my opinion…the impact of the *Young Offenders Act*. *Canadian Journal of Criminology*, 29(2), 205–209.

Reid, S.A. (1986). The juvenile justice "revolution" in Canada: The creation and development of new legislation for young offenders. *Canadian Criminology Forum*, 8(1), 1–14.

Reid, S.A., & Reitsma-Street, M. (1984). Assumptions and implications of new Canadian legislation for young offenders. *Canadian Criminology Forum*, 7, 1–19.

Solicitor General Canada. (1975). *Young persons in conflict with the law*. A report of the Solicitor General's committee on proposals for new legislation to replace the Juvenile Delinquents Act. Ottawa.

Solicitor General Canada. (1977). *Highlights of the proposed new legislation for young offenders*. Ottawa.

LEGISLATION

Bill C-192, *An Act Respecting Young Offenders and to Repeal the Juvenile Delinquents Act, 3d Sess., 28th Parl., 1970–71–72.*

Juvenile Delinquents Act, Revised Statutes of Canada 1970, c. J–3.

Young Offenders Act, Statutes of Canada 1980–81–82–83, c. 110.

Youth Protection Act, Statutes of Quebec 1977, c. 20.

CHAPTER 2
THE YOUNG OFFENDERS ACT
A LEGAL FRAMEWORK

Nicholas Bala[1]

HISTORY

Since the beginning of legal history, there have been special rules for dealing with young persons who violate the law. Under English common law, the special *doli incapax* (Latin for incapacity to do wrong) defence developed. A child under the age of seven years was deemed incapable of committing a criminal act. For children between seven and 13 years, there was a presumption of incapacity, but this could be rebutted if there was evidence to establish that the child had sufficient intelligence and experience to "know the nature and consequences of the conduct and to appreciate that it was wrong" (*Criminal Code*, 1970, s.13). While the *doli incapax* defence afforded certain protections to children, those children who were convicted faced the same penalties as adult offenders, including hanging and incarceration in such places as the old Kingston Penitentiary.

In the latter part of the 19th century, social movements that sought to promote better treatment of children developed in Britain, the United States and Canada. These movements led to such reforms as the establishment of child welfare agencies and the creation of a juvenile justice system, which had a distinct philosophy and provided facilities separate from the adult system. The reformers of this time considered their paramount objective to be saving destitute and wayward children from a life of crime and destitution. Thus they did not draw a clear distinction between neglected and criminal children. W.L. Scott, one of the principal drafters of Canada's early delinquency legislation stated that:

> there should be no hard and fast distinction between neglected and delinquent children, but...all should be...dealt with with a view to serving the best interests of the child. (Archambault, 1983, p. 2)

The efforts of these early reformers culminated with the enactment of the *Juvenile Delinquents Act* (*JDA*) in 1908. This federal legislation provided that children were to be dealt with by a court and corrections system sep-

[1] The author wishes to thank Deirdre Rice (LL.M. Candidate, Queen's University) for her helpful comments about a draft of this chapter.

arate from the adult system. The *JDA* clearly had a child welfare, or *parens patriae* philosophy. The Latin term *parens patriae* literally means "father (or parent) of the country," but it has come to mean a philosophy of state intervention based on an assessment of a child's best interests. This philosophy was reflected in section 38 of the *JDA* (1908):

...the care and custody and discipline of a juvenile delinquent shall approximate as nearly as may be that which should be given by his parents, and...as far as practicable every juvenile delinquent shall be treated, not as a criminal, but as a misguided and misdirected child...needing aid, encouragement, help and assistance.

The *Juvenile Delinquents Act* created a highly discretionary system, which gave enormous power to police, judges and probation officers, to do whatever they considered in a child's "best interests." There were no legislative guidelines governing judicial sentencing, and youths who were sent to training school (reformatory) were generally subject to indeterminate committals. Release from reformatory occurred when correctional officials felt that rehabilitation had been accomplished. While the system created by the *JDA* in 1908 marked an enormous improvement in the treatment of children and adolescents over earlier times, many serious, interrelated problems still existed, and by the 1960s juvenile justice in Canada was subject to criticism from a variety of different sources.

One major criticism of the *JDA* was that it created a system that tended to ignore the legal rights of children. This was true to such an extent that there were occasions when guilt seemed to be presumed so that "treatment" would not be delayed by "unnecessary formalities." In many parts of Canada, lawyers rarely, if ever, represented youths charged in Juvenile Court, and until relatively recently many of the judges in Juvenile Court lacked legal training. Thus, some critics charged that the juvenile justice system was unfair and unduly harsh with some youths. Other critics, however, pointed out that certain judges exercised their broad powers to promote their perceptions of the best interests of children in such a way that their dispositions were too lenient and did not adequately protect society.

The substantial discretion that the *JDA* gave to juvenile judges and probation officers was not the only reason for criticism. The Act also vested very significant control over the system in provincial administrators. As a consequence, there were enormous disparities across Canada in how juveniles were treated (Bala & Corrado, 1985). The maximum age of juvenile jurisdiction varied from province to province, ranging from the 16th to the 18th birthday, and the minimum age varied from seven to 14 years; children under the minimum age in each province were dealt with exclusively in the child welfare system. There were also great disparities in respect of diversion from the formal juvenile justice system, access to legal representation and use of community-based sentencing options.

The 1965 release of a report on juvenile delinquency in Canada marked the beginning of a lengthy period of debate and gradual reform (Canada, Department of Justice, 1965). Some provinces, most notably Quebec, took steps to change their juvenile justice system by, for example, ensuring that young persons had access to lawyers and establishing a formal system of juvenile diversion. Other provinces lagged behind. On a federal level, discussion papers and draft legislation were released and commented upon, but no action was taken. The constitutional entrenchment of the *Canadian Charter of Rights and Freedoms* in 1982 gave a greater sense of urgency to federal reform efforts. Many of the provisions of the *JDA* appeared to ignore the legal rights guaranteed in the *Charter* and the provincial disparities invited challenge under section 15 of the *Charter*, a provision that guaranteed Equality Rights and was scheduled to come into force in April 1985. As a result, in 1982, with the support of all political parties, the *Young Offenders Act* received Parliamentary approval. Most of the *YOA* came into force April 2, 1984. Some parts of the legislation gave rise to controversy from the moment of their initial introduction in Parliament. Most notably, a number of provinces were dissatisfied with the establishment of a minimum age jurisdiction of 12 years, and a maximum age jurisdiction running to the 18th birthday. The proclamation of the uniform maximum age provisions was delayed until April 1, 1985, to allow all provinces sufficient time to adapt. It soon became apparent that there were a number of problems with the *YOA* and in 1986 some relatively minor amendments were enacted through the passage of Bill C-106. These did not alter the philosophy or basic provisions of the Act, but did facilitate implementation.

PRINCIPLES OF THE YOUNG OFFENDERS ACT

The *YOA* constitutes a clear departure from the *JDA*. There is a uniform national age jurisdiction of 12 through 17 years, as of the date of the offence, and the *YOA* is unmistakably criminal law, not child welfare legislation. The discretion of police, judges and correctional staff is clearly circumscribed by the *YOA*. The only justification for state intervention under the *YOA* is the violation of criminal legislation, and this must be established by due process of law. Society is entitled to protection from young offenders, and young offenders are to be held accountable for their acts. However, the *YOA* is not simply a "Kiddies' Criminal Code." It establishes a justice and corrections system separate and distinct from the adult system, and it recognizes that young persons have special needs as compared with adults, require special legal protection, and are not to be held as fully accountable as adults for their violations of the criminal law.

In section 3 of the *YOA*, Parliament offers an express Declaration of Principle for those responsible for the implementation of the Act.

> **3.** *Policy for Canada with respect to young offenders.*
>
> (1) It is hereby recognized and declared that
>
> (a) while young persons should not in all instances be held account-able in the same manner or suffer the same consequences for their behaviour as adults, young persons who commit offences should nonetheless bear responsibility for their contraventions;
>
> (b) society must, although it has the responsibility to take reasonable measures to prevent criminal conduct by young persons, be af-forded the necessary protection from illegal behaviour;
>
> (c) young persons who commit offences require supervision, disci-pline and control, but, because of their state of dependency and level of development and maturity, they also have special needs and require guidance and assistance;
>
> (d) where it is not inconsistent with the protection of society, taking no measures or taking measures other than judicial proceedings under this Act should be considered for dealing with young per-sons who have committed offences;
>
> (e) young persons have rights and freedoms in their own right, includ-ing those stated in the *Canadian Charter of Rights and Freedoms* or in the *Canadian Bill of Rights*, and in particular a right to be heard in the course of, and to participate in, the processes that lead to deci-sions that affect them, and young persons should have special guarantees of their rights and freedoms;
>
> (f) in the application of this Act, the rights and freedoms of young per-sons include a right to the least possible interference with freedom that is consistent with the protection of society, having regard to the needs of young persons and the interests of their families;
>
> (g) young persons have the right, in every instance where they have rights or freedoms that may be affected by this Act, to be informed as to what those rights and freedoms are; and
>
> (h) parents have responsibility for the care and supervision of their children, and, for that reason, young persons should be removed from parental supervision either partly or entirely only when measures that provide for continuing parental supervision are in-appropriate.

Some commentators have suggested that the principles articulated in section 3 are inconsistent and hence offer no real guidance for the imple-mentation of the *YOA*. One youth court judge commented that section 3 reflects, if not "...inconsistency, [then] at least ambivalence about [what] approaches should be taken with young offenders..." (Thomson, 1983, p. 27). It is apparent that there is a level of societal ambivalence in Canada about the appropriate response to young offenders. On the one hand there is a feeling that adolescents who violate the criminal law need help to enable them to grow into productive, law-abiding citizens; this view is frequently reflected in media stories about inadequate facilities for treating young offenders. On the other hand, there is widespread public concern about the need to control youthful criminality and protect society. This view is reflected in media stories and editorials commenting on the inadequacy of the 3-year maximum disposition that can be applied to young offenders, a particular public concern in regard to those youths who commit very serious, violent offences.

While it is not inaccurate to suggest that the Declaration of Principle reflects a certain societal ambivalence about young offenders, it is also important to appreciate that it represents an honest attempt to achieve an appropriate balance for dealing with a very complex social problem. The *YOA* does not have a single, simple underlying philosophy; there is no single, simple philosophy that can deal with all situations in which young persons violate the criminal law. When contrasted with the child welfare oriented philosophy of the *JDA*, the *YOA* emphasizes due process, the protection of society, and limited discretion. In comparison to the adult *Criminal Code*, however, the *YOA* emphasizes special needs and the limited accountability of young persons. There is a fundamental tension in the *YOA* between such competing ideals as due process and treatment; in some situations the Act gives precedence to due process, while in others treatment is emphasized at the expense of due process. The underlying philosophical inconsistencies and tensions in the *YOA* reflect the very complex nature of youthful criminality. There is no single, simple philosophy and no single type of program that will "solve" the "problem." Judges and the other professionals who work with young persons who violate the criminal law require a complex and balanced set of principles like those found in the *YOA*.

The balance of this chapter will be devoted to a consideration of the substantive provisions of the *Young Offenders Act*, with a discussion of how they reflect the principles found in section 3 of the Act and of how the courts have interpreted these principles in different contexts.

ARREST AND POLICE QUESTIONING

In addition to those rights guaranteed to all under the *Charter of Rights*, the *YOA* affords special rights and protections to young persons who are arrested. Some of these provisions are premised on the notion that many young persons lack the maturity and sophistication fully to appreciate their situation, and hence require special legal rights; other provisions are intended to involve parents in the process, both to protect the rights of their children and to recognize their supportive role.

The *Charter of Rights* provides:

> **s.8** Everyone has the right to be secure against unreasonable search or seizure.

> **s.9** Everyone has the right not to be arbitrarily detained or imprisoned.

> **s.10** Everyone has the right on arrest or detention
> (a) to be informed promptly of the reason therefor;
> (b) to retain and instruct counsel without delay and to be informed of that right; and
> (c) to have the validity of the detention determined...and to be released if it is not lawful.

The rights that are guaranteed to all under the *Charter* may be of special significance to young persons, as they are particularly prone to police supervision and even harassment in certain situations. In *R. v. Ina Christina V.* (1985, p. 7211) a police officer observed a 15-year-old girl chatting quietly on a street corner in a place known by the officer to have an "...almost magnetic appeal for children who have run from home, some of whom have become the so-called 'street kids' and acts as a focal point for many persons involved in prostitution and drug trafficking." The officer concluded she was either "loitering" (not a criminal offence) "or possibly a runaway," and purported to arrest her under provincial child welfare legislation. A struggle ensued and the girl was charged with assaulting the police officer. In acquitting the girl of this charge, the judge observed:

> On the basis of the evidence presented, there is more than sufficient to find that Christina V.'s rights were infringed under ss. ...8 and 9 of the Charter and denied under para.10(b) of the Charter. In regard to the latter, although she was advised of her right to retain and instruct counsel without delay, there is no evidence that she was provided with the opportunity and means to do so. In advance of that, she was deprived of her liberty, the security of her person was invaded, her property was unjustly seized and searched and she was arbitrarily detained and imprisoned. These gross violations of her fundamental rights were totally out of proportion with the situation and prescribed nowhere by law. Even if the law had provided for such interference, it would be unreasonable to find that such was demonstrably justified in a free and democratic society....

> The phenomenon of the runaway child is, in the first instance, a social problem. Left unaddressed, it too often escalates into a legal issue involving either or both child welfare authorities and law enforcement officers. The magnitude of the problem as it relates to downtown Toronto...requires an urgent response. Undoubtedly, as a result of pressure from concerned parents, politicians and business people in the area, the Metropolitan Toronto Police Department has felt obliged to provide that response. Unfortunate-

ly, the standard law enforcement approach to the problem is woefully inadequate as well as improper.

As was exhibited in this case, good faith and a sense of duty on the part of the police falls far short of adequately addressing the situation. The runaway child who has been reported missing but has not committed any criminal offence, *may* indeed be a child at risk. That is the issue that must be addressed first and it can only be accomplished in a competent and caring fashion by trained child care workers. (*R. v. Ina Christina V.*, 1985, p. 7212)

In addition to the protections afforded under the *Charter of Rights*, special provisions found in section 56 of the *YOA* are intended to ensure that there is no improper questioning of young persons by police and other persons in authority:

> **s.56(2)** *When statements are admissible.* —No oral or written statement given by a young person to a peace officer or other person who is, in law, a person in authority is admissible against the young person unless
> (a) the statement was voluntary;
> (b) the person to whom the statement was given has, before the statement was made, clearly explained to the young person, in language appropriate to his age and understanding, that
>> (i) the young person is under no obligation to give a statement,
>> (ii) any statement given by him may be used as evidence in proceedings against him,
>> (iii) the young person has the right to consult another person in accordance with paragraph (c), and
>> (iv) any statement made by the young person is required to be made in the presence of the person consulted, unless the young person desires otherwise;
> (c) the young person has, before the statement was made, been given a reasonable opportunity to consult with counsel or a parent, or in the absence of a parent, an adult relative, or in the absence of a parent and an adult relative, any other appropriate adult chosen by the young person; and
> (d) where the young person consults any person pursuant to paragraph (c), the young person has been given a reasonable opportunity to make the statement in the presence of that person.

Section 56 is based on the recognition that young persons may lack the sophistication and maturity to fully appreciate the legal consequences of making a statement, and so require special protection when being questioned by police. It is also premised on the notion that some youths are easily intimidated by adult authority figures, and may make statements that they believe those authority figures expect to hear, even if the statements are false. It is hoped that consultation with a parent or lawyer will preclude the making of such false statements.

Section 56 has been invoked in a number of cases by the courts to exclude statements made by young persons. In *R. v. M.A.M.* (1986) a 16-year-old youth with a learning disability was charged with gross indecency. The police officer who arrested the youth purported to inform him of his rights by reading from a form that recited the words used in section 56. The young person then waived his right to have a lawyer or parent present. In ruling the statements inadmissible, the British Columbia Court of Appeal wrote:

> ...it appears...that the learned trial judge was confronted with the requirements of s.56 and concluded that having the contents of the two forms read to him, the young person did not know what to do in the circumstances and did not know why a lawyer would be necessary....
>
> In my opinion, the course followed by the police officer in the present case did not meet the requirements of s.56 of the *Young Offenders Act*. The forms themselves appear to be clear, but Parliament indicated the requirement that before the statement was made there must be a clear explanation to the young person. I am not persuaded that reading the contents of those two forms met the requirements imposed by Parliament before the statement could be taken from the young person....
>
> Parliament has paid special attention to the needs of young people for protective advice and has called on the police to provide it. There should be a genuine endeavour by the person in authority to describe the function of the lawyer and the benefits to the young person of having a lawyer, or parents, or relatives, or an adult friend present. That endeavour should be designed to lead to an appreciation on the part of the young person of the consequences of the choices that he makes.
>
> Even had this young person been a person without any learning disability, the mere reading over of these two statements and then asking the young person to sign them, without any explanation to him whatsoever, would not, in my opinion, have been compliance with ss.(2)(b) and (c) of s.56 of the *Young Offenders Act*. (*R. v. M.A.M.*, 1986, p. 571 & 573)

An interesting and difficult issue that has arisen in some cases is the extent to which individuals such as school teachers, principals or social workers may be "agents of the state" and hence should be expected to comply with the requirements of the *Charter of Rights* and section 56 of the *YOA*. In *R. v. H.* (1985) a 13-year-old boy was charged with theft and the prosecutor sought to have the court hear statements made by the youth to his teacher and the school principal. Prior to the statements being made, the teacher promised that if the money was returned, nothing further would happen. Not surprisingly, neither the teacher nor the principal complied with the Charter or section 56 of the *YOA*. The court ruled the statements inadmissible because of the violation of the *YOA* and section 10 of the *Charter of Rights*. *R. v. H.* does not require school personnel to afford young persons the right to counsel in all situations, but it does indicate that if this right is not afforded a youth prior to questioning, statements that are made may later be ruled inadmissible in youth court proceedings.

A somewhat different approach was taken in *R. v. J.M.G.* (1986), where a 14-year-old boy was charged with possession of a small amount of marijuana that had been discovered by his school principal after a search of the youth. The Ontario Court of Appeal emphasized that the search was carried out in the context of the principal's normal duties of maintaining discipline in the school, and hence did not constitute a violation of the *Charter of Rights*. The Court recognized that while the relationship between student and principal was not like that of policeman and citizen, "there may come a time when such [significant legal] consequences are inevitable and the principal becomes an agent of the police in detecting crime" (*R. v. J.M.G.*, 1986, p. 712). In such a situation a school principal or teacher might be expected to strictly comply with the warning requirements of the *Charter*. *R. v. H.* and *R. v. J.M.G.* illustrate that the courts will closely scrutinize each situation to determine the extent to which a principal or other person should be treated as an agent of the state. It may also be significant that *R. v. J.M.G.* involved the seizure of physical evidence, which was clearly indicative of the fact that the crime in question had been committed, while *R. v. H.* only involved a statement and the *YOA* has special provisions in regard to statements.

Section 9 of the *YOA* provides that if a young person is arrested or detained, a parent must be notified "as soon as possible." A parent must also be notified in writing of any youth court hearings. If a parent is not available, notice may be given to an adult relative or other appropriate adult. The Act also allows a youth court to order that a parent attend any proceedings if such attendance is considered "necessary or in the best interests of the young person." While parents are not parties to youth court proceedings, they have a statutory right to address the court prior to disposition, disposition review or possible transfer to adult court.

Paragraph 3(1)(h) of the Declaration of Principle recognizes the role of parents in the lives of their children, and sections 9 and 56 ensure that parents have notice of arrest, detention and youth court proceedings. These provisions are premised on the notion that parents will normally provide emotional support and ensure that a youth's legal rights are protected. It should be emphasized that under section 56(2) it is the youth who has the right to decide whether or not a parent will be present during police questioning. Some youths may be unwilling to have parental involvement, and there may be cases where such involvement is clearly not appropriate. Parents will normally not be considered "persons in authority," and statements made to them by their children will usually be admissible, despite the absence of any form of caution (*R. v. A.B.*, 1986; *YOA*, 1982, s. 56(6)).

There may, however, be cases in which parental questioning will amount to duress, and a statement in such circumstances could be ruled inadmissible. In *R. v. S.L.* (1984), the judge felt that a father who became actively involved with the police in the questioning of his son about a suspected homicide became a "member of the investigation team." The court ruled the youth's confession inadmissible, saying:

> There is no doubt that most well-thinking parents in a situation involving the death of a youngster would be anxious to co-operate in finding the truth, but when that involves co-operating with the police and obtaining some incriminating evidence against their own child, and without being made aware of all the information that the police had against the child, it is, I feel, not a rightful situation and can constitute an abuse of the very special relationship of authority and influence that a parent has on his child. (*R. v. S.L.*, 1984, p. 4085)

Youths who are arrested for relatively minor charges are normally released pending a hearing, but those charged with more serious offences, with long records of convictions, or who might not appear for trial, may be detained pursuant to the order of a youth court judge or a justice of the peace. The law governing pre-trial detention of young persons is generally the same as that applicable to adults, but section 7 of the *YOA* specifies that such detention will normally be separate from adults. The *YOA* allows for detention with adults only if a court is satisfied that this is necessary for the safety of the youth or others, or if the youth is in a remote location and no youth detention facilities are available within a reasonable distance. While pre-trial detention is normally separate from adults, youths awaiting trial are often kept in the same facilities as young offenders who are serving sentences in custody.

Pre-trial detention has the potential of being extremely disruptive to a young person, as it may result in sudden removal from familiar surroundings and placement in an often intimidating, institutional environment. Such detention will usually interfere with schooling or employment, and with familial and peer relationships. To minimize such disruptions, section 7.1 of the *YOA* allows a youth court judge or justice of the peace to order that a young person who would normally be detained be placed under the care and control of a "responsible person"; a "responsible person" would normally be a parent or other friendly adult. This will only be done if the "responsible person" undertakes in writing to exercise control over the youth and satisfy such other conditions as may be imposed, for example ensuring that the youth refrain from consuming alcohol pending trial. A "responsible person" who "wilfully fails" to comply with the undertaking may be charged with an offence under section 7.2 of the *YOA*.

The *YOA* provides in section 13 that if there is a question about a young person's mental capacity to stand trial, or if there is an application for transfer of the case to adult court, the youth court may order a medical, psychological or psychiatric assessment prior to trial. In other situations, there is no jurisdiction for a mandatory pre-trial assessment. Assessments and transfer applications are discussed more fully below.

ALTERNATIVE MEASURES

Paragraph 3(1)(d) of the Declaration of Principle recognizes the value of "taking measures other than judicial proceedings" under the *YOA*. Section 4 of the *YOA* creates a legislative framework for "alternative measures," that is to say for dealing with young persons outside the formal youth court process.

Alternative measures are a form of diversion from the court process and are typically used for first-time offenders charged with relatively minor offences. An alternative measures program allows a youth to be dealt with in a relatively expeditious, informal fashion and enables a youth to avoid a formal record of conviction. It is felt that some youths may be unnecessarily harmed by being "labelled" as "young offenders" through the formal court process, and that they may benefit from relatively informal treatment. Use of alternative measures is also consistent with the principle of "least possible interference," which is articulated in section 3(1)(f) of the *YOA*. Further, alternative measures programs may increase the scope for involvement of parents, victims and the community. Such programs may also be less expensive for society to operate than the formal youth court system.

In most provinces, responsibility for alternative measures is given to a community agency with a paid staff or volunteers, though in some provinces, government social workers or juvenile probation staff are responsible (Rabinovitch, 1986). Case referrals must initially be made by the police or Crown Attorney, who must be satisfied that alternative measures would be "appropriate, having regard to the needs of the young person and the interests of society," and that sufficient evidence exists to take the case to court. The program administrator then meets with the young person and proposes some form of alternative measures that might involve, for example, an apology, restitution, some form of volunteer work or a charitable donation. The young person is not obliged to participate, and always has the option of going to youth court for a judicially imposed disposition. Youths must "fully and freely consent" to participating and must "accept responsibility" for the offence alleged to have been committed; if the young person denies responsibility, the matter must go to court for a judicial finding of guilt or innocence. The young person must be advised of the right to consultation with a lawyer prior to participation.

If a young person agrees to participate and successfully completes the alternative measures agreed to, the charges must be dropped. Whether or not there is successful completion, no statement made by a youth, in the process of consideration of whether alternative measures should be imposed, may be used in later court proceedings.

While there is some controversy over the efficacy of alternative measures as opposed to court in terms of reducing future offences (Moyer, 1980), until April 1988, every province except Ontario had implemented section 4 of the YOA. It is generally felt that alternative measures represent a socially useful experiment for dealing with first-time offenders in a humane, socially inexpensive fashion. The failure of Ontario to implement section 4 of the YOA has been successfully challenged in the Ontario Court of Appeal, as a violation of the Equality Rights guaranteed by section 15 of the Charter of Rights. In R. v. Sheldon S. (1988) it was held that the absence of such programs in Ontario constituted a "denial of equal benefit and protection of the law" on the basis of place of residence, and hence was in violation of section 15 of the Charter. This decision is under appeal to the Supreme Court of Canada and it remains to be seen whether the Charter can be invoked to force a provincial government to provide services and programs in accordance with the YOA. Sheldon S. may be a significant precedent for ensuring all youths access to a minimum level of services, regardless of their province of residence.

The Declaration of Principle in section 3(1)(d) mentions "taking no measures" as well as alternative measures. In R. v. David L. (1985) a 13-year-old boy who had been placed in a group home under child welfare legislation was charged with an assault as a result of an altercation in which the boy punched a staff member. The court dismissed the charge, relying in part on section 3(1)(d) of the YOA, and stated that staff who occupy a "parent-like" role should not look to the courts to deal with relatively minor disciplinary matters.

YOUTH COURT PROCEEDINGS

Proceedings under the YOA are conducted in a specially designated "youth court." In a number of provinces, the Family Court, which is responsible for such matters as child protection and adoption, has been designated as the youth court. In other jurisdictions, the Provincial Court, which deals with most adult criminal charges, has been designated as the youth court, although the proceedings must be held at a separate time from those involving adults.

Ontario and Nova Scotia have adopted a two-tier youth court model. As was the practice under the *Juvenile Delinquents Act*, 12- to 15-year-olds are dealt with in Family Court, while 16- and 17-year-olds are proceeded with in the adult Provincial Court, albeit with adult court judges who are nominally sitting as youth court judges. Critics have argued that Ontario and Nova Scotia have simply acted in an expedient fashion and have failed to implement the spirit of the *YOA* by maintaining the court jurisdiction in effect under the *JDA* (Bala, 1987; Stuart, 1987). However, the courts have held that the two-tier implementation model is permitted under the *YOA* and does not violate the *Charter of Rights* (*R. v. R.C.*, 1987).

In section 52, the *YOA* stipulates that proceedings in youth court are to be similar to those governing "summary conviction offences" in adult court. This means that the proceedings are less complex and more expeditious than those applicable to the more serious adult "indictable offences." More specifically, this means that there are no preliminary inquiries, and all trials are conducted by a judge alone; there are no jury trials in youth court. It is felt that it is particularly important for young persons to have the more expeditious resolution of their cases available through summary procedures. The courts have held that the failure to afford young persons an opportunity for trial by jury does not violate the provisions of the *Charter of Rights* that guarantee equality and the right to a jury trial to persons facing imprisonment of five years or more. In *R. v. Robbie L.* (1986) the Ontario Court of Appeal emphasized that the maximum penalty under the *YOA* is three years, as opposed to the life sentence an adult may face for certain serious offences. Justice Morden wrote:

> ...the *Young Offenders Act* is intended to provide a comprehensive system for dealing with young persons who are alleged to be in conflict with the law which is separate and distinct from the adult criminal justice system. While the new system is more like the adult system than was that under the *Juvenile Delinquents Act* it nonetheless is a different system. As far as the aftermath of a finding of guilt is concerned, the general thrust of the *Young Offenders Act* is to provide less severe consequences than those relating to an adult offender....the establishment of the legal regime...for dealing with young persons, which is separate and distinct from the adult criminal justice system, is of sufficient importance to warrant the overriding of the equality right alleged to be infringed in this proceeding.... (*R. v. Robbie L.*, 1986, pp. 219 & 225)

While a young person being tried in youth court is denied the opportunity to a preliminary inquiry and a jury, a youth is afforded all of the procedural protections that are given to an adult who faces a summary charge. There is a constitutionally based presumption of innocence (*Canadian Charter of Rights and Freedoms*, 1982, s.11(d)) with the onus upon the prosecution to prove its case. If a "not guilty" plea is entered, the Crown will call witnesses to establish its case and each witness will be subject to cross-examination. The youth is entitled to call witnesses and to testify, subject to the Crown's right of cross examination, but there is no obligation upon the accused to adduce any evidence or testify. After all the witnesses are called, there may be submissions (or arguments) and the judge then renders a verdict. If the judge is satisfied, beyond a reasonable doubt, that the offence charged has occurred, a conviction is entered, and the case proceeds to disposition under the YOA. Otherwise, an acquittal is entered and this ends the YOA proceedings, though in appropriate cases the youth might still be dealt with under provincial child welfare or mental health legislation.

Most cases under the YOA do not in fact result in trials, but rather result in guilty pleas. Frequently the youth recognizes that an offence has occurred and wishes to plead guilty. If a guilty plea is entered, the Crown Attorney will read a summary of the evidence against the youth. Section 19 of the YOA has a special provision requiring a judge in youth court to be satisfied that the facts read by the Crown support the charge. If they do not, the judge must enter a plea of not guilty and conduct a trial. This provision recognizes that a youth may not appreciate the significance of a guilty plea as fully as an adult.

It is not uncommon for a guilty plea in youth court to be the product of a "plea bargain." A plea bargain is typically the result of informal discussions between the Crown Attorney and the lawyer representing the youth. There is an agreement to plead guilty to certain charges in exchange for dropping of other charges or a request by the Crown to the court for a particular disposition. Though considered controversial by some, plea bargaining is not regarded as unethical or illegal. It should be noted that if there is a plea bargain, the judge is not bound to impose the disposition requested by the accused.

The YOA affords very important rights in regard to the provision of legal representation. Section 11 requires that as soon as a young person is arrested or appears in youth court, the youth is to be advised of the right to counsel. If the young person is "unable" to obtain counsel, the youth court judge shall "direct" that legal representation be provided. While adults have the right to retain counsel, if they are unable to afford a lawyer, they must rely on legal aid, which has fairly stringent criteria for deciding whether to provide representation. The YOA guarantees that whenever a youth is "unable" to obtain counsel, it will be provided. It has been held that when assessing financial ability to retain counsel, the court should not have regard to parental resources (R. v. Ronald H., 1984; R. v. M., 1985). Since few young people have significant financial resources, in practice this means that most youths are represented by lawyers who are paid by the state.

While a youth is not obliged to be represented by a lawyer and may choose to appear unrepresented or assisted by some other adult, like a parent, the effect of the YOA has been to ensure that most youths are represented by counsel. This has proven controversial to some observers, who have argued that securing legal representation often results in unnecessary delays and that lawyers often fail to promote the "best interests" of adolescent clients (Leschied & Jaffe, 1987, p. 428). However, the YOA is clearly criminal law and it is understandable that those subject to potential punishment by the state are entitled to full legal representation; young persons without lawyers are rarely in a position to appreciate the significance of their involvement in the legal system or to protect their rights. It may well be that in some localities administrative difficulties do result in delays in obtaining legal counsel, and that some lawyers involved in the representation of young persons lack the training or sensitivity to provide truly adequate legal services. However, denial of access to counsel does not seem to be an appropriate strategy for dealing with these problems.

The YOA has a number of provisions intended to protect the privacy of young persons involved in the youth court process and to minimize the stigmatization they may face. Section 38 provides that the media cannot publish identifying information about a young person, though there is a special exception if a youth is at large and considered "dangerous to others" by a judge. Section 39 stipulates that while youth court proceedings are generally open to the public, the judge may make an exclusion order if their presence "would be seriously injurious or seriously prejudicial" to the young person. Sections 40 to 46 govern records; access to records of youths involved with the court system is generally restricted. While police may fingerprint and photograph youths charged with indictable offences, the central records of the Royal Canadian Mounted Police must be destroyed five years after the completion of any sentence for an indictable offence, provided the youth commits no further offences in that five-year period. Local police forces and others who have records related to young offenders are not obliged to destroy their records, but their use is severely restricted after the five years have passed. Section 36 of the YOA prohibits employers governed by federal law from asking whether a potential employee has ever been convicted of an offence under the YOA. These provisions recognize the "limited accountability" of young persons and are intended to afford a "second chance" to those who are convicted under the YOA.

DISPOSITION AND DISPOSITION REVIEW

Young persons convicted of offences under the *YOA* receive a "disposition," or "sentence," pursuant to section 20 of the Act. Available dispositions consist of the following:

- an absolute discharge;
- a fine of up to $1,000;
- an order for restitution or compensation;
- an order for up to 240 hours of community service;
- an order for up to two years probation;
- an order for treatment for up to three years;
- an order for custody for up to three years.

For less serious offences, a court may make a disposition immediately after a finding of guilt. However, for more serious offences, the court will normally adjourn to allow preparation of a report to assist the court. Most commonly the youth court will request a "predisposition" report, or social history. A youth court worker will prepare such a report. The worker will interview the youth, the youth's parents, the victim and any other significant individuals, and will summarize the youth's background and provide information about the offence. Frequently the report will include a recommendation about disposition. Although not binding on the court, these recommendations are usually influential. The youth, of course, has the right to challenge the report, and may introduce independent evidence about disposition. Parents also have the right to make submissions prior to disposition.

In more serious cases, or in cases where there is particular concern about a young person, the court may order a psychiatric, medical or psychological assessment to assist in arriving at an appropriate disposition.

Since the enactment of the *YOA*, appellate courts in different Canadian provinces have gradually articulated a dispositional philosophy for young offenders. In *R. v. Richard I.* (1985, p. 523) the Ontario Court of Appeal acknowledged that in comparison to sentencing adults "...the task of arriving at the right disposition may be considerably more difficult and complex given the special needs of young persons and the kind of guidance and assistance they may require." In *R. v. Joseph F.* (1986, p. 304), Justice Morden of the Ontario Court of Appeal wrote:

> While undoubtedly the protection of society is a central principle of the Act...it is one that has to be reconciled with other considerations, such as the needs of young persons and, in any event, it is not a principle which must inevitably be reflected in a severe disposition. In many cases, unless the degree of seriousness of the offence and the circumstances in which it was committed militate otherwise, it is best given effect to by a disposition which

gives emphasis to the factors of individual deterrence and rehabilitation. We do not agree that it puts the matter correctly to say the whole purpose of the Act is to give a degree of paramountcy to the protection of society with the implication that this is to overbear the needs and interests of the young person and must result in a severe disposition.

One controversial issue is the extent to which courts making dispositions under the *YOA* should take into account the principle of general deterrence. In *R. v. G.K.* (1985) the Alberta Court of Appeal declined to impose a custodial disposition on a youth without a prior record who was convicted of armed robbery, emphasizing that a psychiatric report indicated that there was no likelihood of recurrence of delinquent acts. Justice Stevenson wrote:

> We...reject the suggestion that the young offender's sentence should be modelled on the sentence that would be imposed on an adult offender. If a custodial sentence is warranted then it ought not to be lengthier than that which would be imposed on an adult.... In any event, deterrence to others does not, in my view, have any place in the sentencing of young offenders. It is not one of the principles enumerated...in s.3 of the Act which declares the policy for young offenders in Canada. (*R. v. G.K.*, 1985, p. 560)

However, most other appellate courts have held that general deterrence may play a role in the sentencing of young offenders. The Ontario Court of Appeal specifically rejected the approach of the Alberta Court of Appeal in *R. v. G.K.*:

> The principles under s.3 of the *Young Offenders Act* do not sweep away the principle of general deterrence. The principles under that section enshrine the principle of the protection of society and this subsumes general and specific deterrence. It is perhaps sufficient to say that...the principles of general deterrence must be considered but it has diminished importance in determining the appropriate disposition in the case of a youthful offender. (*R. v. Frank O.*, 1986, p. 377)

Another controversial issue is the extent to which courts should consider the promotion of the welfare of a youth as a basis for imposing a custodial sentence. In *R.R. v. R.* (1986) the Nova Scotia Court of Appeal upheld a sentence of five months open custody imposed on a 14-year-old youth without a prior record who was convicted of the theft of a skateboard. The Court felt the youth "desperately requires strict controls and constant supervision" (*R.R. v. R.*, 1986, p. 3461–34). The commission of the offence was considered a justification for imposing needed care, even though the sentence was grossly disproportionate to the offence and far in excess of what an adult would have received for the same offence.

A more common approach, however, has been to reject the use of the *YOA* simply as a route for providing treatment. In *R. v. Michael B.* (1987) the Ontario Court of Appeal overturned an order for five months open custody imposed upon a youth who committed a relatively minor assault and had no prior record. The trial judge had been concerned that the boy was suicidal and neither his family nor the mental health facility he had been staying in wanted to accept him. Justice Brooke concluded that incarceration under the YOA "was not a sentence that was responsive to the offence, but in reality was what seemed at the time a sensible way of dealing with a youth who had a personality problem and needed a place to go" (R. v. Michael B., 1987, p. 574). The Court of Appeal suggested that involuntary mental commitment was the appropriate route to follow; in fact this had occurred by the time the case came before that Court.

As a result of the YOA's distinctive dispositional philosophy and reflecting the fact that many youths involved in the criminal justice system have not committed serious offences, the vast majority of convicted young offenders receive dispositions that keep them in their communities. Section 20(1)(9) of the YOA allows the imposition of an absolute discharge if the court considers "it to be in the best interests of the young person and not contrary to the public interest." This disposition is usually reserved for minor first offenders and results in no real sanction being imposed, other than the fact of conviction. Restitution, community service and fines allow the court to impose a real penalty on the youth, without unduly restricting freedom. In appropriate cases, victims may be compensated by restitution.

The most frequently imposed disposition under the YOA is probation. The nature of a probation order depends on the circumstances and various conditions may be imposed. These might include that a youth maintain a curfew, attend school, or reside with parents. Probation may also entail regular reporting to a probation officer, and might even be used to require a youth to live in a foster home or with a suitable adult person (R. v. W.G., 1985).

The most serious disposition that can be ordered under section 20 of the YOA is placement in a custodial facility. For most offences the maximum custodial disposition is two years, but for offences for which an adult may receive life imprisonment, the maximum is three years. The YOA requires a judge placing a youth in custody to specify whether the sentence will be served in "open custody" or "secure custody."

Section 24.1 of the YOA specifies that an open custody facility means a "community residential centre, group home, child care institution, or forest or wilderness camp, or any other like place or facility" designated as "open" by the provincial government, while "secure custody" means a place "for the secure containment or restraint" of young persons that is designated as secure by the provincial government. The intention of the Act is that judges should have control over the level of restraint imposed on a youth. Provincial governments also retain significant control because they are able to designate the level of facilities. The courts have indicated, however, that they will cautiously review provincial designations. In one case, a Prince Edward Island court ruled that the provincial government could not simply designate as a place of "open custody" one floor of a building that had formerly served as an adult jail and which was then serving as a secure custody facility for young offenders.

> Undoubtedly the physical characteristics are not the only things to be looked at. Other factors which make a place suitable for open custody would include the security that is in place, the number of staff, the qualifications of the staff, bearing in mind that one of their primary functions is to teach young offenders how to better achieve in society. Additionally, a place of open custody will have a program set up for the benefit of the offenders. (*Re L.H.F.*, 1985, p. 46)

A very disturbing trend immediately following the enactment of the *YOA* was a significant increase in the use of custodial placements for young persons who violated the criminal law (Leschied & Jaffe, 1987; Wardell, 1987). This trend can in part be attributed to the attitudes of many youth court judges who initially emphasized the protection of society and the youth's responsibility over recognition of special needs and limited accountability. It also seems that in those provinces where the age jurisdiction was raised, older youths who had been appearing in adult court as "first-time offenders" (their juvenile records being ignored), were appearing in youth court with long records of prior offences. Further, it seems that some youth court judges were making extensive use of open custody as a "middle option" for youths who had not committed serious offences but who "needed some help." Prior to the enactment of the *YOA*, many of these youths had been helped through the child welfare system.

It remains to be seen whether this trend toward increased use of custody will continue. There is some evidence that there may be a decline in the use of custody. In most provinces, the appellate courts have rendered decisions that reduce the length of custodial dispositions for young offenders, and emphasize limited accountability and recognition of special needs. As originally enacted, the *YOA* placed certain restrictions on the use of custody, requiring a predisposition report before any custodial disposition was made, and restricting the use of secure custody to cases where a more serious offence occurred or where there was a record of prior offences. In amending the *YOA* in 1986, Parliament also provided that a youth court should not place a young offender in open or secure custody unless this was considered "necessary for the protection of society...having regard to the seriousness of the offence and...the needs and circumstances of the young person" (Section 24(1)). Under the original legislation, this consideration only applied to secure custody. It is to be hoped that these signals from the appellate courts and Parliament may be having the effect of curbing the excessive use of custodial placements by the youth courts.

When a youth is ordered into custody, provincial correctional officials have significant control over the youth's placement. While the youth court specifies a level of custody, correctional officials select the specific facility a youth will reside in and can move the offender from one facility to another in that level. Provincial officials may also permit the temporary release of the youth from custody, either to engage in employment, education or other activities, or to return home for a specified period of time. Correctional officials also have the authority under the *YOA* to transfer a youth from an open to a secure custody facility for up to 15 days. A youth may be transferred if there has been an escape or attempted escape, or if in their opinion, this is "necessary for the safety of the young person or...others" in the open custody facility. Section 24.5 of the *YOA* allows correctional officials to apply to a youth court judge to transfer a young offender who has reached 18 into a provincial adult correctional facility for the remainder of the youth's custodial sentence. Such a transfer shall only be allowed if the youth court, after a hearing, is satisfied that it is "in the best interests of the young person or in the public interest."

The *YOA* provides that once a disposition has been imposed on a young offender, the youth court retains the authority to conduct a review hearing to ensure that the disposition remains current and appropriate to the needs of the youth. For youths placed in custody, there is a mandatory review hearing by the court after one year, with the possibility of an earlier review, but there is no parole for young offenders. Correctional officials may release a youth from custody into probation or may transfer a youth from secure to open custody, but these decisions are subject to the approval of a youth court judge; normally these processes can be carried out without a hearing, though sometimes one is required. At a review hearing, the youth court cannot increase the level of security that was specified in the original disposition, though if there has been a wilful failure to comply with a disposition, such as a breach of probation or an escape from custody, this would constitute an offence for which a new disposition can be imposed.

One of the most controversial dispositional provisions of the *YOA* deals with "treatment orders," which allow a youth to be placed in a psychiatric hospital or other "treatment facility" instead of custody. Such orders may only be made on the recommendation of a psychiatric or psychological report ordered under section 13, and only if the youth consents; normally parents must also consent to such an order being made. The requirement that the youth consent has been criticized, as relatively few youths are prepared to admit that they need treatment even if they are highly disturbed, and very few of these orders have been made. Some critics have advocated removal of the requirement for a youth's consent to such a treatment order, although they acknowledge that "the efficacy of compulsory treatment for young offenders is an area laden with considerable debate" (Leschied & Jaffe, 1987, p. 427). It should be noted that forms of rehabilitative services, therapy and counselling are provided in most custodial facilities. Also, in cases of severely disturbed youths, the insanity provisions of the *Criminal Code* or provincial mental health legislation may be invoked to require that a youth be involuntarily confined in a mental health facility.

TRANSFER TO THE ADULT SYSTEM

The most serious thing that can happen to a young person charged with an offence is transfer to the adult system. Such a transfer can only occur after a youth court hearing, which must be held prior to an adjudication of guilt or innocence. If a youth court judge orders transfer, there will be a trial in adult court. If there is a conviction in an adult court, sentencing will be in accordance with the principles applicable to adults. Although it is theoretically possible for a youth to seek transfer in order, for example, to have the benefit of a jury trial, it is invariably the Crown that seeks transfer in order to subject the young person to the much more severe maximum penalties that can be imposed in adult court. Usually transfer applications are made where the adult maximum of life imprisonment is considered a more appropriate response than the three years under the *YOA*.

Under section 16 of the *YOA* an application for transfer can be made in regard to any serious indictable offence alleged to have been committed by a young person 14 years or older at the time of the alleged offence. Transfer is only to be ordered if the youth court "is of the opinion that, in the interest of society and having regard to the needs of the person" it is appropriate. In deciding whether to transfer a case, section 16(2) instructs the courts to consider: the seriousness of the alleged offence; the age, character and prior record of the youth; the adequacy of the *YOA* as opposed to the *Criminal Code* for dealing with the case; the availability of treatment or correctional resources; and any other relevant factors.

Transfer hearings are adversarial in nature, but are not formal criminal trials. The rules of evidence are greatly relaxed, and the court will receive hearsay (or second-hand) evidence about the youth's background and the circumstances of the alleged offence. The court need not be satisfied beyond a reasonable doubt that an offence occurred, but rather decides what is the appropriate forum for the trial and disposition of the charge in question (*R. v. S.J.H.*, 1986). Witnesses are often called to describe the differences between the likely fate of the youth if placed in custody under the *YOA* as opposed to incarceration pursuant to the *Criminal Code*. A predisposition report must be presented at a transfer hearing and there is usually a section 13 psychiatric report prepared as well. Often, a central issue at transfer hearings is the amenability of the youth to rehabilitation within the 3-year period prescribed as the maximum *YOA* disposition.

There has been substantial judicial disagreement about the appropriate interpretation of the *YOA*'s standard for transfer, "the interest of society...having regard to the needs of the young person." The courts have compared this to the standard articulated under section 9 of the *Juvenile Delinquents Act*: that transfer was to occur only if "the good of the child and the interest of the community demand it."

Justice Monnin of the Manitoba Court of Appeal wrote:

> The test under this Act [the *YOA*] is different than that under the old *Juvenile Delinquents Act*.... In the new test there is at least a slight emphasis on the interest of society having regard to the needs of the young person. (*R. v. C.J.M.*, 1985, p. 229)

Another Manitoba decision commented:

> With the advent of the *Young Offenders Act* the transfer provisions ensure a more realistic approach to transfer. The fact that transfer exists in certain cases for those over the age of fourteen, by implication, considers that in some instances those youths will face a period of adult incarceration. While the primary concern has now shifted so that the interests of society would appear to be of primary importance, the needs of the young person are still to be addressed and these needs might well be so addressed with the treatment available in an adult institution. (*R. v. J.T.J.*, 1986, p. 3409–32)

The Manitoba approach has led to a relatively high transfer rate, not only for such offences as murder and attempted murder, but also for such offences as robbery.

The approach of the Manitoba Courts can be contrasted with the more restrictive approach taken in a number of other jurisdictions. In *R. v. Mark Andrew Z.* (1987) the Ontario Court of Appeal refused to transfer a youth who, at the age of 15, shot and killed his mother and sister. Justice MacKinnon observed that "a charge of murder does not automatically remove a youth from the youth court" (*R. v. Mark Andrew Z.*, 1987, p. 158). The judge stressed the amenability of this youth to treatment and wrote:

> In light of s.3 [of the *YOA*] I do not think that the interests of society or the needs and interests of the young person are to be given greater importance one over the other. They are to be weighed against each other having regard to the matters directed to be considered in subs.16(2). (*R. v. Mark Andrew Z.*, 1987, p. 162. See also *R. v. N.B.*, 1985 and *R. v. E.E.H.*, 1987)

In *Mark Andrew Z.*, the Ontario Court of Appeal did note that in a case such as this, involving first-degree murder, the court was faced with a choice between the 3-year maximum disposition under the *YOA* and the possibility of life imprisonment with no opportunity for parole for at least 25 years. While deciding against transfer, Justice MacKinnon stated:

> Put bluntly, three years for murder appears totally inadequate to express society's revulsion for and repudiation of this most heinous of crimes.... This is obviously an area for consideration and possible amendment by those responsible for the Act. (*R. v. Mark Andrew Z.*, 1987, p. 162)

A leading juvenile forensic psychiatrist, Dr. Clive Chamberlain, has supported the view that for homicides, judges acting under the YOA should be able to impose sentences of longer than three years, noting that for a few highly disturbed youths it may be necessary to have five to 10 years of treatment in a secure setting. Dr. Chamberlain commented on the problem with the YOA's three-year maximum disposition, saying that it

> ...puts pressure on the Crown to move these kids into the adult court, where a 25 year murder sentence is available. As a result some of them will wind up in the adult prison population, where there is no treatment for them and where they just get worse.... Society would be better served, I believe, if the three-year maximum term of the youth system of which the greater part involves counselling—were extended in the rare cases where kids kill somebody. (Bagley, 1987, p. 61)

CONCLUSION

The *Juvenile Delinquents Act* came into force close to the start of the 20th century, and by the 1980s major reforms were inevitable. The *Young Offenders Act* created a relatively uniform, national scheme for dealing with adolescents who violate the criminal law. While these youths are not afforded a child welfare approach, used for children under 12 whose behaviour may be a threat to others, nor are they subject to the full rigours of the adult criminal justice system.

The YOA has clearly achieved certain objectives, most notably protecting the legal rights of young persons, and provides recognition of the right of society to appropriate protection. It seems unlikely for the foreseeable future that Parliament will engage in a major revision of the YOA or change its fundamental principles. However, there remain many issues for the courts, provincial administrators, and the federal Parliament to address before we will have achieved a system of youth justice truly worthy of the close of the 20th century. Our search for a youth justice system that fairly balances the needs and rights of young persons while adequately protecting society must be an ongoing one.

REFERENCES

Archambault, O. (1983). *Young Offenders Act: Philosophy and principles. Provincial Judges Journal, 7*(2), 1–7.

Bagley, G. (1987). "Oh, what a good boy am I": Killer angels chose when friends die. *The Medical Post,* December 8, 1987, 9 & 51.

Bala, N., & Corrado, R. (1985). *Juvenile justice in Canada: A comparative study.* Ottawa: Ministry of the Solicitor General of Canada.

Bala, N. (1987). Annotation to *R. v. Robert C., Young Offenders Service,* 7353–3 to 7353–6.

Canada, Department of Justice, Special Committee on Juvenile Delinquency. (1985). *Juvenile Delinquency in Canada.*

Leschied, A., & Jaffe, P. (1987). Impact of the *Young Offenders Act* on court dispositions: A comparative analysis. *Canadian Journal of Criminology, 30,* 421–430.

Moyer, S. (1980). *Diversion from the juvenile justice system and its impact on children: A review of the literature.* Ottawa: Ministry of the Solicitor General of Canada.

Rabinovitch, P. (1986). Diversion under section 4: Is there a future for it in Ontario? *Young Offenders Service,* 7533–7542.

Stuart, D. (1987). Annotation to *R. v. R.C., Criminal Reports* (3d), 56, 185–186.

Thomson, G. (1983). Commentary on the *Young Offenders Act. Provincial Judges Journal, 7*(2), 27–29, 34.

Wardell, W. (1987). The *Young Offenders Act*: A Report Card 1984–86. *Journal of Law and Social Policy, 2,* 39–72.

LEGISLATION

An Act to Amend the Young Offenders Act, the Criminal Code, the Penitentiary Act and the Prisons and Reformatory Act (Bill C–106), Statutes of Canada 1984–85–86, c.32.

Canadian Charter of Rights and Freedoms, Part I of the *Constitution Act, 1982,* being Schedule B of the *Canada Act 1982* (U.K.), 1982, c.11.

Criminal Code, Revised Statutes of Canada 1970, c. C–34.

Juvenile Delinquents Act, Revised Statutes of Canada 1970, c. J–3.

Young Offenders Act, Statutes of Canada 1980–81–82–83, c.110.

CASES

R. v. A.B. (1986), 50 *Criminal Reports* 247 (Ont. C.A.).

R. v. Michael B. (1987), 36 *Canadian Criminal Cases* (3d) 572 (Ont. C.A.).

R. v. N.B. (1985), 21 *Canadian Criminal Cases* (3d) 374 (Que. C.A.).

R. v. R.C. (1987), 53 *Criminal Reports* (3d) 185 (Ont. C.A.).

R. v. Joseph F. (1986), 11 *Ontario Appeal Cases* 302.

Re L.H.F. (1985), 57 *Newfoundland & Prince Edward Island Reports* 44 (P.E.I.S.C.).

R. v. J.M.G. (1986), 56 *Ontario Reports* (2d) 705, *Young Offenders Service* 86–135 (Ont. C.A.).

R. v. W.G. (1985), 23 *Canadian Criminal Cases* (3d) 93 (B.C.C.A.).

R. v. H. (1985), *Young Offenders Service* 4140 (Alta Prov. Ct-Youth Div.).

R. v. E.E.H. (1987), 35 *Canadian Criminal Cases* (3d) 67.

R. v. Ronald H. (1984), *Young Offenders Service* 3319 (Alta Prov. Ct).

R. v. S.J.H. (1986), 76 *Nova Scotia Reports* (2d) 163 (N.S.S.C.).

R. v. Richard I. (1985), 17 *Canadian Criminal Cases* (3d) 523.

R. v. J.T.J. (1986), *Young Offenders Service* 3409–31 (Man. Prov. Ct-Fam. Div.).

R. v. G.K. (1985), 21 *Canadian Criminal Cases* (3d) 558 (Alta C.A.).

R. v. David L. (1985), *Young Offenders Service* 3103 (B.C. Prov. Ct).

R. v. Robbie L. (1986), 52 *Criminal Reports* (3d) 209 (Ont. C.A.).

R. v. S.L. (1984), *Young Offenders Service* 4085 (Ont. Prov. Ct-Fam. Div.)

R. v. M. (1985), *Young Offenders Service* 3322 (Ont. Prov. Ct-Fam. Div.).

R. v. C.J.M. (1985), 49 *Criminal Reports* (3d) 226 (Man. C.A.).

R. v. M.A.M. (1986), 32 *Canadian Criminal Cases* (3d) 567 (B.C.C.A.).

R. v. Frank O. (1986), 27 *Canadian Criminal Cases* (3d) 376 (Ont. C.A.).

R.R. v. R. (1986), *Young Offenders Service* 3461–34.

R. v. Sheldon S. (1986), *Young Offenders Service* 7375 (Ont. Prov. Ct-Fam. Div.); affirmed (1988), as yet unreported decision, summarized in *The Lawyers Weekly*, April 1, 1988, p. 1 (Ont. C.A.).

R. v. Ina Christina V. (1985), *Young Offenders Service* 7211 (Ont. Prov. Ct-Fam. Div.), per Main Prov. J.

R. v. Mark Andrew Z. (1987), 35 *Canadian Criminal Cases* (3d) 144.

CHAPTER 3

THE FEDERAL GOVERNMENT'S ROLE IN IMPLEMENTING THE YOUNG OFFENDERS ACT

Jim Coflin

This chapter examines the role played by the federal government in the development and implementation of juvenile justice reform in Canada.[1] As that role is largely circumscribed by the constitutionally defined powers of the federal and provincial governments, a discussion of the jurisdictional circumstances of the juvenile justice system, first under the *Juvenile Delinquents Act* (1970) and then under the *Young Offenders Act* (1982), is necessary.

JURISDICTIONAL ISSUES

The federal and provincial governments share constitutional jurisdiction in the field of criminal justice. Specifically, the federal government, pursuant to section 91(27) of the *Constitution Act* (1982), has jurisdiction to legislate in the area of criminal law and procedures, while the provinces have jurisdiction to administer justice. Thus, provincial responsibilities consist of policing, prosecution, court administration and corrections. Of course, there are variations in this pattern. For example, responsibility for the administration of prison sentences of two years or more imposed in the cases of adult offenders and the prosecution of drug statutes rests with the federal government. Other policy areas impinging on the juvenile justice system are comparatively straightforward. For example, the provincial governments have exclusive jurisdiction over such matters as welfare,

---

[1] When the federal government initiated the review of the juvenile justice system in the early 1960s, the responsibility for the *Juvenile Delinquents Act* rested with the Department of Justice. In 1966, with the creation of the Department of the Solicitor General of Canada, responsibility for juvenile justice reform, along with responsibility for federal corrections and policing were located in the new Department. The responsibility for juvenile justice policy generally and the *YOA* was, however, returned to the Department of Justice in April 1987 following a clarification of the respective criminal justice policies of the two federal departments.

education and health. In the past, however, the federal government has exercised its spending powers in order to participate, albeit indirectly, in these areas of exclusive provincial jurisdiction.

The *Juvenile Delinquents Act* (*JDA*), while a creation of the Parliament of Canada and a matter of criminal law and procedure, was founded upon a philosophy that emphasized the virtues of a "child welfare" rather than a "criminal" response to the deviant behaviour of children and youth. This philosophical orientation was clearly expressed in the Act's interpretive provision:

> 38. This Act shall be liberally construed in order that its purposes may be carried out, namely, that the care and the custody and the discipline of a juvenile delinquent shall approximate as nearly as may be that which should be given by his parents, and that as far as practicable every juvenile delinquent shall be treated, not as criminal, but as a misdirected and misguided child, and one needing aid, encouragement, help and assistance. (*Juvenile Delinquents Act*, 1970)

The child welfare orientation of the juvenile justice system before 1984 was more than a guiding principle. It was given explicit form in two specific provisions of the *JDA* which directly incorporated the provincial statutes governing the child welfare system:

> 21.(1) Whenever an order has been made under section 20 committing a child to a children's aid society, or to a superintendent, or to an industrial school, if so ordered by the provincial secretary, the child may therefore be dealt with under the laws of the province in the same manner in all respects as if the order had been lawfully made in respect of a proceeding instituted under authority of a statute of the province; and from and after the date of the issuing of such order except for new offences, the child shall not be further dealt with by the court under this Act.
>
> (2) The order of the provincial secretary may be made in advance and to apply to all cases of commitment mentioned in this section. R.S., c. 160, s. 21.

> 39. Nothing in this Act shall be construed as having the effect of repealing or overriding any provision of any provincial statute intended for the protection or benefit of children; and when a juvenile delinquent who has not been guilty of an act that is under the provisions of the *Criminal Code* an indictable offence, comes within the provisions of a provincial statute, he may be dealt with either under such statute or under this Act as may be deemed to be in the best interests of the child. R.S., c. 160, s. 36. (*Juvenile Delinquents Act*, 1970)

Thus it is apparent that the very provisions of the *JDA* placed the entire juvenile justice system in a rather complex jurisdictional environment where the shared and concurrent powers of the federal and provincial governments in the area of criminal justice and the exclusive provincial jurisdiction for welfare overlapped. Any proposal intended to replace the JDA would affect not only the areas of shared jurisdiction, but also areas of exclusive provincial jurisdiction, particularly the field of child welfare. Thus, from the outset, the provinces had a strong interest in the nature of the reforms.

The extent to which the child welfare orientation had been adopted by provincial juvenile justice systems varied from province to province. Saskatchewan and Quebec had fully integrated their child welfare and juvenile justice systems. Saskatchewan, for example, had established a policy of integration in the late 1950s and adopted that orientation in its *Family Services Act* (1978), which provided for the automatic placement of those found delinquent in the care of the child welfare authority. Child welfare intervention at earlier stages of the process were encouraged through a range of formal and informal procedures.

Quebec's *Youth Protection Act* (1977) gave child welfare officials authority to determine, in some cases, whether prosecutions would proceed, although this practice was later amended. Other provinces, such as New Brunswick, Ontario and British Columbia maintained systems that, while making extensive use of welfare services and programs, nevertheless maintained a greater measure of distinction between children brought into care because of delinquency and those in need of protection.

The merging of the child welfare and the juvenile justice systems was further encouraged by the JDA provision that a child could be found to be a "juvenile delinquent" for reasons other than offences defined in criminal law. No clear distinction was made between truancy, traffic offences and serious criminal acts. Given that the declared mandate of the system was to act in the best interests of the child, virtually any child could be brought within the scope of the juvenile justice system on the way to the child care system. However, the assertion has been vigorously debated. In some measure, the integration of the criminal justice and child welfare systems through the JDA provided the impression, at least, that the juvenile justice system served as a comparatively simple intake process for the child welfare system.

Integration of child welfare and juvenile justice also provided the opportunity for the indirect exercise of federal spending powers in the field of criminal justice. While the federal government has generally refrained from applying its spending powers in the area of criminal justice matters falling within provincial jurisdiction, it has exercised those powers in other social program areas. In the 1960s the federal government passed the *Canada Assistance Plan Act* (1970), which established a cost-sharing program providing for federal financial contributions to a variety of provincial welfare services, including child welfare. As children who had been found delinquent under the provisions of the *JDA* could, pursuant to section 21 of the Act, be transferred to the jurisdiction of provincial legislation and dealt with "...in all respects as if the order had been lawfully made in respect of a proceeding instituted under authority of a statute of the province...," they were, for purposes of the Canada Assistance Plan, defined as being in receipt of welfare services. The provincial government was therefore able to claim federal financial support for those services. Consequently, many provincial governments were effectively able to obtain federal financial benefits for what might be generally considered as a criminal justice activity. Not all provinces, however, chose to utilize the provisions of section 21 on a routine basis, resulting in some measure of interprovincial disparity in terms of federal transfer payments.

In the early 1970s, in the interest of maintaining equity, the federal government entered into special agreements with the provinces that did not integrate provincial child welfare and juvenile justice systems. These agreements were separate from the Canada Assistance Plan, but paralleled its benefits. As a result federal spending powers were extended to cover a significant proportion of juvenile correctional services. Thus, the federal government had, and continues to have, clear jurisdiction to legislate in the area of juvenile justice; in contrast, the provinces had a unique interest in the nature and implications of juvenile justice reforms because of the jurisdictional complexities occasioned by the *JDA*.

CONSULTATIVE PROCESS

Early steps toward legislative reform of the juvenile justice system were initiated in 1963 with the formation of a federal committee to examine the operation of the *JDA*. The committee tabled its report (Committee on Juvenile Delinquency, 1965) and the proposals contained in that report led to introduction, in 1969, of Bill C–192 to replace the 1908 Act. The Bill was, however, abandoned in the face of opposition from a number of sources. Many child welfare and juvenile justice commentators found the proposals objectionable because they served to criminalize juvenile delinquency and criticized the federal government for its failure to consult adequately with those responsible for the juvenile justice services and institutions. Provincial authorities echoed this criticism, observing that the federal government, in proposing juvenile justice reforms, had failed to recognize provincial interests and jurisdiction in the area or to sufficiently consider the financial implications of the proposed reforms.

Demands by the provinces for full participation in juvenile justice reform arose partly from the nature of the distribution of constitutional powers in the area of criminal justice. However, the integration of the criminal and child welfare systems under the *JDA* brought the issue of federal financial responsibilities to the fore; such an issue had not previously arisen and this factor lent greater impetus to provincial demands. When efforts to develop acceptable reforms were re-instituted in the early 1970s, there were clear expectations that the federal government would consult broadly and give active consideration to provincial concerns respecting the financial implications of reforms. The review process that was undertaken by the federal government was indeed characterized by a greater degree of provincial participation than had been the case in the 1960s. In particular, a federal-provincial committee was established to facilitate adequate consultation.

In 1975, following extensive preparatory discussions, a set of proposals for comprehensive reform was released (Solicitor General Canada, 1975) and became the focus for study and vigorous debate amongst professional groups concerned with criminal and juvenile justice. These groups consisted of: police; the Bar; judges; child welfare authorities; civil liberties groups; and a broad range of non-governmental organizations. The consultative process continued at various levels of intensity until 1981 when Bill C–61 was tabled in Parliament. This process was highlighted by the release of modified proposals in 1977 (Solicitor General Canada, 1977) and various ministerial statements reflecting the results of the ongoing study and debate that had followed the earlier federal-provincial consultations.

In addition to consulting with the public and the provinces throughout the decade preceding the introduction of legislative proposals, the federal government had supported initiatives undertaken by provincial governments and community organizations. These initiatives served to demonstrate and test the impact of some of the proposed reforms, especially those related to alternative measures and community-based, non-custodial sentencing options, such as community service orders and restitution programs. These demonstration projects and research activities complemented similar activities supported by provincial governments. The private sector assisted the consultative process by opening the juvenile justice system to greater public scrutiny and providing a larger range of people with the opportunity to participate in the debate concerning juvenile justice reform.

With the eventual passage of the *Young Offenders Act* (*YOA*) in 1982, the federal government undertook a series of programs intended to facilitate the full implementation of both the reforms that had been developed over the previous decade and those that were possible only through legislation. These implementation activities fell under the following headings: training and orientation; federal-provincial cost-sharing arrangements; funding program development; information systems development; and, a process of ongoing policy review.

TRAINING AND ORIENTATION

The *YOA* was passed by Parliament in the summer of 1982, but was not immediately proclaimed for a number of reasons, not the least of which was the fact that the new law represented a virtually complete change in the orientation and procedures of the juvenile justice process. In addition, the child welfare orientation of the *JDA* had permitted the development of juvenile justice in each province to follow a distinct path. These inter-provincial variations added to the complexity of the implementation task and the need for those involved in the administration of the system to become knowledgeable about the new procedures and requirements and to establish new and appropriate procedural and program guidelines and standards to comply with the Act. The federal implementation program, responding to the evident need of juvenile justice professionals for information that would assist them in formulating their own responses to the new legislation, focused on making detailed information about the Act available to professionals and agencies before the Act's proclamation. An important element of the federal program was the publication of the manual *The Young Offenders Act: Annotated* (Bala & Lilles, 1982).

This document was widely distributed to members of the judiciary, police, Bar and juvenile justice agencies. It was also made available to academic institutions, training facilities, provincial training programs and other organizations. In addition to making the manual as widely available as possible and distributing copies of the Act itself, the federal government provided financial, organizational and consultative support to train and provide orientation programs for juvenile professionals, whether these were organized by professional groups and associations or provincial agencies. As one aspect of this training venture, a national training conference was held in Ottawa in early 1983. This multi-disciplinary event provided an opportunity for key personnel and program planners from across Canada to begin the task of examining the implementation requirements of the new legislation. It also provided insight into the operational, training and program developments that would be required when the Act was proclaimed in force.

The pre-proclamation orientation and training activities were supplemented by a continuing emphasis on such activities in the months following proclamation on April 2, 1984. As was the case in the period before the Act came into force, the federal role in the post-proclamation period focused on assisting those directly responsible for administration of the Act, through funding and consultative assistance, to organize and provide seminars and training sessions designed to incorporate information relevant to the implementation strategies that had been adopted in that particular jurisdiction.

Implementation of the *YOA* was accompanied by a general effort, undertaken largely in cooperation with provincial agencies and local organizations, to provide legal information to the public about the new procedures and requirements. Some of this effort was directed specifically at young people who fell under the jurisdiction of the *YOA*. The information needs of parents, other significant adults, such as teachers, and the general public were also targeted. These public legal information activities were of particular importance because the juvenile justice system had become largely invisible to the public under the *JDA*, which emphasized the confidentiality of the juvenile court. Although there had been some movement toward opening the juvenile process to greater public scrutiny, the nature and extent of juvenile crime and the juvenile justice process were effectively hidden from public view. While the consultation and debate that had preceded the passage of the *YOA* had exposed many people to the issues involved, the fact that the new legislation opened the courts and the process to public view and removed juvenile justice from the privacy of the family court stimulated interest in and concern about juvenile crime and juvenile justice and a need to ensure that accurate and reliable information was generally available.

FEDERAL—PROVINCIAL FINANCIAL ARRANGEMENTS

As noted above, one of the concerns identified by the provincial governments by the late 1960s related to the financial implications of juvenile justice reform. In the consultations leading to the adoption of the *YOA*, those governments sought and obtained a commitment that the federal government would continue to provide financial support to provincially administered juvenile justice programs and services. The establishment of a mutually acceptable financial arrangement, therefore, became a priority of both levels of government in the period between the passage of the legislation in June 1982 and its coming into force in April 1984.

Historically, the federal government has not participated in the financing of criminal justice activities outside its area of constitutional jurisdiction. As noted earlier, however, the juvenile justice system was and continues to be an exception. The reason for this variation is that the *JDA* included provisions to allow for the transfer of cases from the juvenile court to the child welfare system following a finding of delinquency. The procedures and programs developed in many provinces through the 1950s and 1960s have subsumed the administration of juvenile corrections, particularly the institutional programs, into child welfare programs administered under provincial statutes. This overlap between criminal justice and child welfare created a set of circumstances under which juvenile justice became the subject of federal financial support of welfare services, not criminal justice services. As the legislative reforms incorporated in the YOA eliminated the provision for transfer to child welfare authorities, it also eliminated the basis for cost sharing under the Canada Assistance Plan, which specifically excludes the extension of its benefits to correctional services.

Under the JDA, federal transfer payments were made in respect of services associated with dispositions consisting of placements in the care of child welfare authorities or in industrial schools; i.e., paragraphs 20(1)(h) and (i) and where an appropriate order was made pursuant to section 21 or where a province had entered into a special agreement which paralleled the Canada Assistance Plan. Other dispositions, such as probation, were not eligible for federal support because they were considered as correctional services for the purposes of the Canada Assistance Plan. The only services eligible for cost sharing involved the removal of the juvenile delinquent from his or her home to a child welfare facility or program of some nature. In other words, these services involved some measure of institutionalization, the equivalent of custodial orders under the YOA.

The federal-provincial agreements established in the negotiations that preceded the proclamation in force of the YOA provide for federal contributions toward the costs of both open and secure custodial services, on much the same terms as those that were applicable to similar services under the JDA and the Canada Assistance Plan. Specifically, the federal government contributes 50% of the operating costs incurred in the delivery of such services and programs. In addition, the agreements provide for federal contributions of approximately 50% of the costs associated with the development and delivery of alternative measures programs, as provided for in section 4 of the Act, review boards as defined in section 32 and judicial interim release programs. Judicial interim release programs are perhaps more commonly described as "bail supervision programs," and are directed toward minimizing the need for pre-trial detention, just as they do in the adult system. Finally, the agreements provide for federal contributions toward the "increased costs" incurred for the supervision of non-custodial dispositions made pursuant to section 20 of the YOA, pre-trial screening programs, the preparation of predispositional reports (section 14) and assessments (section 13). The restriction to "increased" costs in these cases is intended to limit federal contributions to new costs arising from the implementation of the legislation.

Under the financial agreement, the federal government transferred to provincial governments approximately $78 million for fiscal year 1984–85, $117 million for 1985–86, $135 million for 1986–87 and $140 million for 1987–88. The significant increase in transfer payments over this 4-year period is largely attributable to the additional costs incurred by those provinces and territories that had maintained the maximum age limits under the *JDA* at under 16 or under 17. It is estimated that the transfer of 16- and 17-year-olds from the adult or ordinary courts to the jurisdiction of the youth courts effectively doubled the number of custodial spaces and non-custodial services required by the juvenile justice system. The extent of the impact of this major reform is clearly suggested by the increments in the size of annual transfers under the cost-sharing arrangements described above.

The present cost-sharing arrangements were negotiated in 1983–84 and will be in effect until the end of the 1988–89 fiscal year. Accordingly, a second round of financial negotiations will be undertaken to determine the terms of the federal-provincial cost-sharing arrangement in this area into the 1990s.

PROGRAM DEVELOPMENT FUNDS

There was a great deal of program experimentation and development across Canada in the years preceding the proclamation of the *YOA*; program development experience varied considerably from one jurisdiction to another. The introduction of the new legislation provided the opportunity, even the need, for further experimentation and development. In the interest of supporting the continuing process of exploration and innovation under the Act, the federal government established a Program Development Fund. This initiative, under which project funds are made available to provincial governments and non-governmental organizations at the local and national levels, was originally projected to have a life span of three years (1984–1987). However, the significant changes required by the new Act resulted in a slower pace of development than had been forecast and in 1986–87, the program was extended to March 1989.

The Program Development Fund had three principle objectives. The first was to support the replication and adaptation of non-custodial programs and services that were required or encouraged under the new legislation and that had demonstrated their effectiveness through earlier developmental work. The second objective was to support innovative approaches to implementing the community and non-custodial provisions of the new Act and to provide for evaluation of such undertakings. The third objective, and a priority in the period immediately following the proclamation of the Act, was to foster professional development through an interdisciplinary and interprovincial exchange of experience and expertise. This activity partly consisted of directing financial support towards seminars, workshops and conferences with the aim of exposing juvenile justice personnel to the implementation and program strategies underway or planned in individual provinces and nationally.

Nationally, the funds supported such activities as the preparation of an inventory of community-based juvenile justice programs by the Canadian Council for Children and Youth and the planning and development efforts of organizations such as the John Howard Society of Canada and the Salvation Army. It also facilitated training and information efforts undertaken in response to the needs of groups, such as clinical psychologists and those concerned with learning disabilities, whose objectives and interests are broader than the criminal justice system. Provincially, funding assistance was offered to major development activities such as Manitoba's "Working Together" project, a province-wide community mobilization initiative focusing upon the development of community youth justice committees, alternative measures programs, non-custodial disposition and alternatives to custody. Similar initiatives were undertaken in Nova Scotia and Newfoundland.

Local projects supported by the fund included: the Juvenile Intensive Supervision Project sponsored by the Lower Mainland Correctional Society, which has explored special supervision strategies as alternatives to pre-trial custodial remand; the probation project sponsored by the Dakota-Ojibway Tribal Council in Manitoba, which sought to develop a comprehensive community correctional program managed by the community; a rural victim-offender reconciliation project sponsored by the Province of Quebec and Plaidoyer Victime; Saskatchewan's Conditional Release and Intensive Supervision Project, which has focused efforts to accelerate the return to the community of youth who had received custodial dispositions; and the development of Prince Edward Island's Youth Court Clinics.

INFORMATION SYSTEMS DEVELOPMENT

In developing its implementation support programs, the federal government made a major commitment to the design and implementation of automated information systems to support the administration of the records provisions of the YOA and the management and statistical information needs of the juvenile justice system. More than $12 million was allocated to this program area over a 3-year period; like the Program Development Fund, this was later extended to a 5-year period. These funds facilitated the creation of the young offenders criminal records registry provided for in section 42 of the Act. The great majority of the funds (more than $10 million), however, have been dedicated to creating, modifying or enhancing provincial information systems.

The development of automated systems has been partly driven by the comprehensive records requirements of the YOA, which are not simply concerned with the "criminal history" files that identify an individual's history of charges, convictions and sentences, but all documents in which a specific individual is identified as having been dealt with under the *YOA*. This scheme, therefore, affects the records management activities of any individual or organization dealing with young people as accused or convicted offenders and places upon all such record holders the responsibility to ensure that they are made available to others only in the circumstances set out in the legislation. These circumstances include the requirement that records not be used for any purpose under certain conditions, such as the acquittal of an accused youth or the satisfaction of a crime-free period. A variety of factors, many of which are not immediately apparent in a particular document or file, determine who may have access to records and when records are simply not available for any purpose. Thus the ability to obtain accurate and timely information about the status of young offenders and the possible location of records argues for the implementation of effective information systems, particularly automated systems.

The development or enhancement of automated systems, with the assistance of federal funds, has been undertaken in most provinces and territories. However, it has proven to be an arduous and complex process. The major difficulty has been to develop automated information systems that allow for the interaction of numerous organizations with varying needs, program objectives and, in some cases, legally-prescribed access privileges. In addition to the funding that has been made available to the provinces and territories, the development of young offenders information systems has been assisted by the Canadian Centre for Justice Statistics, an agency of Statistics Canada which operates under the policy direction of a federal-provincial body known as the Justice Information Council and provides technical support to both federal and provincial departments.

ONGOING REVIEW AND CONSULTATION

The proclamation of the *YOA* culminated almost two decades of study, debate and consultation, but did not bring an end to these processes. The dimensions and often innovative character of the reforms required that the implementation and impact of the legislation be monitored on an ongoing basis. In support of this ongoing process, the federal government undertook research and evaluation activities, established juvenile justice as a permanent subject of policy development and agreed to the formation of a formal mechanism for federal-provincial consultation.

The research activities undertaken in support of ongoing policy review processes were, in fact, initiated in the late 1970s in anticipation of the implementation of the *YOA*. The *National Study of the Functioning of the*

Juvenile Court had as its primary objective the establishment of a body of baseline data that could facilitate subsequent evaluation of the new legislation. The study utilized observation and file reviews to document 2,500 cases involving 8,000 charges dealt with in juvenile courts located in Vancouver, Edmonton, Winnipeg, Toronto, Montreal and Halifax, as well as several smaller communities in Quebec, Alberta and British Columbia. Three reports, based on the data collected by the study have been published and additional work is currently underway (Bala & Corrado, 1985; Moyer, 1985; Moyer, Kopelman & Carrington, 1985).

Since the implementation of the *YOA*, the federal government has contributed to a number of smaller research and evaluation projects, particularly projects associated with innovative program initiatives supported under the Program Development Fund. However, the federal government has focused primarily on the development of a national information base in support of the implementation and ongoing development of juvenile justice reform. The Youth Court Survey managed by the Centre for Justice Statistics experienced significant implementation difficulties but provides a source of data for research studies. In addition, the federal government cooperated closely with provincial governments to support a major study that will provide a detailed description of the juvenile justice system of each province and jurisdiction. The first phase of the Qualitative Description Study, which deals with the "correctional" sector of the juvenile justice system, is expected to provide a database that will facilitate the interpretation and analysis of national statistics and a context in which to better understand and assess the products of specific research initiatives in the future.

Mechanisms established to ensure the continuing review of the juvenile justice system include a federal-provincial committee structure headed by the deputy ministers of departments involved in the administration of the major components of the system. The Committee of Deputy Ministers Responsible for Juvenile Justice (28 members in total) is supported by a committee of officials and, as necessary, special working groups. This structure was the focal point of the consultation process that preceded the introduction in 1986 of Bill C–106, *An Act to Amend the Young Offenders Act*. In response to a range of difficulties encountered in the implementation of the Act, the Committee of Deputy Ministers developed an inventory of concerns and proposals for amendments which served as a basis for the proposals adopted by Parliament in 1986. The work carried out by the federal-provincial committees and work groups was augmented by consultations with concerned national, regional and local organizations and submissions from a variety of concerned groups and individuals.

This review process and the development of options for further reform and refinement of the juvenile justice process has continued through the federal-provincial mechanisms established in 1984. In the spring of 1987, the Minister of Justice and Attorney General of Canada met with provincial and territorial ministers. Together they established an agenda for the review and study of a number of issues, including: the provisions of the *YOA* governing the admissibility of statements given by young persons to "persons in authority" (section 56); the two-tiered custodial system (section 24); the implications of the provisions for transfer to ordinary court (section 16) as they interact with the maximum duration of dispositions set out in section 20(4); the implications of the treatment order disposition (section 20(1)(i)); and the decriminalization of the behaviour of children under 12 years of age. These and other matters affecting the treatment of young people as accused and convicted offenders will be the subject of federal-provincial study and broader consultation as progress is made in the ongoing review process.

REFERENCES

Bala, N., & Corrado, R.R. (1985). *Juvenile justice in Canada: A comparative study* (Technical Report No. 5). Ottawa: Ministry of the Solicitor General.

Bala, N., & Lilles, H. (1982). *The Young Offenders Act: Annotated*. Kingston: Ministry of the Solicitor General.

Committee on Juvenile Delinquency. (1965). *Juvenile delinquency in Canada: The report of the Department of Justice Committee on juvenile delinquency*. Ottawa: Queen's Printer.

Moyer, S. (1985). *The attitudes of Canadian juvenile justice professionals towards the Young Offenders Act* (User Report No. 1985–22). Ottawa: Ministry of the Solicitor General.

Moyer, S., Kopelman, F., & Carrington, P.J. (1985). *The relationships between the age of the accused young person and other personal and case characteristics* (User Report NO. 1985–43). Ottawa: Ministry of the Solicitor General.

Solicitor General Canada. (1975). *Young persons in conflict with the law. A report of the Solicitor General's Committee on proposals for new legislation to replace the Juvenile Delinquents Act. Ottawa: Ministry of the Solicitor General*.

Solicitor General Canada. (1977). *Highlights of the proposed new legislation for young offenders*. Ottawa: Ministry of the Solicitor General.

LEGISLATION

An Act to Amend the Young Offenders Act, the Criminal Code, the Penitentiary Act and the Prisons and Reformatories Act (Bill C–106), Statutes of Canada 1984–85–86, c. 32.

Bill C–192, *An Act Respecting Young Offenders and to Repeal the Juvenile Delinquents Act, 3d Sess., 28th Parl., 1970–71–72*.

Canada Assistance Plan Act, Revised Statutes of Canada 1970, c. 45.
Constitution Act, 1982, being Schedule B of the *Canada Act 1982* (U.K.), 1982, c. 11.
Criminal Code, Revised Statutes of Canada 1970, c. C–34.
Family Services Act, Revised Statutes of Saskatchewan 1978, c. F–7.
Juvenile Delinquents Act, Revised Statutes of Canada 1970, c. J–3.
Young Offenders Act (Bill C–61), Statutes of Canada 1980–81–82–83, c. 110.
Youth Protection Act, Statutes of Quebec 1977, c. 20.

CHAPTER 4

IMPLEMENTING THE YOUNG OFFENDERS ACT
AN ALBERTA PERSPECTIVE

Brian Mason

PLANNING FOR IMPLEMENTATION OF
THE YOUNG OFFENDERS ACT IN ALBERTA

On March 28, 1983, a senior committee of the Alberta Government Cabinet made the decision to transfer program responsibility for the management of young offenders from the Department of Social Services to the Department of the Solicitor General. Prior to proclamation of the *Young Offenders Act* (1982), the Department of Social Services had joint responsibility for both child welfare and juvenile delinquency matters. To ensure the successful implementation of this decision, the Cabinet Committee directed representatives from the two departments as well as the Department of the Attorney General to prepare a coordinated plan for the transfer of facilities and resources from the Department of Social Services to the Department of the Solicitor General.

The Department of the Solicitor General had been responsible for the administration of adult corrections in Alberta since its creation in 1973. As such, it was experienced with administering adult correctional centres, the adult probation system and for introducing numerous innovative corrections programs such as Fine Option, Temporary Absence, Pre-trial Release, Community Residential Centres and community service work. Since the adult age of criminality in Alberta had, prior to the *Young Offenders Act* (*YOA*), been age 16 (*Child Welfare Act*, 1980) for both boys and girls, the Department of the Solicitor General was experienced at dealing with the older, young offender group. In fact, subsequent bed space reviews would show that the department had been responsible for between 200 and 300 inmates ages 16 and 17 before the introduction of the *YOA*. Four years after proclamation, internal studies show that 75% of young offenders in custody in Alberta are age 16 and older.

Once the decision was made to transfer responsibility for *YOA* programs to the Department of the Solicitor General, a coordinated and intensive planning effort was begun. At the time of the March 1983 decision, it was not known precisely when the *YOA* would be proclaimed, although it was anticipated that it might be done as early as the summer of 1983.

The planning exercise, in other words, had to be done within a context of uncertainty with respect to the proclamation date. It was decided early in the planning phase to take advantage of the sections of the *YOA* that allowed provinces to phase in the age provisions, first for the 12- to 15-year-old group inclusive and, one year after proclamation, to extend the Act to the 16- and 17-year-old group. This decision was made because it would have been impossible to build or arrange suitable resources and programs to accommodate such a large scale transfer at one time.

In addition to the interdepartmental committee responsible for developing the coordinated plan, the Department of the Solicitor General took three important steps to organize the planning phase:

1. Commissioned a private consulting firm to conduct a custody bed space analysis, which was completed in November 1983. This internal study was based on data prepared by the Departments of the Solicitor General and Social Services.

2. Established 15 separate task groups, each charged with planning a designated aspect of the *YOA* implementation. These task groups were struck in May 1983.

3. Established in December 1983, an implementation committee to coordinate the work of the 15 task groups and ensure all implementation duties were completed in time for the now expected proclamation in April 1984. By this time, the position of Provincial Director of the Young Offender Program had been created and filled. This person chaired the implementation committee.

Many critical path models were identified and flow charts prepared early in the planning phase to ensure that the enormous number of separate duties and activities were well coordinated and completed as required in order to meet the implementation deadline. A review of the type of work completed by each task group appears below and provides an appreciation of the magnitude of the planning exercise.

1. *Capital Planning* This committee was responsible for meeting the immediate and long-term bed space needs of the young offender custody population. Further it had to ensure that provincial resources were in place to house the expected number of temporary detention, secure custody and open custody young offenders. In this work, the committee made extensive use of the bed space analysis completed by the private consulting firm. In addition, the committee worked with the Department of Social Services in identifying resources such as institutions and group homes that would have to be transferred to the Department of the Solicitor General to coincide with proclamation of the *YOA*. This group also began the long pro-

cess of planning for the construction of new, purpose-built young offender facilities. Several years of lead-time are required before any major facility can be designed and constructed. Until new facilities could be built (a 128-bed Edmonton Young Offender Centre and a 112-bed Calgary Young Offender Centre to open in 1988), facilities that had previously been used to house child welfare clients or in some cases, adult inmates, would have to be converted for use by the young offender population. Consequently this group also examined the extent of renovations that would be required in these temporary facilities.

2. *Policies and Procedures* This task group was responsible for developing departmental policies and guidelines for use by staff who would be working in young offender centres, probation offices, group homes and private custody homes.

3. *Escort Services* This group worked with the Alberta Correctional Escort Service (ACES), the RCMP and city police forces to ensure a coordinated plan would be ready to escort young offenders to and from courts and places of custody. The needs of the young offender system would make it imperative that an efficient escort and placement system be developed to ensure that newly sentenced young offenders were placed in the most suitable facility for the type of custody received. This committee developed the idea of a central placement authority, consisting of one person located in Edmonton, who would function like an "air traffic controller" by making immediate decisions for the initial placement of all young offenders remanded or sentenced to custody. The placement authority now works extensively with probation officers from around the province in selecting the place of custody that is closest to the young offender's home and that provides the best program and level of custody to meet the needs of the young person.

4. *Information Systems* Since federal cost-sharing dollars were made available to assist with the development of automated information systems, this group worked to develop such systems for use in community corrections and custody facilities. The result is an on-line tracking and information system that can be used to assist in placement, research and tracking of young offenders. It is now being expanded into a comprehensive management information system with the inclusion of administrative and personnel data.

5. *Community Corrections Staffing/Office Space Requirements* In addition to planning custody facilities, there was an equally important need to ensure staff and other resources were in place to provide Community Corrections programming, such as probation, community

service and the preparation of predisposition reports. This task group was also involved in coordinating the transfer of some community-based resources from the Department of Social Services.

6. *Centre Program Delivery* This group planned the casework and living unit programs for implementation in the young offender centres. Extensive internal documentation was prepared covering every aspect of a centre's program such as casework, living unit routines, recreation, health services, mental health services and educational programs.

7. *Legislation, Regulations and Amendments* A lengthy Order in Council was prepared to ensure that facilities were properly designated as places of open or secure custody or temporary detention, and that staff were designated as youth workers or provincial directors, as required (Alberta Regulations 101/85 and subsequent Designation Order Amendments).

8. *Cost Sharing* This group ensured that all financial documentation systems would be in place to take advantage of the federal cost-sharing agreement. It also helped negotiate the terms of the initial 5-year agreement.

9. *Documentation* This was the paperwork task group which ensured that all required forms and documents for young offender centres and Community Corrections offices were properly designed and printed in time for the proclamation date.

10. *Alternative Measures* This was a joint planning group formed by the Departments of the Solicitor General and Attorney General. The group's principal task was to develop guidelines, procedures and policies for a province-wide Alternative Measures Program. This program was eventually introduced in 1985 for first offenders.

11. *Contracts* This group was responsible for negotiating any new contracts required for overseeing the transfer of existing contracts from the Department of Social Services.

12. *Staff Training* This group built on the work of many of the other committees such as those dealing with policies and procedures and documentation. The resources of the Department's Staff Training College in Edmonton were used to develop schedules and lesson plans for the numerous training courses that eventually were delivered in the two months preceding proclamation of the Act. Youth workers in custody centres, probation officers and group home operators all required training in the various legal aspects of the *YOA* and departmental policies. This group oversaw the design and delivery of all such training courses.

The three remaining task groups dealt with internal administrative and financial issues such as payroll, staffing patterns and related personnel issues. To ensure that the work of the task groups was properly focused, a Mission Statement was developed shortly after the March 1983 transfer decision. This statement derived its philosophy from the Declaration of Principle in the federal *Young Offenders Act* and provided tactical guidelines for those planning for implementation, as well as for those who would be working in young offender programs. The Mission Statement was published and issued to the public and interested private groups. It has been revised several times and was most recently reissued in September 1987 with the title, *Towards the community: A statement of purpose, programs and services for young offenders* (Alberta, Department of the Solicitor General, 1987).

IMPLEMENTATION OF THE YOUNG OFFENDERS ACT IN ALBERTA

Because of the work done in the planning phase, the Department of the Solicitor General was ready for implementation of the *YOA*, at least as ready as an organization can be for the introduction of a major piece of legislation that would fundamentally change the way in which Canadian society dealt with delinquent youth. Several important features were already in place in the department, and these facilitated the implementation. These included a diversified network of community corrections district offices in over 50 locations across the province. Probation officers in these locations were accustomed to working within the guidelines established by provincial policies, which ensured that key aspects of the work were done consistently and to a high standard across the province. This was especially important with respect to report writing (predisposition reports), supervision standards and casework planning.

This existing staff and office network, in addition to some community staff transferred from the Department of Social Services, was used to carry out the community program mandate under the *YOA*. In rural areas, probation officers commonly carried a mixed caseload of adult and young offenders, while in the larger centres of Calgary, Edmonton, Red Deer and Lethbridge, a degree of specialization was made possible by young offender caseload concentrations. In February 1984, specialized young offender offices were created in Calgary and Edmonton.

The idea of using the existing organizational structure during the months following proclamation was also carried through at the more senior levels of the bureaucracy. Although a Provincial Director, Young Offender Program position was created together with a small head office complement, this position did not have line authority over community or centre operations. The Provincial Director position was used for the first two and one-half years to develop policies, procedures and innovative programs. Line authority flowed from senior Regional Directors who oversaw community and centre operations for both adult and young offenders. This reliance on the existing organizational structure served the program well during the early implementation phases. It was not altered until November 1986, when a separate Young Offender Branch with its own Executive Director was created. The new Branch has operational and policy responsibility for all young offender operations in the province. This evolution acknowledged that young offender programming and operations must not only appear to be distinct from adult corrections but in fact must be distinct.

There was some early concern expressed by related professional groups that the Department of the Solicitor General might not have the proper orientation or expertise to deal with young persons. Part of this concern was expressed as a fear that the department would place too much emphasis on custodial options at the expense of treatment and community programs. In fact, the department had a long history of developing non-custodial programs for adult offenders. Considering also that it took over many of the staff, contracts and programs from the Department of Social Services and had, as previously noted, lengthy experience in dealing with the older young offender group, the Department of the Solicitor General was in a good organizational position to assume responsibility for young offenders.

The first year of implementation (April 1, 1984–March 31, 1985) went relatively smoothly, a situation made easier by the comparatively low number of young offenders in the 12- to 15-year-old age group. The increased demand on facilities, procedures and staff came in April 1985 when the 16- and 17-year-olds were introduced to the system. The number of young offenders in custody in Alberta jumped from approximately 240 in April 1985 to a high of about 520 in May 1986 (Alberta, Department of the Solicitor General, 1985–1988). The numbers in custody increased significantly every month for over a year once all age groups were included in the system, and only began to level out in October 1987. The custody system is now relatively stable with an average daily population of 106 in temporary detention (remand), 128 in secure custody and about 240 in open custody. The system is now well equipped for dealing with these numbers on a routine basis, but the rate of increase after April 1985 created a severe demand on available resources, resulting in occasional overcrowding in the larger centres during part of 1986.

The older, bigger young offenders also taxed the physical security of the temporary or converted young offender centres. There were challenges to staff from the larger young offenders until staff learned that their routine child care skills were equally applicable to this older group. Two of the converted centres—Bow River Young Offender Centre in Calgary (formerly a minimum security adult facility) and Edmonton Youth Development Centre (a former child welfare institution)—underwent further security enhancements during 1986 in order to provide adequate physical security for the 16- and 17-year-olds.

In time for proclamation, the department was able to have a wide range of custody facilities in place to accommodate the temporary detention and secure and open custody populations. The objective was to establish resources of each type in as many locations as was practical and affordable, so that young offenders could be placed as near their home community as possible. This resulted in some sharing of facilities with the Department of Social Services, since neither department had sufficient demand under its mandate—child welfare or young offender—to justify the provision of separate facilities in all areas of the province. This arrangement applied in particular to temporary detention beds in smaller towns or cities such as Fort McMurray, Lac La Biche and Red Deer and to shared group homes in a variety of locations. Experience has now shown that the child welfare and young offender populations do not easily mix under the same roof because of the different mandates and policies of the two departments as well as the different needs of the children involved. Most of the shared-use agreements have now been cancelled but they served a purpose during the early years of implementation by giving the Department of the Solicitor General time to establish its own resources.

A broad range of custody facilities is provided. Examples include: multi-purpose institutions such as the 150-bed Edmonton Youth Development Centre; the 64-bed open custody Strathmore Youth Development Centre, numerous group homes ranging in size from six to twelve beds; custody homes (contracted private homes accommodating one or two offenders each in a family setting); forestry and wilderness adventure camps; and treatment beds. Virtually all facilities provide accommodation for both male and female young offenders. As of September 1987, the department had over 600 beds in the three categories of temporary detention, secure custody and open custody.

The Edmonton and Calgary Young Offender Centres will commence operations in 1988. These are the first facilities in Canada designed and built specifically for use by young offenders. Residents will be accommodated in small 16-bed living units in a combination of mostly single and some double bed rooms. Each facility will incorporate ample room for educational, vocational, recreational, medical and other programs. Although both Centres will have built-in security features, these will be mostly non-obtrusive in favour of a well-lit, spacious and comfortable living environment.

The department established the private custody home program in mid-1986 to complement its range of custody options. Custody homes are similar to foster homes insofar as a contract is signed with a set of private parents or a single parent to provide accommodation for one or two open custody young offenders. The home itself is designated by an Order in Council as a place of open custody. Operators are well screened, properly trained and then closely monitored by a probation officer during their term with the program. They receive a small *per diem* fee to cover the cost of caring for the young offenders. There are approximately 30 custody home beds in the province.

Another focus has been the development of treatment oriented beds for the special needs or mental health population. The Alberta Hospital in Edmonton opened its Turning Point program, a 19-bed forensic unit for young offenders, in the summer of 1986. It provides mental health assessments for use in court and also a treatment program for the custody population. Additionally, an eight-bed mental health group home was established in Edmonton in 1985 and the department has contracts for custody beds with two major treatment providers in Calgary.

This range of custody resources is necessary in spite of the principle of the least restrictive level of intervention in the *YOA*. There is a need to provide custody services for young offenders who commit serious offences, are repeat offenders or who pose a danger to society. Nevertheless, the department believes that young offenders usually are best dealt with in community settings with the least level of intervention consistent with the needs of the young person and the safety of society. Most young offenders can benefit from community programs such as Alternative Measures, Pre-Trial Supervision, Probation and Community Service. For those in custody, the least restrictive type of facility should be used unless the offender's behaviour poses a serious risk to the community. There is little evidence to suggest that institutionally-based care is effective or more effective than community programs in dealing with the problems of young offenders. At best, a short stay in an institution for the more serious young offenders is the first step in a progressive reintegration process.

CURRENT OPERATIONS

The Department of the Solicitor General's involvement with young offenders often begins at the pre-sentence stage when its staff are asked to prepare predisposition reports to assist the court in determining the most suitable disposition. Predisposition reports provide a thorough,

well researched social history of the young offender, cover
tails as his or her family upbringing, experiences in school, p.
involvement, the results of any psychological testing conduct
formation about the young person's past or present involven
other social service agencies. This information forms the basis c   ..s-
sessment used to compile the case plan for work with the young person,
should he or she be sentenced to custody, placed on probation or ordered
to complete community service work. The objective is to establish individualized goals for young offenders—goals that they have helped establish and that address their own particular behavioural and developmental
problems.

For those sentenced to a period of open or secure custody, the report is
used by a probation officer in discussing with the provincial placement
authority a suitable placement for the young person. Every effort is made
to place the young person in a facility close to his or her home, provided
such a facility has the right type of security and programs to meet the
needs of the young person. The objective is to work with those in custody
and progressively move them from more secure to less secure settings
and, as soon as possible, from custody to probation. This is done by having the original disposition reviewed in court and demonstrating that
progress towards attaining case goals has been made.

DEVELOPMENTAL ISSUES

One of the biggest challenges for staff involved with implementing the
YOA was learning how to administer the complex and interrelated sections of the legislation. The Act introduced a number of concepts that were
new to those experienced in dealing with the adult and juvenile criminal
justice systems. Items such as treatment orders, review applications, alternative measures, different levels of custody and progress reports were
but a few of the challenging and innovative aspects of the new Act.
Although the Act resolved many of the problems associated with the
Juvenile Delinquents Act (1970), it stopped well short of having young
offenders treated in the same way as adults in the criminal justice system.
For example, young offenders given a custody disposition, unlike their
adult counterparts, are not eligible for earned remission, parole or any
form of extended temporary release from custody. Any alteration to the
intended impact of the disposition is clearly a judicial function under
sections 28 and 29 of the YOA. Any adjustment to the original disposition
must be made by the youth court upon application for review by the Provincial Director or other designated party.

These features were new challenges for the police, crown, defence
counsel, judiciary and correctional authorities. Although efforts were

made to coordinate responses, there were many occasions when one part of the criminal justice system had to wait for another part to come to terms with its mandate with respect to one of the new features. Review applications are one example of a feature that has at times brought the mandate of each part of the system into conflict.

The Department of the Solicitor General has taken the position that the provisions of the temporary release and review sections of the *YOA* are appropriate instruments to use in properly managing the young offender population. The department believes that it has the obligation and right to take a case back before the courts for a review as soon as the young person has demonstrated that he or she meets one of the conditions for review in the *YOA*. Although the review provisions are technically complex, involving considerable paperwork, notice and scheduling demands, the department has brought forward a high number of reviews each month. The emphasis has been on generating reviews to move a young person from either open or secure custody to probation. An average of 30 to 35 such applications are initiated every month. Many of these review applications have been submitted prior to the 6-month point of a custody disposition such that leave of the youth court is required in order for the application to proceed.

The department also briefly used extended or back-to-back 15-day temporary releases for a 6-month period during 1986. It was felt that young persons in custody were inadvertently being treated more onerously than their adult counterparts. In other words, because young offenders were not eligible for parole, earned remission or extended temporary absences, and instead had to rely on the review provisions of the legislation, they were spending longer periods of time in custody than were adults. In mid-1986, review applications were cumbersome to process and few in number. Consequently, back-to-back or extended temporary releases were introduced as a method to manage the custody population and meet the objectives of the department. The program proved that a large number of young offenders could be safely released under strict supervision with an excellent chance of completing their custody disposition in the community. In September 1986, the Department of the Solicitor General requested a formal legal opinion on the practice of granting these renewable temporary releases and were subsequently advised to discontinue the program. The department now depends solely on the review process as a means to meet program objectives and carry out its mandate.

The province-wide alternative measures program for first offenders is now being reviewed by the Department of the Solicitor General and Attorney General to determine whether it is being consistently applied and meeting its objectives. The program is jointly administered by the Departments of the Solicitor General and Attorney General. The program is open to first-time offenders who commit one of a number of relatively minor offences. The investigating police agency makes a program recommendation but a decision for formal referral to the program is made by the local Crown prosecutor. The young person is then referred to a probation officer or contracted agency to develop an alternative measures agreement. The agreement involves such elements as an apology to the victim, community or personal service work, restitution and sometimes an orientation tour of an adult correctional facility.

Initial research into the program shows that a high proportion of offenders are female and most offences are shoplifting. Males, especially native male offenders, are under-represented. The program review will focus on reasons for the low rate of participation by native young persons and recommend ways to increase their participation.

Another major focus for the department has been the development of specialized custodial and community-based programs for native young offenders. Internal studies have indicated that native young offenders consistently comprise between 35 and 40% of the custody population, and approximately 20% of the community corrections caseload (probation, community service and fine option). Native young persons comprise less than 5% of the general population of young people in Alberta, so it is obvious that they are significantly over-represented in the young offender system. Further, they are especially over-represented in the custody population.

The department recognizes that there is a strong aspiration on the part of native people and communities to take care of, and be responsible for, their own young people. This aspiration is consistent with two of the fundamental principles stated in section 3 of the YOA, which recognize parental responsibility and, to the greatest extent possible, that young persons should be dealt with in their community and family environment. The department is therefore committed to ensuring that programs and services are appropriate to native young offenders; that policies, guidelines and standards reflect the native young offenders' unique familial, cultural, social and spiritual heritage; that cross-cultural staff training is provided; and that native staff and agencies are recruited to deliver programs in native communities.

The department is now working to establish a range of custody facilities that provide specialized programming for natives. Additionally, it is developing community programs that provide a sentencing alternative for use by the youth court. The presence of effective community alternatives may help lower the number of native young offenders in custody. The department works closely with the well established Native Counselling Services Association of Alberta (NCSA) in developing its programs for native young offenders. The department has contracted with NCSA to operate a province-wide native youth court worker program modelled after its successful similar program for adult offenders; two specialized open custody native group homes located in Edmonton and Slave Lake; supervision of native young offender probationers in Edmonton, Grande Prairie, Gleichen, Wetaskiwin and High Level; and the operation of a pilot attendance centre (day supervision program) on the Assumption Reserve near High Level. The latter initiative represents the first of what is hoped will be a series of attendance centres in isolated locations in northern Alberta to provide effective community alternatives for the youth court. The pilot program in Assumption involves the establishment of a youth services centre on the Reserve staffed by local native persons under contract to NCSA. The youth services centre offers a variety of life skills programs, camping activities, community service work and alcohol and drug abuse counselling. Participants attend as a condition of probation or other community disposition. Negotiations are now underway with other government departments to expand the mandate of these youth services centres beyond young offenders to other high-risk native youth.

Another tentative plan involves the establishment of a special native-operated and native-oriented custody centre. The proposed centre would be located in northern Alberta and would provide both a residential and day school for native youth. Approximately half the population would be young offenders in open custody and the rest would consist of high risk native youth referred by Child Welfare, parents or nearby bands. One objective in mixing the two populations would be to allow young offenders, if they so choose, to continue their education after their custody disposition has expired. Efforts are also underway to develop a formalized native elders visitation program at young offender centres.

Another issue is the need to develop casework protocols with the Department of Social Services to ensure good case planning whenever a young person has both a child welfare and young offender status. Internal reviews have shown that approximately 21% of the custody population currently has a child welfare status. Senior officials from both departments are working to develop policies and protocols to guide the casework of their respective staffs. Although field staff in the two departments have already established effective working relationships, there is a need to review and formalize the practices that have evolved thus far to deal with joint cases.

CONCLUSION

The Department of the Solicitor General relied on an extensive planning exercise to facilitate the implementation process. Although the first few years following proclamation were challenging, the problems were neither unexpected nor insurmountable. All departments and agencies that were directly or indirectly involved—Attorney General, Social Services, Hospitals and Medical Care, Community and Occupational Health, Alberta Alcohol and Drug Abuse Commission and Solicitor General—worked closely together to implement the provisions as well as the spirit of this major new legislation. The Declaration of Principle in section 3 of the *YOA* has served as a beacon to guide everything from the design of new facilities and programs to the development of policies and funding priorities. Although the interpretation of the Declaration of Principle and its connection to specific sections in the Act can be subject to debate, it nevertheless has served well as a general guideline. By constantly keeping it in mind, Alberta will continue to develop innovative, effective programs to meet the challenge of youth crime.

REFERENCES

Alberta, Department of the Solicitor General. (1985, 1986, 1987, 1988). *Alberta correctional services management information summary*. Edmonton: Department of the Solicitor General, Correctional Services Division.

Alberta, Department of the Solicitor General. (1987). *Towards the community: A statement of purpose, programs and services for young offenders*. Edmonton: Department of the Solicitor General, Correctional Services Division.

LEGISLATION

Alberta Regulations 101/85.
Child Welfare Act, Revised Statutes of Alberta 1980, c. C–8.
Young Offenders Act, Statutes of Canada 1980–81–82–83, c.110.
Juvenile Delinquents Act, Revised Statutes of Canada 1970, c. J–3.

CHAPTER 5

IMPLEMENTING THE YOUNG OFFENDERS ACT IN ONTARIO
CRITICAL ISSUES AND CHALLENGES FOR THE FUTURE

Alan W. Leschied and Peter G. Jaffe

This chapter will address issues arising out of Ontario's experience in implementing the *Young Offenders Act* (1982). Contentious issues related to accusations that Ontario has only minimally ascribed to the spirit of the *Young Offenders Act* (*YOA*) will be presented and reviewed, reflecting the impact of *YOA* policy on juvenile justice practice.

THE LEGACY OF THE JUVENILE DELINQUENTS ACT

Within the spirit of the *Juvenile Delinquents Act* (1970), judges were allowed considerable discretionary power in responding to juveniles in conflict. The court had access to child welfare and children's mental health services and to the correctional system. Dispositions did not necessarily have to fit the *crime* as much as they had to fit the *need* of the young person. Under the legislation, 7-year-old law breakers could be brought into the justice system not as criminals but rather as children in need of the court's guidance and direction. Similarly, truant youths or sexually promiscuous females could suffer the same judgment as youths convicted of a property offence or, indeed, murder. For example, it was possible for a truant 14-year-old to find himself sharing a room at training school with an adolescent convicted of serious assault if, in the view of the court, the needs of the two youths were similar.

Such potential abuses of power and skepticism concerning the positive effects that might accrue from such a system led many to question the relevance and utility of the *JDA*. Leon (1977) suggests that the Ontario juvenile justice system was simply not working, a popular opinion that began to emerge in Ontario in the early 1970s. Data suggested that Ontario's training schools could do no better than keep 25% of their wards out of further legal difficulty (Birkenmeyer & Polonski, 1976). Further, there was a growing concern that placing status offenders—offenders, who if they were of adult age, would not have been charged, i.e. for offences such as truancy and sexual promiscuity—alongside more serious offenders may have a negative effect by promoting delinquency among the status offenders.

Aside from questionable effectiveness of the *JDA*, issues had also arisen regarding abuses of young persons' rights within a *parens patriae* social welfare court. Bala (1986, p. 241) captures this concern in the following summary:

> Juveniles were often detained prior to trial in circumstances where adults would be released on bail, often on the pretext that a youth might benefit from a "short, sharp shock," or because it was felt that adequate care would not otherwise be available. Sometimes fundamental legal rights, like the right of appeal or the right of access to counsel, were effectively denied.

The frequency of rights abuses under the *JDA* has not been established. Whether the issue was the extent of actual abuse or the potential for abuse, reformers sought to codify the right of access to counsel and right to appeal for young people.

Provincial legislative amendments in Ontario, to address some of these concerns, began to take effect in the mid- to late 1970s. For example, the validity of section 8 of the Ontario *Training Schools Act* (1975) was repealed in 1975; as a result, status offenders could no longer be placed in training schools (Grant, 1984). Coincidentally, by 1977 the Ontario Ministry of Community and Social Services combined all children's services within one governmental branch, the Children's Services Division (CSD), which consolidated programs affecting children. The aim of this reorganization was to rationalize children's services at a policy level and, at the community level, to provide the impetus for coordination of services reflected in such things as the establishment of local children's services coordinating committees.

Two initiatives that grew out of the Children's Services Division were specific to young offenders. The first related to a goal of deinstitutionalization and was reflected in the establishment of community-based intervention programs. As a result of such programs, the number of training schools in Ontario was reduced from 13 to seven from 1970 to 1980; the average number of beds per facility declined from 115.2 to 74.4 in the same time period (Ministry of Community and Social Services, 1983).

The second initiative for young offenders that grew out of the CSD was in the area of detention. Beginning in 1977, the province produced a series of discussion papers on detention (Ministry of Community and Social Services, 1977a; 1977b; 1978). These discussions prompted a move to provide temporary detention services to the court within a range of four security levels: secure; semi-secure; open; and home detention. Recommendations were made in reaction to a concern that too many youths were being housed in detention and to the perception that youths who required temporary housing while before the court could be accommodated in something less than a secure facility. This policy was also in anticipation of judicial decisions which invoked application of the *Bail Act* (1980) with juveniles. Based on these reforms and in accordance with *YOA* requirements, the current practice for young offenders in Ontario requires that youths for whom the court may consider detention have a hearing to consider release on bail. For youths who are committed to detention, a provincial director may consider whether the youth meets the requirements under Ontario's *Child and Family Services Act* (1984) for placement in a secure detention facility.

The decision to order secure or open detention is based on section 89(2) of the *Child and Family Services Act*, which indicates that secure detention may be applied if:

...the young person is charged with an offence for which an adult would be liable to imprisonment for five years or more and,

(a) the offence includes causing or attempting to cause serious bodily harm to another person;

(b) the young person has, at any time, failed to appear in court when required to do so under the [*Young Offenders Act*] or the *Juvenile Delinquents Act* (Canada) or escaped or attempted to escape from lawful detention; or

(c) the young person has, within the twelve months immediately preceding the offence on which the current charge is based, been convicted of an offence for which an adult would be liable to imprisonment for five years or more...

Prior to ordering secure custody, the Provincial Director (as designated under section 24(2) of the *YOA*) must also be satisfied that it is necessary to detain the young person in a place of secure temporary detention, to ensure the young person's attendance in court and to protect the public interest or safety.

Some observers of Ontario's juvenile justice system have suggested that the ills that the *Young Offenders Act* were to redress had in fact already been rectified by provincial legislation and practice during the decade leading to the proclamation of the *YOA*. It has also been suggested by some outside Ontario that the policies of the *YOA* actually over-corrected past excesses and may have created more problems than they solved (Hackler, 1986). Whatever conclusion is arrived at, all sides would agree that the *YOA* rhetoric has been "hot" and the issues have been actively debated.

In summary, it is suggested that Ontario's initiatives with Children's Services, and especially with young offenders, during the 1970s and 1980s, anticipated some of the children's rights and deinstitutionalization initiatives of the *YOA*.

IMPLEMENTING THE YOA IN ONTARIO:
RELUCTANCE AND DEL.' (S

Three specific areas of contention in the province in implementing the *YOA* were: the minimum age for accountability, the maximum age for accountability, and implementation of the alternative measures section.

Minimum Age of Accountability

The *YOA* raised the age of criminality from seven to 12 years of age. This rested on the belief that the youth court should serve as a criminal court, not as a means of addressing the social welfare needs of children who broke the law. With the injunction of the youth court as a criminal court, Dalby (1985) and others questioned whether children under 12 years of age could developmentally meet the requirements of appreciating the nature and intent of their behaviour. Furthermore, our data show that children under 12 years were not being well serviced by the *JDA*, insofar as the measures provided by the *JDA* did not prevent further difficulty (Leschied & Wilson, 1988). Lowry (1983) has suggested that raising the age of criminality from seven to 12 years was a "vote of confidence" for children's aid societies. It de-criminalized behaviour problems for this age group and placed responsibility for resolving such problems with the child, family and social welfare system.

Chief among dissenters of this policy were Ontario's police forces, which argued that considerable anti-social behaviour was being practiced by children under 12. Indeed, representatives of the Toronto Police Force argued for a mechanism to bring children under 12 to court. Such a measure would be analogous to section 16 of the *YOA*, which allows for transfer of young offenders to adult court (Metro Children's Advisory Group, 1985). Apart from the police, there appears to be little support in Ontario for changes to the minimum age policy.

Maximum Age of Accountability

Prior to the *YOA* the provinces had failed to agree on the age at which adolescence ended and adulthood began. Ontario limited access to family court to young offenders under the age of 16 years. Increasing the age of jurisdiction for the young offender system to 17 years inclusive was not warmly received in Ontario, where it was believed that 16- and 17-year-olds could not be dealt with in the same system as 12-year-olds. Also, the province felt that the cost of providing the necessary court and dispositional services would be prohibitive. As a result, Ontario was granted a 1-year "grace" period in implementing the increased age provision. Furthermore, Ontario continues to service older youths within a different ministry; a system referred to as "split jurisdiction." This method of implementing the increased age provision has been extremely controversial.

Since the enactment of the *YOA*, Ontario has perpetuated the two-tiered system, or split jurisdiction, in dealing with young offenders. This response by Ontario to the *YOA* has been one of the most controversial and has emerged not as a well conceived long-term plan but, rather, as a neglectful plan based on minimal compliance with the spirit of the *YOA*. Two government ministries, The Ministry of Community and Social Services (COMSOC) and the Ministry of Corrections, administer respectively tier one (12- to 15-year-old young offenders) and tier two (16- and 17-year-old young offenders) within their existing mandates. Although external debate has suggested that one ministry should take full responsibility for the *YOA* to ensure a co-ordinated and consistent approach to young offenders, the Ontario cabinet has decided not to organize in this way.

The two ministries are very different in terms of their mandates and responsibilities. COMSOC funds a range of children's services, including daycare, children's aid societies, children's mental health centres and juvenile correctional facilities. The Ministry of Corrections, for the most part, is responsible for all offenders serving two years less a day in provincial jails and for community programs operated through probation offices. Many of the correctional resources are available only after incarceration.

The result of split jurisdiction is that 15- and 16-year-old young offenders with the same charge and same needs may be treated very differently, because each has access to a different court (Provincial Court—Family Division or Criminal Division) and each comes under the authority of a different ministry. For example, compared to a 16- or 17-year-old young offender, a 12- to 15-year-old young offender is at least 10 times as likely to receive a medical/psychological predisposition assessment because of emotional or learning problems (Leschied & Jaffe, 1987).

This differential treatment based on age has seemed ripe for a clear, legal challenge ever since the two-tiered system was implemented on April 1, 1986, with full implementation of the *YOA* in Ontario. Only one challenge has resulted, however. This challenge cited section 15 of the *Canadian Charter of Rights and Freedoms* (1982), and argued discrimination on the basis of age, when co-accused 15- and 16-year-old youths appeared in different courts (*R. v. C.(R.)*, 1987). However, the Ontario Court of Appeal ruled in February 1987 that no meaningful basis of discrimination could be demonstrated in these circumstances. Although the two-tiered system was seen by the court as based on "unjustifiable political, monetary and administrative considerations," and "contrary to the spirit of the aim of the [*YOA*] of uniformity for young offenders across Canada," the court concluded that "Given the enormousness and complexity of demonstrating unevenness between separate court systems, the accused had a near-impossible burden" (R. v. C.(R.), 1987, p. 186).

Alternative Measures

Ontario has only recently implemented the alternative measures section of the YOA as a result of a Court of Appeal decision. The previous rejection of this section reflected primarily the Ontario Attorney General's belief that: (a) it is necessary to reduce anti-social behaviour by bringing the power of the court to bear in deterring crime; (b) the use of alternative measures may jeopardize the protection of a youth's civil rights by having them take part in programs following a finding of "guilt" without due process; and (c) alternative measures programs may "broaden the net" by including some young persons in programs and services, when they may be better "serviced" through non-intervention.

The alternative measures issue has a long history. Diversion from the formal juvenile system had been well recognized prior to the YOA being implemented in Ontario. For example, both Windsor and Kingston had programs diverting many first-time offenders into volunteer programs (Jaffe et al., 1986). There was broad acceptance of the concept because it was perceived to be cost efficient and to encourage community involvement in the problems of delinquent youth. However, in early 1984, the Attorney General of Ontario took a definite stand against the legality of diversion and any alternative measure. Alternative measures were deemed to compromise a young person's rights to a fair trial and the court's opportunity to decide on appropriate disposition. The fear was expressed that an "undercover" system of juvenile justice could develop without the protection afforded by the public scrutiny and accountability characteristic of the court system. Concern was also expressed that young persons could face double jeopardy because if they accepted a diversion program but did not comply fully with it, then they could face the original charge again.

Three years after the YOA became law, Ontario still refused to develop alternative measures. However, changes have recently occurred, partly as a result of court decisions that did not support the Attorney General's position. Two recent youth court decisions found youth not guilty of particular offences as a result of Ontario's failure to provide alternative measures [R. v. Sheldon S. (1986); R. v. Brian P. (1987)]. In passing judgment, the judges in both instances noted that the accused had experienced rights violations by virtue of residing in a province that had not authorized alternative measures pursuant to Section 4(1)(a) of the YOA. The judge in one case stated that subsections 3(1)(d) and (f) required the province to authorize some program of alternative measures (R. v. Brian P.,

1987). Since the Attorney General did not authorize the development of these programs, the young person missed an opportunity available to young offenders in eight other provinces.

IMPACT OF YOA POLICY ON PRACTICE

Until April 2, 1984, when the YOA was first implemented in Ontario, many of the debates between the federal government and Ontario centered on hypothetical issues. How were the citizens of the province to be protected from the crimes of youth? How would the YOA actually affect youth? How much would the Act cost to implement properly? Many of the debates defied simple answers and did not allow for meaningful closure. While the debates have continued, some clear trends have emerged. The trends are apparent by comparing the family court system under the JDA to the youth court under the YOA.

Principles of the YOA emphasize young persons being held accountable for their actions and the right of society to be protected. Therefore one could hypothesize that dispositions (sentences) may be more severe under the YOA than under the JDA. As well, the YOA (section 3(1)(c)) states that young offenders "...require supervision, discipline and control but, because of their state of dependency and level of development and maturity, they also have special needs and require guidance and assistance." Therefore one could hypothesize that certain services would be utilized more under the YOA than under the JDA, because of the provisions made by the YOA to deal with special needs. (See, for example, sections 13 and 22, which deal with "Medical and Psychological Reports" and "Consent for Treatment Order" respectively.)

These hypotheses were tested by the authors. Data were collected from family courts (under the JDA) and youth courts (under the YOA); the sample was limited to young persons aged 12 to 15 years in southwestern Ontario. The area studied extends from Hamilton to Windsor and north to Owen Sound; approximately half the adolescents in the province live in southwestern Ontario. The court data are summarized in Table 1, which provides an overview of system data before and after the implementation of the YOA.

The data suggest that, under the YOA, youths are being held more responsible for their offences. Focusing on residential committals, for example, compare open and secure custody dispositions under the YOA (13.4% of all dispositions in 1986) to JDA committals to training school (5% in 1983). Additionally, special needs are not receiving increased attention under the YOA. The requests for psychological and psychiatric assessments have decreased by more than half from 11.8% in 1983 to 5.1%

TABLE 1
YOUNG OFFENDERS ACT DISPOSITIONS
IN SOUTHWESTERN ONTARIO[1]
12- TO 15-YEAR-OLDS
(April 1, 1986 to November 30, 1986)

Dispositions[2]	Number	%
Probation	1,964	46.5
Open Custody	339	8.0
Secure Custody	230	5.4
Community Services	679	16.1
Restitution	174	4.1
Compensation	34	.8
Fine	149	3.5
Absolute Discharge	570	13.5
Other Sentences	88	2.1
Total	**4,227**	

[1]Includes courts in Sarnia, London, Windsor, Chatham, Owen Sound, St. Thomas, Stratford, Woodstock, Goderich, Brantford, Orangeville, Cayuga, Milton, Simcoe, Kitchener, Guelph, Hamilton, Welland and Walkerton; based on data available from Courts Administration Division,Ontario Ministry of the Attorney General.

[2]Based on a total of 5,143 charges under the *Criminal Code* (Canada).

in 1986. Table 2 provides a further breakdown of *YOA* dispositions. Orders for treatment are notable by their absence.

Comparable data are not yet available from the Ministry of Correctional Services, which is responsible for 16- and 17-year-old young offenders. Comparing the fate of these offenders to pre-*YOA* times would require access to Adult Criminal Court records and an analysis of sentences for 16- and 17-year-old adults before April 1, 1985. Clinical experience and common sense suggest that the *YOA* exerted an even more dramatic effect on this population than on the 12- to 15-year-old young offenders. Before 1985, 16- and 17-year-olds were the youngest of the offenders seen by criminal court judges, and tended to receive relatively lenient sentences compared to older offenders, because they were seen to be first-time offenders who showed the greatest potential for change. After April 1, 1985, 16- and 17-year-old offenders comprised the upper range of the young offender population. Therefore, they have a greater likelihood of prior offences and failed prior dispositions, and hence may be seen as more likely to need custody. There is no evidence that an equal emphasis

TABLE 2
SOUTHWESTERN ONTARIO[1] COURT DISPOSITIONS
FOR 12- TO 15-YEAR-OLDS UNDER
THE JUVENILE DELINQUENTS ACT (1983)
AND YOUNG OFFENDERS ACT (1984/85)

	JDA (Apr. 1/83 – Nov. 30/83)	YOA		
		(Apr. 1/84 – Nov. 30/84)	(Apr. 1/85 – Nov. 30/85)	(Apr. 1/86 – Nov. 30/86)
Charges	3,944	3,989	3,404	5,143
Dispositions	2,750	2,585	3,178	4,227
Probation	1,178 (42.8%)	1,203 (46.5%)	1,196 (37.6%)	1,964 (46.5%)
Children's Aid Society	121 (4.4%)	–	–	–
Open Custody	–	149 (5.8%)	159 (5.0%)	339 (8.0%)
Training School /Secure Custody	138 (5.0%)	134 (5.2%)	106 (3.3%)	230 (5.4%)
Psychological Psychiatric Reports (S. 13)	325 (11.8%)	143 (5.5%)	146 (4.6%)	219 (5.2%)
Ratio of S. 13 Reports to S. 14 Reports[2]	1:1.2	1:3.8	1:3.8	1:3.4

[1]Includes courts in Sarnia, London, Windsor, Chatham, Owen Sound, St. Thomas, Stratford, Woodstock, Goderich, Brantford, Orangeville, Cayuga, Milton, Simcoe, Kitchener, Guelph, Hamilton, Welland and Walkerton; based on data available from Courts Administration Division, Ontario Ministry of the Attorney General.

[2]A medical, psychiatric or psychological report may be ordered under Section 13 of the YOA, while a social history report may be ordered under Section 14 of the YOA.

on rehabilitation, which recognizes adolescents' "state of dependency and level of development and maturity," has occurred.

CONSENT TO TREATMENT

Section 22 of the YOA requires a youth court judge to obtain the consent of a young offender before any order for medical and/or psychological treatment can be made. This section has sparked considerable controversy (Leschied & Hyatt, 1986). Under the JDA, a judge who found a young person to be in a "state of delinquency" could order the offender into a treatment centre as a term of probation. The JDA focus was the young person's needs rather than the offence. Critics of the JDA suggested that much of the "treatment" may have been well-intentioned but misguided in its length and intensity, and represented an infringement on the child's and family's rights to the least level of intrusion.

The present debate has polarized two viewpoints. At one extreme, supporting the present legislation, it has been argued that juvenile justice legislation is not mental health legislation. Young persons should not have to break the law in order to have access to the resources that they require in their community. Ordering treatment may be a futile exercise because it may not result in rehabilitation and it also infringes on a young person's right not to face a more severe intervention than an adult would if charged with a similar offence.

The other extreme suggests that many young persons who require counselling are unable to provide consent because of the very nature of their particular problems (Leschied & Jaffe, 1986). Focusing solely on the offence, without recognizing a young person's special needs may ignore an underlying principle of the YOA and simply turn the youth court into a mini criminal court. Juvenile justice was born out of a belief that young offenders could and should be rehabilitated. The Court was seen as having an opportunity to impact on the underlying social, emotional, education, and familial conditions that promote anti-social behaviour. The section 22 requirement that the youth's consent must be obtained for treatment to be provided is seen as anti-rehabilitative. Numerous legal safeguards exist to protect a youth from unnecessary or inappropriate treatment: (a) the production of a section 13 assessment outlining needs and available resources; (b) consent of the treatment resource; (c) legal counsel and cross-examination of the section 13 reports and its author; and (d) a youth court judge's final decision to order treatment based on an assessment, other evidence, and submissions by defence and crown counsel. The authors of section 22 seem to view child and adolescent resources as seeking clients to treat involuntarily; in reality this is unlikely, given that resources for the most troubled youth are limited.

Changes to section 22 seem inevitable. Even adolescents do not understand why they should be given the right to veto a counselling order that is part of a judge's reasoned decision (Jaffe, Leschied & Farthing, 1987). Ultimately, a compromise may evolve out of several factors: (a) a clearer definition of treatment with an explicit exclusion of extraordinary measures such as electro-convulsive therapy; (b) limiting treatment periods to comparable custody periods for the same offence; and (c) developing a more definite child welfare alternative through provincial legislation similar to Quebec's *Youth Protection Act* (1977).

TRUANCY

In response to the *YOA*, Ontario has had to develop provincial legislation to address areas that are no longer covered under the federal legislation. One issue that has been ignored for almost four years is truancy or habitual absence from school under the *Education Act* (1980). The *Education Act* clearly indicated that all *JDA* dispositions were available after a finding of guilt. Prior to the introduction of the *YOA*, several cases received notoriety through the media when truants were found to have been committed to training school. Both the Minister of Education and Minister of Community and Social Services expressed outrage that missing school could lead to incarceration, although the facts suggested these circumstances to be isolated and highly unusual. Additional fuel has fired this issue through a post-*YOA* court decision by Judge Steinberg (*R. v. L.*, 1985) who ruled that in the absence of replacement legislation for truancy, the statute that existed prior to the *YOA* can be applicable. Hence, some judges currently hear truancy cases under Judge Steinberg's decision, bringing *JDA* dispositional alternatives to bear. Other judges however, have ruled truancy to be *ultra vires* of the court and refuse to hear truancy cases in the absence of appropriate legislation.

Decriminalization of truancy has occurred without the development of an alternative. The needs of the extreme cases of truancy suggest some young persons require more radical intervention than what is presently offered (Leschied, 1986). The *Education Act* has not been amended to provide for the alternatives. Are truant children in need of educational services within the mandate of child welfare, mental health, and/or correctional resources? Non-compliance by truant youths with school authorities and alternative programs may suggest that more than a voluntary intervention is necessary. There seems to be a lack of any public outcry or professional consensus on this issue to wake the Ministry of Education out of its slumber, although some pressure is being applied by the provincial association of attendance counsellors, whose members are experiencing increasing frustration in serving this population.

SUMMARY

In Ontario, the YOA seems to have offered little relief from the complex and controversial problems of youth crime. Civil libertarians in Ontario have heralded the YOA as progressive legislation. Interventionists, however, have argued that law makers did not give adequate attention to the ultimate effect the law would have on youths, that it is legislation grounded in process, not outcome. Also, the belief that due process was already guaranteed and did not require a federally legislated mandate was pervasive in Ontario. Ontario officials would no doubt agree with Hackler (1986) that "the legislation [YOA] would have been more profitable had it been less detailed...[and] would have made better use of innovation that takes place at the local level."

Neither has the YOA been spared from the historical federal-provincial conflicts between Ottawa and Ontario. Ontario reluctantly implemented the Act but sought and received a 1-year delay in implementing the increased age provision. The alternative measures section has only recently been implemented in Ontario. The split-jurisdiction issue is used as further confirmation that the province is only in minimal compliance with the Act. Added to these concerns are findings suggesting that incarceration rates may have increased with the legislation (Leschied & Jaffe, 1987) and that concern regarding fairness in sentencing may still be an outstanding issue (Leschied & Thomas, 1988).

Four years after implementation, Ontario continues to wrestle with revisions to the juvenile justice system. This coincides with heightened concern about other issues pertinent to children, such as the implications of the high incidence of divorce, exposure to family violence and increased reports of sexual abuse. These issues are often factors in the early development of some young offenders. Expecting legislation to resolve these issues is, of course, foolhardy. However, what must be addressed is the extent to which legislation should facilitate intervention and the extent to which autonomy of the family and protection of civil rights should be legislation's central theme.

Ontario's reluctance towards supporting the YOA may be symptomatic of the divergent views on the role society should play in controlling the behaviour of individuals. Juvenile justice legislation may simply serve as a focus for debate. It should therefore come as no surprise that Ontario has given at best a lukewarm reception to the YOA. The province has tailored some of its laws to conform to the spirit of the YOA, but has also chosen to demonstrate its independence by rejecting some aspects of the law, citing uniqueness and progressiveness as its defence.

In other ways, Ontario shares with the rest of the country the dilemma of adjusting to new juvenile justice law. As in other parts of the country, there is the dilemma for the courts in disposing of cases where the concept of equitable justice may run contrary to the acknowledgement of children's "best interests." For example, in *R. v. Teresa C.* (1987), Judge Grant Campbell who, having committed a particular 13-year-old girl known to have been prostituting herself in Toronto to a 6-month secure custody placement for a rather minor offence, stated:

> ...I do not perceive that there is a separation between society's social concerns for [her] lifestyle and that of her criminal behaviour... Twelve and thirteen year-olds cannot be expected to use the experience of criminal court in as effective a manner as eighteen year-olds nor are they as aware of themselves and their potential and the realities of the streets of downtown Toronto.

In this particular case, the disposition was appealed and overturned at the District Court level by a judge who cited problems in the disproportionality of disposition in regards to the presenting offence.

Bill C–106 (1986) represents an attempt by the federal government to refine the initial law. No attempt has been made to fundamentally change the original Act. Concerns that the law is too narrow and restricts intervention have been countered by the argument that provincial child welfare and mental health legislation should be amended to be more enabling, and that the province should not look to federal law to provide direction in this area. Should this continue to be the case, Ontario may look to amending its provincial *Child and Family Services Act* to fill the gap. However, it seems that the latest round of amendments to the provincial *Child Welfare Act* were undertaken to be more in step with the federal government's leadership in civil rights and limited intervention. Quebec's model of countering the federal *YOA* with more liberalizing provincial child-related legislation may serve as a model to be more closely scrutinized and emulated. In contrast, only time and further debate will force Ontario to develop a clear and consistent response to the *YOA*. The ultimate hope lies in Ontario taking a more proactive response to these problems rather than awaiting further crises and higher court decisions.

REFERENCES

Bala, N.M.C. (1986). The *Young Offenders Act*: A new era in juvenile justice? In B. Landau (Ed.), *Children's rights in the practice of family law* (pp. 238–254). Toronto: Carswell.

Birkenmeyer, A.C., & Polonski, M. (1976). *Trends in training school admissions: 1967–1975*. Toronto: Ministry of Correctional Services.

Dalby, J.T. (1985). Criminal liability in children. *Canadian Journal of Criminology*, 27(2), 137–145.

Grant, I. (1984). The 'incorrigible' juvenile: History and prerequisites of reform in Ontario. *Canadian Journal of Family Law*, 4(3), 293–318.

Hackler, J. (1986). *The life and death of a new role in juvenile justice: A lesson for policy workers.* Paper presented to the American Society of Criminology, Atlanta.

Jaffe, P.G., Kroeker, B.J., Hyatt, C., Misceuick, M., Telford, A.G., Chandler, R., Shanahan, C., & Sokoloff, B. (1986). Diversion in the Canadian juvenile justice system: A tale of two cities. *Juvenile and Family Court Journal*, 37(1), 59–66.

Jaffe, P.G., Leschied, A.W., & Farthing, J.L. (1987). Youth's knowledge and attitudes about the *Young Offenders Act*: Does anyone care what they think? *Canadian Journal of Criminology*, 29(3), 309–316.

Leon, J.S. (1977). The development of Canadian juvenile justice: A background for reform. *Osgoode Hall Law Journal*, 15(1), 71–106.

Leschied, A.W. (1986). *The use of court for compulsory school attendance.* Unpublished manuscript.

Leschied, A.W., & Hyatt, C.W. (1986). Perspective: Section 22(1), consent to treatment under the *Young Offenders Act*. *Canadian Journal of Criminology*, 28(1), 69–78.

Leschied, A.W., & Jaffe, P.G. (1986). Implications of the consent to treatment section of the *Young Offenders Act*: A case study. *Canadian Psychology*, 27(3), 312–313.

Leschied, A.W., & Jaffe, P.G. (1987). Impact of the *Young Offenders Act* on court dispositions: A comparative analysis. *Canadian Journal of Criminology*, 29(4), 421–430.

Leschied, A.W., & Thomas, K.E. (1988). Reviewing the needs of youths committed to secure custody: Why it's necessary to recreate the wheel for Canada's juvenile justice policy makers. Manuscript submitted for publication.

Leschied A.W., & Wilson, S.K. (1988). Criminal liability of children under twelve: A problem for child welfare, juvenile justice, or both? *Canadian Journal of Criminology*, 30(1), 17–29.

Lowry, G. (1983). *Youth, opportunity, action.* Toronto: Central Toronto Youth Services.

Metro Children's Advisory Group (1985). *Kids not cons: A problem in search of a policy, children under twelve in conflict with the law.* Toronto.

Ministry of Community and Social Services (1977a). *Operational review, observation and detention homes: Where we are.* Toronto: Queen's Printer.

Ministry of Community and Social Services (1977b). *Operational review: A plan for observation and detention homes: Recommendations.* Toronto: Queen's Printer.

Ministry of Community and Social Services (1978). *Operational review: A plan for observation and detention services for children in Ontario.* Toronto: Queen's Printer.

Ministry of Community and Social Services (1983). *Three decades of change: The revolution of residential care and community alternatives in children's services.* Toronto: Queen's Printer.

LEGISLATION

An Act to Amend the Young Offenders Act, the Criminal Code, the Penitentiary Act and the Prisons and Reformatories Act (Bill C–106), Statutes of Canada 1984–85–86, c. 32.

Bail Act, Revised Statutes of Ontario 1980, c. 36.

Canadian Charter of Rights and Freedoms, Part I of the *Constitution Act, 1982*, being Schedule B of the *Canada Act 1982* (U.K.), 1982, c. 11.

Child and Family Services Act, Statutes of Ontario 1984, c. 55.

Child Welfare Act, Revised Statutes of Ontario 1980, c. 66.

Criminal Code, Revised Statutes of Canada 1970, c. C–34.

Education Act, Revised Statutes of Ontario 1980, c. 129.

Juvenile Delinquents Act, Revised Statutes of Canada 1970, c. J–3.

Training Schools Act, Statutes of Ontario 1975, c. 21.

Young Offenders Act, Statutes of Canada 1980–81–82–83, c. 110.

Youth Protection Act, Statutes of Quebec 1977, c. 20.

CASES

R. v. C.(R.) (1987), 56 *Criminal Reports* (3d), 185 (Ont. S.C.).

R. v. Teresa C. (1987). Judgement unreported (Ont. Prov. Ct Fam. Div.), Campbell, G.

R. v. L. (1985), *Young Offenders Service*, 6686 (Ont. Unif. Fam. Ct), Steinberg J.

R. v. Brian P. (1987), 2 *Weekly Criminal Bulletin* (2d), 121 (Ont. Prov. Ct Fam. Div.).

R. v. Sheldon S. (1986), 17 *Weekly Criminal Bulletin*, 399 (Ont. Prov. Ct), Bean, J.

CHAPTER 6

THE QUEBEC PERSPECTIVE ON THE YOUNG OFFENDERS ACT
IMPLEMENTATION BEFORE ADOPTION

Marc LeBlanc and Hélene Beaumont[1]

In Canada, the Province of Quebec has always been somewhat regarded as an "enfant terrible." Regardless of the political or social question involved, Quebec either leads or refuses to follow the other provinces. This holds true for legislation on juvenile delinquents, notably for the most recent related act, the *Young Offenders Act* (1982). Most *Young Offenders Act* (*YOA*) regulations were implemented in Quebec before the law was adopted by the federal government. Some of the various legislative and administration events that preceded or accompanied introduction of the *YOA* in Quebec can be identified before turning to Quebec's experience with implementing the *YOA*.

BACKGROUND

The federal *Juvenile Delinquents Act* (*JDA*) was passed in 1908 and only slightly modified in 1929; it remained more or less unchanged until 1982, despite attempted reform in 1970 with Bill C–192. Even though Quebec did not pass its first youth protection act until 1951, it pushed ahead with radical changes over the next few years. A law for the protection of abused children was enacted in 1974 and in 1977, the *Youth Protection Act* (*YPA*) was passed.

The *YPA* represented a radical departure from the preceding philosophy of juvenile justice. A clear distinction was made between protection and delinquency; such distinction was lacking in the *JDA*. The *YPA* was introduced over two years, from 1977 to 1979, providing adequate time to inform and train those in the field, and transform organizations dealing with children.

As could be expected, this innovative law sparked acrimonious debate and differences of interpretation between legal and social authorities. In 1982, a special Parliamentary Commission was set up to investigate prob-

---

[1] The data in this chapter are derived from the National Study on the Functioning of the Juvenile Courts in Canada, research subsidized by the Department of the Solicitor General of Canada.

lems that had come to light under the *YPA*. The Commission's report (Charbonneau, 1982) suggested that specific changes be made to the *YPA* in light of the *YOA* that the federal government was in the process of finalizing. Thus, Quebec updated the definition and treatment of juvenile delinquency before the federal government clearly defined its legislative proposal. The nature of the changes introduced are outlined below.

FEATURES OF QUEBEC'S YOUTH PROTECTION ACT

With its new *YPA*, Quebec brought in changes that overlapped clauses in the *JDA*, touching on such areas as defining the court's mandate, limiting legal intervention, separating decisions from the execution of measures, and changing the role of the Crown Prosecutor. These regulations had significant impact on the functioning of the court. We shall examine the 1977 changes, as well as those introduced beginning in 1979, using data from the study on the functioning of the juvenile courts in Quebec (Marceau & LeBlanc, 1980; Marceau et al., 1982; LeBlanc & Beaumont, 1985a, b).

Juvenile Court

In Quebec, section 106 of the *Courts of Justice Act* (1964), was modified by section 140 of the *YPA* to specify that the jurisdiction of the juvenile court replace that of the social welfare court. The section stated that:

> The Youth Court is competent to take cognizance of:
> (a) cases of juvenile delinquents within the meaning of the *Juvenile Delinquents Act* (Revised Statutes of Canada, 1970, chapter J-3);
> (b) cases of adoption within the meaning of the *Adoption Act* (1969, chapter 64);
> (c) cases of offences against an act or a regulation of Quebec;
> (d) the other cases it is seized of under the *Youth Protection Act* (1977, chapter 20).

Before the *YOA* was implemented, the *JDA* and *YPA* applied in principle to all children under 18 years of age. The *YPA* defined "child" as "any person under the age of eighteen years," whereas according to the federal *JDA* when applied in Quebec, "child" meant "any boy or girl apparently or actually under the age of eighteen years."

The *YOA* adopted the same upper age limit as Quebec when it made 18 years the mandatory limit for all provinces. But it went on to set the new minimum age for criminal responsibility at 12, compared with seven years under the *JDA* and 14 years in Quebec's *YPA*. A survey of social and legal practitioners showed that most granted general approval to *YOA* regulations governing minimum and maximum ages (LeBlanc, 1984a, b, c, d).

Limiting Legal Intervention

During the 1960s, several diversion programs were begun in the United States. The diversion doctrine was widely publicized and hotly debated among Canadian specialists in juvenile delinquency and justice for minors during the 1970s. In Canada, Bill C–192 (1970) was formulated to replace the *JDA*; it proposed a diversion formula following referral to the courts. At the same time, Quebec's youth protection legislation was being scrutinized in the province. The diversion doctrine had an impact on Quebec's *YPA*, which sought to coordinate social and legal interventions according to the situation and needs of the young person, whether that young person was a child in need of protection or a delinquent. Recognizing that children had a number of rights, particularly the right to be kept in their natural environment insofar as possible, this Act pursued the objective of diversion, by limiting court intervention to cases where such intervention was absolutely necessary, and by promoting the use of "voluntary measures."

Consistent with these principles, the *YPA* proposed mechanisms for screening cases to be brought before the court. It stated that a child should only appear in court if: (a) his/her safety or development was considered to be compromised; (b) he/she was suspected by the "Directeur de la protection de la jeunesse" ("Youth Protection Director," or YPD) of an infraction of a law or regulation in effect in Quebec; and (c) the youth was at least 14 years old.

The YPD could not refer children under 14 years of age to court simply because they might have contravened a law or regulation in effect in Quebec. However, this provision of the *YPA* was contested in court. In 1981, a Supreme Court of Canada ruling declared *ultra vires* the provisions that prevented any person, in this case a victim, from bringing a matter of delinquency before the juvenile court when the YPD and the person appointed by the justice minister refused to take legal action (*The Attorney General of the Province of Quebec v. Lechasseur et al.*, 1981). However, the provincial law did provide parents and youth with limited access to the juvenile court if they did not agree with the decision of the YPD concerning the orientation of the child or the extension of voluntary detention.

The YPD could impose emergency measures even if the child or parents objected. In this case, the director would be required to refer the case to court as quickly as possible. The YPD could not invoke emergency measures for more than 24 hours without first obtaining a court order.

In the exceptional cases that did call for court intervention, the *YPA* attempted to ensure the best possible coordination of the various laws likely to apply, by specifying which provisions would actually be applicable according to the nature of the grounds for intervention. If a child were charged with breaking a law or regulation in effect in Quebec, the applicable provisions would vary depending on whether it was a law or a provincial statute, the latter also encompassing municipal by-laws. In the first case, the *JDA* applied; in the second case, the *Summary Convictions Act* (1964) applied providing it was not incompatible with the YPA. In protection cases the *YPA* applied, and the court was to be referred to "by the filing of a sworn declaration containing, if possible, the names of the child and his parents, their addresses, their ages and a summary of the facts justifying the intervention of the Court" (*Youth Protection Act*, 1977, section 75).

The *YPA* sought to restrict, as much as possible, application of the *JDA*. The federal law was invoked only where a child 14 years of age or older was charged with infraction of a law or federal statute in effect in Quebec and/or the YPD and the representative of the Justice Minister considered it inappropriate to close the file or to limit action to voluntary measures, or such measures did not receive the consent of the child or his parents. The other cases were dealt with under Quebec law, whether provisions adapted from the *Summary Convictions Act* (*SCA*) in the case of children 14 and over suspected of breaking a law or a provincial statute or municipal by-law, or the *YPA* in all other cases, including offences committed by children under 14 years of age.

These restrictions placed on the *JDA* were brought in as provided for in section 39 of the federal act, which stated that provisions of a provincial statute intended for the protection or benefit of children could be opted for in the case of a committed offence, except in the instance of an indictable offence under the *Criminal Code* (1970), and on condition that such action is in the best interest of the child.

By introducing alternative measures, the *YOA* recognized the principle of diversion and at the same time diminished the problems of coordination between the *YPA* and *YOA*. Alternative measures, like the voluntary measures in the *YPA*, could be proposed for an adolescent found guilty of an infraction of the Criminal Code or other federal statutes when the Attorney General ruled that there was sufficient proof. The *YOA* also reduced coordination problems between the federal and provincial acts by making only infractions of the Criminal Code and some other federal statutes punishable; this initiative endorsed Quebec's *YPA* option that clearly distinguished between protection and delinquency. Thus, the two main sources of friction between federal and provincial legislation were ironed out.

By 1982, there were few social and legal practitioners in the Province of Quebec who did not support the principle of limiting legal intervention (LeBlanc, 1984a, b, c, d). Four out of five practitioners agreed with the main conditions proposed in the *YOA* for applying alternative measures. These conditions were that: (a) the sufficiency of proof be established before negotiating such measures; (b) the adolescent not deny having committed the infraction in question; (c) the adolescent freely demonstrate his firm intention to collaborate; and (d) the adolescent declare his wish not to appear before the court. According to the Charbonneau Commission report (Charbonneau, 1982), practitioners supported and abided by these regulations.

Separating Decisions from the Execution of Measures

When a case came before the juvenile court by virtue of the *JDA*, the court could take one or more of the several courses of action set out, in rather general terms, in section 20 of the federal act. (Exceptional cases were referred to the ordinary criminal courts.) Under the *YPA*, the court could order various measures set out in the provincial law; some of these measures were rather general while others were more specific.

As for executing these measures, the Quebec law provided for the social affairs minister to assume the role of provincial secretary for the purposes of section 21 of the *JDA*. The minister could thus order that children who were committed under section 20 to a children's aid society, a superintendent, or an industrial school, were to be dealt with under provincial law. The *YPA* ensured that whenever the court ordered a measure concerning a minor (except a fine), the most appropriate resource was selected. It was also stated in section 92 that the court's decisions and rulings were to be carried out immediately and that "any person named therein must conform to the law without delay" (*Youth Protection Act*, 1977, section 93).

The court could revise or modify the measures adopted under the *JDA*, according to section 20 (3) (4) of this law. The *YPA* also stated that the YPD, the child's parents, or the child himself, if 14 years of age or over, could ask the court to revise its decision or order in light of new information. Court decisions and orders could also be appealed under the *JDA* but an appeal under the provincial law was not as exceptional as one under the old federal law.

The *YOA* confirmed the separation between decisions and the execution of measures. Juvenile court judges, sitting under the *YOA*, can order that an adolescent be placed under supervision and stipulate whether custody is to be open or closed. However, as had been the case with Quebec's *YPA* prior to 1982, it is up to the provincial director (or his representative) to specify the facility the youth is to be referred to, in accordance with the level of supervision ordered by the court. The *YOA* stipulates that a minor cannot be transferred from one level of custody to another without the court's authorization.

Furthermore, any supervision order is reexamined by the court one year from the date of the decision, at which time a progress report of the adolescent's behaviour is required. The report would also contain additional information on the background and the present situation of the child and his family; in this respect, the YOA is more precise than the YPA.

The principle of separating decisions and the execution of measures introduced in the YPA and confirmed by the YOA was far from universally accepted (LeBlanc, 1984a, b, c, d). The vast majority of social and legal practitioners agreed to the YOA requirement of submitting reports. Social practitioners, however, would have preferred a greater role in making the decision, while their legal counterparts would have liked to retain total control of that aspect of the process. Virtually all judges and prosecutors agreed that judges should decide whether supervision should be open or closed; less than half of those in social services were of the same opinion. However, neither social nor legal practitioners were overwhelmingly in favor of the provincial director deciding on the appropriate location for supervision.

Role of the Crown Prosecutor

Before the YPA came into effect, the deputy public prosecutor was requested by the police to begin legal proceedings. Office staff completed the complaints after checking the evidence and the relevant regulations, and sent the parents written notice by way of a copy of a hearing notice (see Marceau & LeBlanc, 1980; Trépanier & Gagnon, 1984). This department of the former Social Welfare Court of Montreal was dismantled after the YPA came into effect.

The YPA, with its goal of diversion, contained a mechanism designed to provide an initial analysis of all cases involving children in need of protection or children suspected of an offence. At this stage, agreement on the implementation of voluntary measures was strongly encouraged, and only those cases where court intervention appeared necessary continued in the system. Since all protection and delinquency cases were, in principle, to be first submitted to this screening process, the role formerly played by the deputy public prosecutor's office in screening cases was considerably reduced. The YPD had taken over this vital role.

The YPD played a major role in both screening cases to be submitted to the court and coordinating the use of resources. A YPD was to be named in each of the social service centres, as established in *An Act Respecting Health Services and Social Services* (1971), by the centres' administrative councils after they had consulted organizations working in the area. Thus, there was at least one YPD in each of the health and social service regions of the province. The YPD came under the authority of each centre's director-general. Under the YPA, the YPD had certain responsibilities that he could, in turn, delegate in writing, in whole or in part, to a person, establishment or organization recognized by Quebec. He was responsible primarily for defending rights, promoting interests, and improving the living conditions of minors. His responsibilities, as set out in section 33, were as follows:

- to analyze the situation of any child whose safety or development could be considered as compromised (as defined in section 38) or who was charged with committing an infraction of a law or regulation in effect in Quebec;
- to take emergency measures as required by the situation, provided such measures did not exceed 24 hours in duration, without a court order;
- to decide on the orientation of the child or to participate in this decision with a person appointed by the Minister of Justice;
- to take charge of any child whose safety or development was compromised or who was charged with committing an infraction of a law or regulation in effect in Quebec, and to propose and see to the application of voluntary measures, when the parents of a child over 14 years of age gave their consent;
- to see to the execution of measures ordered by the court.

Thus the police notified the YPD of all infractions. The YPD would analyze each case with the help of the person appointed by the justice minister, and decide on the possibility of applying alternative measures. If such measures did not seem appropriate, he filed a complaint with the court through the deputy public prosecutor's office. This diversion mechanism was harshly criticized for fundamental reasons and because of the practical problems investigated at length by the Charbonneau Commission (Charbonneau, 1982). On the one hand, it was argued that the mechanism failed to respect both the basic rights of the individual and principles of criminal law, such as the right to be considered innocent and the necessity to establish the sufficiency of proof. On the other hand, this mechanism gave rise to a large number of practical problems: occasionally a YPD would request that proceedings be started without sufficient proof, for a stipulated infraction, or he would apply alternative measures to adolescents who would later be found not guilty by the court.

In the face of such difficulties, the Charbonneau Commission reviewed the diversion mechanism (Charbonneau, 1982). The report proposed that the deputy public prosecutor receive all requests from the police to start proceedings and, after analyzing the sufficiency of proof, forward the most serious complaints to the court. For the remaining infractions, the minor would be referred to the YPD, who would then analyze the possibility of applying alternative measures. This mechanism has prevailed since the *YOA* came into effect.

Impact on the Functioning of the Court

With the 1973 introduction of Legal Aid to the juvenile courts and the implementation of the *YPA*, Quebec experienced a strengthening of juvenile court procedures. One of the practices introduced by the *YPA* and taken up in the *YOA* was the recognition of minors' rights and the rights and responsibilities of parents. A study of the Montreal court (LeBlanc & Beaumont, 1985a) found that minors were accompanied by a lawyer for almost all criminal infractions. In most cases, parents were informed of the arrest, detention, charging, indictment and appearance of their adolescent before the court. However, no more than half the parents were present at the hearings.

The survey of practitioners indicated that they accepted and supported legal representation for minors at all stages of the proceedings; they did not, however, accept that any adult should take the place of a lawyer if the adolescent did not have one (LeBlanc, 1984a, b, c, d). This opinion was shared by over 90% of all legal and social practitioners surveyed; it is interesting to note that only 65% of the police held this view. The study also revealed virtual unanimity on the question of notifying parents at the time of arrest and at the beginning of court procedures; again, however, the police were alone in seeing less need for such action.

In short, the *YPA* resulted in increased respect for minors' and parents' rights, even before the *YOA* came into effect. Moreover, in 1980 and 1981, the preparation of social and psychological evaluations (if necessary) was common practice. Preparation of these reports was also to be provided for by the *YOA*; although the reports were rarely mentioned in hearings, they were circulated among legal practitioners.

Marceau and LeBlanc (1980) and LeBlanc and Beaumont (1985a) found that three procedures were not explicitly practiced in Quebec before the *YOA* came into effect: (a) establishment of jurisdiction; (b) reading of the facts; and (c) registration of the plea. The *YOA* paid particular attention to these procedures. According to the 1985 study, justice was administered slowly but was seldom contested. Moreover, trials were rare and decisions, which generally followed few adjournments, were usually based on guilty pleas.

Detention was seldom imposed in Quebec, even before the *YOA* was brought in. The spirit of the *YOA* was already respected; detention was only used for serious offences committed by a chronic delinquent. As early as the beginning of the 1980s, the province of Quebec generally conducted legal proceedings according to the regulations that would later be required under the YOA.

IMPLEMENTATION OF THE YOUNG OFFENDERS ACT IN QUEBEC

In light of the changes described in the preceding section, it is clear that the introductory phase of the YOA was not as complicated as it might have been, since many transformations had already taken place. From the mid-1970s until the mid-1980s, Quebec experienced a flurry of activity in the form of bills, new legislation, implementation, studies, symposia, commissions of inquiry, and so on. This activity in the areas of youth protection and juvenile delinquency contained a strong planning component. The adoption of the YPA in 1977 allowed for a 2-year establishment period; its implementation was followed by a Parliamentary Commission of Inquiry (Charbonneau, 1982).

The first inter-departmental (Justice and Social Affairs) establishment commission, working from 1977 to 1979, performed two tasks: it informed the public about the YPA, trained practitioners whose task it would be to apply it, and coordinated the work of the various committees that were to put the law into operation. Later, the commission was transformed into a consultation committee (Table centrale de consultation et de concertation) that supervised the work of various committees. Representatives from the organizations involved in applying the YPA sat on each of the committees as well as on the central committee.

It was at one of the central committee meetings in December 1981 that the idea of establishing a Quebec commission for the implementation of the new federal Young Offenders Act first arose. The federal act was not adopted until July 7, 1982 and it was not until the following October that the central committee created a subcommittee responsible for submitting proposals for implementing the YOA in Quebec. In December 1982, the central committee suggested to the Deputy Ministers of Social Affairs and Justice that a Quebec commission should be established and given the responsibility of implementing the new federal law and eventual amendments to the provincial Youth Protection Act.

The commission began its work quickly in the fall of 1983, but was soon stopped because of uncertainty as to when the YOA would be introduced. It was not until the following spring that the commission resumed intensive work, the official announcement of the introduction of the YOA having been made, and amendments having been made to the YPA.

The commission's main achievements, according to its June 1985 report, were on three levels: it ensured general understanding of the legislative changes; allowed for relevant training of practitioners; and provided adequate and coherent information (Mission québécoise d'implantation, 1985). To ensure general understanding of the legislative changes, the commission supervised the production and distribution of the following documents: a general model of the functioning of the YOA; an overall presentation of the YOA principles; as well as an overall presentation of the YPA principles, with the accent on recent amendments to it; and a presentation of some of the central ideas behind the YPA.

To provide for relevant training of practitioners, the commission adapted for Quebec a video produced by the federal government on the judicial process of the YOA. It also produced and distributed two videos on social intervention in applying the YOA and collaborated in producing six brochures for training of social practitioners.

The commission prepared adequate and coherent information concerning the YOA and the YPA. Information was made available through radio messages, a video distributed to secondary schools, a pamphlet and poster available in locations frequented by young people, and four pamphlets aimed at young offenders already involved in the justice system. Leaflets and a television campaign were prepared for parents and the general public was reached through the newspapers and a public relations effort.

Upon submitting its June 1985 report, the commission noted that the following matters were still unresolved: (a) confidentiality of information, particularly the relationship between the YPA, YOA and the Act Respecting Access to Documents Held by Public Bodies and the Protection of Personal Information (1983); (b) community participation, especially the conditions for applying alternative measures by community organizations; and (c) application of the YPA and YOA in the native community.

The contribution of the Quebec YOA implementation commission was thus mainly one of providing information. It played no specific role with regard to youth services for two reasons. First, the services for minors under 18 years of age were generally sufficient and diversified, as a result of social service transformations of the 1960s and 1970s. Second, since there had been a whole series of modifications between 1979 and 1982 that fundamentally changed justice for minors, there was already a diversion mechanism in place, a distinction was made between open and closed supervision and the separation of court decisions and the execution of measures was commonplace.

CONCLUSION

The implementation of the YOA was not a difficult process in Quebec; it required very few changes. It was not necessary to change people's thinking because social and legal practitioners had already generally accepted the principles of decriminalization, diversion, due process, and deinstitutionalization. The new philosophy proposed in the YOA fit in well with the changing Quebec perspective. The new legislation contained no surprises, since it had been preceded by modifications to the YPA that closely reflected the regulations contained in the YOA.

There was no need for changed thinking and provincial legislation concerning minors easily fit with the YOA. Debate between legal and social interest groups was a thing of the past. From 1975 to 1982, the two groups had entered into lengthy discussions on limiting legal intervention and separating decisions from the execution of measures and a consensus had emerged from these discussions.

Also entering into the equation was the fact that the YOA had little effect on institutions and services. The functioning of the juvenile courts, following gradual changes, already conformed to the YOA regulations; judges had progressively seen their role evolve from that of a benevolent "father" to that of a moderator of legal debate. During the same period, services for juvenile delinquents had become diversified and more specialized, so that introduction of the YOA did not necessitate any abrupt reorganization.

In short, the Province of Quebec is atypical because it introduced the principles of a law before its adoption: essentially, the YOA was established in Quebec before the federal parliament adopted it. The regulations of the future law were thus enforced at the provincial level before they became official. This is surely a unique situation—one which only a federal system such as ours could allow. It is all the more anomalous when one realizes that while legislation usually follows changes in thinking, it seldom follows its own practical application.

REFERENCES

Charbonneau, J.P. (1982). *Rapport de la Commission Parlementaire Spéciale sur la protection de la jeunesse.* Québec: Assemblée Nationale du Québec.

LeBlanc, M. (1984a). La Loi sur les jeunes contrevenants et les intervenants du système de justice pour mineurs au Québec. *Annales de Vaucresson*, 21, 67–92.

LeBlanc, M. (1984b). L'opinion des juges, avocats de la défense et procureurs de la couronne sur le système de justice pour mineurs et la Loi sur les jeunes contrevenants. *Revue de d* 4(2), 591–624.

LeBlanc, M. (1984c) iers, la Loi sur les jeunes contrevenants et le système de justi Criminologie, 17(1), 91–116.

LeBlanc, M. (19 de relations humaines des CSS, la Loi sur les jeunes contrever système de justice pour mineurs. *Service Social*, 33(2–3), 323–356.

LeBlanc, M., & Beaumont, H. (1985a). *Description du fonctionnement du Tribunal de la jeunesse de Montréal entre mai 1981 et avril 1982*. Montréal: Consultation, evaluation et recherche sur l'inadaptation juvénile.

LeBlanc, M., & Beaumont, H. (1985b). *Description du fonctionnement de Tribunaux de la jeunesse en milieu rurbain entre mai 1981 et avril 1982*. Montréal: Consultation, evaluation et recherche sur l'inadaptation juvénile.

Marceau, B., & LeBlanc, M. (1980). *Description du Tribunal de la jeunesse de Montréal: Rapport final*. Montréal: Groupe de recherche sur l'inadaptation juvénile, Université de Montréal.

Marceau, B., LeBlanc, M., Lacombe, P., & Trudeau-LeBlanc, P. (1982). *La cueillette des données auprès des tribunaux de la jeunesse du Québec: rapport technique et annexes*. Montréal: Groupe de recherche sur l'inadaptation juvénile, Université de Montréal.

Mission québécoise d'implantation Loi sur les jeunes contrevenants, Loi sur la protection de la jeunesse (1985). *Rapport des activités de la mission québécoise d'implantation de la Loi sur les jeunes contrevenants et des amendements apportés à la Loi sur la protection de la jeunesse*. Québec: Table centrale de consultation et de concertation Loi sur la protection de la jeunesse.

Trépanier, J., & Gagnon, R. (1984). *La déjudiciarisation à la Cour du Bien-Être social de Montréal*. Montréal: École de criminologie, Université de Montréal.

LEGISLATION

Act Respecting Access to Documents Held by Public Bodies and the Protection of Personal Information, Statutes of Quebec 1982, c. 30, as am. *Public Service Act*, Statutes of Quebec 1983, c. 55, s. 34.

Adoption Act, Statutes of Quebec 1969, c. 64.

An Act Respecting Health Services and Social Services, Statutes of Quebec 1971, c. 48.

Bill C–192, *An Act Respecting Young Offenders and to Repeal the Juvenile Delinquents Act*, 3d Sess., 28th Parl., 1970–71–72.

Courts of Justice Act, Revised Statutes of Quebec 1964, c. 20.

Criminal Code, Revised Statutes of Canada 1970, c. C–34.

Juvenile Delinquents Act, Revised Statutes of Canada 1970, c. J–3.

Summary Convictions Act, Revised Statutes of Quebec 1964, c. 35.

Young Offenders Act, Statutes of Canada 1980–81–82–83, c. 110.

Youth Protection Act, Statutes of Quebec 1977, c. 20.

CASES

The Attorney General of the Province of Quebec v. Lechasseur et al. (1981), [1981] 2 Supreme Court Reports 253.

CHAPTER 7
YOUTH COURT COMMITTEES IN MANITOBA

Joseph C. Ryant and Catherine Heinrich

INTRODUCTION

The *Young Offenders Act* (*YOA*) was passed by Parliament in 1982, proclaimed in 1983 and came into effect in 1984. The *Young Offenders Act* replaced the *Juvenile Delinquents Act* of 1908. It signifies major changes in programs and services for youth. The Act aims to involve communities, victims and parents in the dispositions or measures for youth. Section 69 of the *YOA* refers to youth justice committees as one means of involving the community:

> **69.** The Attorney General of a province or such other Minister as the Lieutenant Governor in Council of the province may designate, or a delegate thereof, may establish one or more committees of citizens, to be known as youth justice committees, to assist without remuneration in any aspect of the administration of this Act or in any programs or services for young offenders and may specify the method of appointment of committee members and the functions of the committee.

Section 69 was introduced to further encourage community involvement in dealing with juvenile offenders, an existing practice in some provinces and communities. Legislative support for this earlier citizen participation came from sections 27 and 28 of the *Juvenile Delinquents Act* (1970):

> **27.**(1) There shall be in connection with the juvenile court a committee-of citizens, serving without remuneration, to be known as the "juvenile court committee."

> **28.**(1) It is the duty of the juvenile court committee to meet as often as may be necessary and consult with the probation officers with regard to juvenile delinquents, to offer, through the probation officers and otherwise, advice to the court as to the best mode of dealing with such delinquents, and, generally to facilitate by every means in its power, the reformation of juvenile delinquents.

Each Act differs in the source of authority for the committee. Under the *Juvenile Delinquents Act* (*JDA*), the committee was authorized by, and subservient to, the Juvenile Court. Under the *YOA*, committees are designated by the provincial Attorney General or his/her delegate and operate independently of the court. These differences in source of authority and relationship to the court lead to other differences between the activities and procedures of the newer youth justice committees and those under the *JDA*.

THE MANITOBA RATIONALE FOR
YOUTH JUSTICE COMMITTEES

The province of Manitoba was well suited for community participation in juvenile justice for a variety of reasons. One reason was its population distribution: half the population of approximately 1,000,000 people live in Winnipeg. The non-Winnipeg population lives either in five cities ranging in size from 10,000 to 30,000 people or in widely scattered settlements of much smaller size. One way to prevent domination by the only major population centre was to develop a tradition of local initiative in governance.

Forms of youth justice committees existed in a number of communities in the province prior to the *YOA*. These were formed when the interests of community members in finding consequential, but non-judicial, ways of dealing with juvenile delinquents coincided with the desire of probation staff to encourage community participation. The *YOA* provided greater opportunity to elaborate on this existing system and federal project funding provided an incentive to do so.

Staff of some probation units in Manitoba held a professional commitment to community development. This was reflected in probation activities encouraging the use of volunteers and citizens. This commitment to citizen participation and community involvement lay behind the establishment of early juvenile court committees, the first of which was formed in 1975 in Dauphin. Other committees were subsequently established in both rural and urban settings across the province. Sometimes the initiative for the formation of committees came from probation workers and sometimes from members of the community.

Under the *JDA*, committee activities were linked to the juvenile courts, which sometimes consulted committees about dispositions for particular juvenile offenders. The committee would make a recommendation to the court based upon the facts presented to it and judges could, at their discretion, incorporate these recommendations into their sentences. This procedure involved no contact between the court committee and the juvenile offender (Bracken & Loewen, 1983).

The public attention generated by these committees resulted in an interest within the probation service in their expansion. Some probation officers established a working group to discuss the relative merits of increasing the commitment to a community development approach within the probation program. The coincident passage of the *YOA* provided stronger legislative support for local lay involvement than existed under the *JDA*.

In summary, two factors intrinsic local interest in citizen participation, particularly outside Winnipeg, and professional commitment to community development within the probation service provided much of the rationale for a provincial proposal entitled "Working Together." The introduction of Working Together codified and elaborated upon activities and intentions that were already part of the juvenile justice system in parts of the province.

Formal planning for Working Together began in 1984. Contribution agreements between Canada and Manitoba for joint funding were signed in April 1985 and the project was formally implemented in October 1985. "The program's mandate is to promote effective implementation of community youth justice programming based on the principles of the *Young Offenders Act*" (Manitoba Community Services and Youth Corrections, 1986, p. 2). This programming is organized around the formation of youth justice committees, the creation and use of a variety of alternative measures based on community participation, the provision of community education and community awareness programs, and the involvement of young people themselves in crime prevention programs. The funding provides for a number of community facilitator positions, which were allocated to all regions of the province.

The Working Together proposal (Manitoba Community Services and Youth Corrections, 1985) offered two reasons for locating the project in Manitoba. First, compared to other provinces, Manitoba had relatively few referrals for alternative measures. Second, in some parts of the province, there continued to be a high reliance on custody for young offenders. Greater community participation, nurtured by the Working Together project, was seen as a way to address these problems within the community participation focus of the *YOA*.

PROGRAM DESCRIPTION

An evaluative component of the Working Together project was a condition of federal participation in the funding of Working Together and the authors were engaged to evaluate the project for the federal Department of Justice The evaluation comprised three tasks: (a) an overall description of the Working Together project; (b) detailed descriptions of the project in eight selected communities; and (c) the development and field-testing of recording systems for both community facilitators and youth justice committees.

Working Together is a program of the provincial Department of Community Services and Corrections, which has administrative responsibility for the probation service in Manitoba. It is an attempt to implement extensive citizen participation in the administration of the federal *YOA*. The major intention is to establish a large number of youth justice committees. These committees are meant to receive referrals of young offenders from a probation officer, the police, or the Crown attorney and to design appropriate, but non-judicial, dispositions for these young people. The youth justice committees are also expected to implement public education activities and sponsor crime prevention programs for young people.

As noted above, expansion of the youth justice committee concept is only one component of the Working Together project. Working Together also seeks to increase community participation through the use of volunteer probation officers and victim-offender mediation. A further goal of Working Together is to achieve successful crime prevention through public education directed both to young people and the general community. To achieve these other goals, Working Together facilitators engage in inter-agency networking, public speaking and community mobilization, and also support the emergence of youth justice committees.

The objectives of the youth justice committees are pursued through two major activities: (a) the design and implementation of dispositions for particular young offenders; and (b) more general community programs. Youth justice committees tend to concentrate on the first activity. This may be because the more general activities also coincide with the duties of probation staff and because committee members enjoy direct work with young offenders.

Most referrals from the probation office are cases designated for alternative measures rather than those set for trial in the youth court. Eligibility for referral to the youth justice committee is usually reserved for first-time offenders. The nature of the offence is typically limited to the minor end of the continuum break-and-enter, theft under $1,000 and, occasionally, assault. Young offenders have the right to not accept referral to a youth justice committee and the decision to appear connotes admission to the charge. Thus, the youth justice committee does not become involved in deciding guilt or innocence; rather, its role is to determine the consequences that will be attached to an already acknowledged offence. Dispositions must be within the range of alternative measures, such as financial restitution, community service work, mediation between the victim and offender and letters of apology. The youth justice committee ordinarily monitors compliance with its orders so that it can either discharge a young offender as having met his or her obligations or report non-compliance to a probation officer so that further action might be taken.

PROGRAM STRUCTURE

The Manitoba Department of Community Services and Corrections offers services to young offenders through a structure characterized by centralized program management and decentralized service delivery. Central control is exercised by the Assistant Deputy Minister of Corrections, the Executive Director of Community and Youth Corrections and the Program Manager of Working Together. For administrative purposes, the province is divided into eight regions, each of which is sub-divided into a number of district sub-offices. Staff in these sub-offices are required to serve a number of communities within the district. Each region has one manager responsible for all social services offered by the Department; there is also a regional manager (area director) for each major service category, such as probation services. While all staff are ultimately responsible to central office, the operational level of accountability is at the regional level. This dual accountability is a source of both tension and innovation.

Working Together staff are even more subject to dual accountability. Of the 12 1/2 staff-year allocations designated as the community facilitator staff complement, 10 positions are allocated to regional operations. However, Working Together responsibilities are often split into half-time positions, requiring the incumbents to divide their time equally between Working Together and regular probation duties. The line of accountability to the central office program manager is both short and direct because of the special project nature of Working Together. Local accountability is in no way diminished by special project status, however, because work is done under the supervision of an area director.

Working Together activities are operationally defined at the regional level, resulting in variation between the regions. Regional managers and local staff are free to put their own particular imprint upon the program. The overall design functions more as a permissive envelope than as a call to more precisely defined action.

OBSERVATIONS

There are currently over 40 youth justice committees in Manitoba at various stages of development. Not all of them have, as yet, been officially designated by the Minister of Community Services and Corrections. Consistent with the decentralized character of program delivery and field management, there is considerable variability in the procedures, operations and activities of youth justice committees. Some committees meet directly with youth, while others maintain a more distant relationship. Some committees routinely include victim-offender mediation as part of the disposition, while others do not. Some committees meet as a group with the young offender, while others delegate the work with a young offender to an individual member or sub-committee. Committees also vary in the extent to which they are involved with public education activities. Finally, the relationships between committees and youth court also vary. The project manager accepts this variability as consistent with the *modus operandi* of departmental organization and with a community development ideology that stresses responsiveness to community needs and preferences.

Committee members seem pleased to be involved in youth justice. There is a sense of a return to earlier, less complicated times when communities, not governments, solved local problems. Members report that they are convinced that their volunteer activities help young people. For example, many who use victim-offender mediation feel that this measure helps to integrate the young person into the community by stressing accountability to one's neighbours for offences against them.

Regional response to the Working Together project varies. Some regions view Working Together as additional to regular, mandated probation duties. In these regions, program activities tend to be limited to the activities of the Working Together facilitator. Others use Working Together as an opportunity to reconceptualize the entire approach to corrections work and attempt to integrate Working Together goals into daily practice, permitting a partial diffusion of Working Together activities and philosophy throughout the region. This was most completely observed in the Thompson region. In this northern area, the full range of community participation possibilities was exploited by the regional staff.

Within Manitoba, three general types of committees urban committees, rural non-native committees and rural-native committees can be observed. They tend to differ in membership composition and the degree of community legitimization. For example, native committees almost always draw their members from social service workers and other official "helpers" in the community. It is unclear whether their membership on a committee reflects a personal commitment to the concept of youth justice committees or is tied to their work responsibilities. By contrast, in the non-native communities, membership is ostensibly unrelated to work roles and tends to be drawn from the same middle-class levels of the community that provide volunteers to other community organizations.

Committee membership in urban areas is more heterogeneous. Some committees include criminology or social science students who volunteer in order to acquire practical experience or to gain entry to the corrections field. Other committees have a high proportion of social services personnel. This is considered by them to be a problem, however, and efforts are being made to recruit members who are more representative of the general population.

Reserve communities are unique in the extent to which the support of the band council is necessary to legitimate youth justice committees. We found no equally important legitimation function in the governance structures of either non-native rural communities or the cities. We believe that it would be impossible for youth justice committees to operate without at least *pro forma* approval of band councils. However, in the native communities studied, band council support was minimal; committees were certainly allowed to operate but overt interest in committees was minimal.

Judicial opinions of youth justice committees range from enthusiastic support to passive acceptance to mild disdain. Some judges claim to want to know as little as possible about youth justice committees since alternative measures are statutorily outside their jurisdiction. Sometimes judges include youth justice committees as part of their own dispositions after having been made aware of them. The judges' greatest concern is that youth justice committees might overstep their authority and/or neglect to observe due process, thereby compromising the protection of an individual's rights. Judges point out that the YOA takes greater account of due process than did the JDA and that this aspect of the new Act must be protected. However, the new legislation renders judicial opinions of youth justice committees of little consequence, since committees are totally independent of youth court sanction.

PROBLEMS AND ISSUES

Working Together community facilitators are influenced by several external factors. Their access to communities is limited by regular probation work duties such as attendance at court sessions, supervision of probationers and preparation of court reports. Furthermore, for budgetary reasons, travel is sometimes restricted. These factors limit the attention that facilitators can pay to community development and sometimes results in youth justice committees getting less staff attention than they should.

The organizational structure creates two lines of authority one to the program manager and one to the regional manager. When the wishes and demands of these two managers are similar, the community facilitator has clear direction and consistent administrative support. However, when these two key actors differ in respect to Working Together, conflict is created for community facilitators, especially those with half-time probation duties. Usually, a facilitator forced by work circumstances to choose one authority over the other pays more attention to the preferences of the regional manager.

The organization of the community facilitator's work leads to other problems. Facilitators are often assigned probation responsibility for certain communities within the region as well as responsibility for Working Together for the entire region. In a community where the facilitator has full responsibility for both Working Together and probation, project philosophy can be incorporated into the regular probation work. In a community where the facilitator does not have probation jurisdiction, however, Working Together ideals and philosophy can only be introduced with the consent of that community's probation officer. If the two staff members have similar ideas and values about the project, conflict does not emerge. If the regular probation officers do not fully accept Working Together, and find ways to resist its progress, little community development work can be accomplished and the development of youth justice committees is somewhat retarded.

Community experience with youth justice committees also affects the work of the community facilitators. In communities where youth justice committees existed prior to the formal initiation of Working Together, the facilitator's job was dictated as much, if not more, by the committees as by the area directors or central manager. As more contact develops between committees through informal communication and/or occasional provincial conferences, youth justice committees may more regularly wish to pursue an orientation independent of probation service advice. As Lotz (1969) points out, community workers are ultimately responsible to the communities they serve. This third line of responsibility may generate additional conflicting demands for community facilitators. However, as the probation service is the source of referral to youth justice committees, recalcitrant committees could find that they no longer are sent referrals. This limits the degree to which committees can be fully autonomous.

Differences in community characteristics have even greater consequences for the emergence and operation of youth justice committees. Highly disorganized and disintegrated communities tend to experience a greater number of offences by young people but, outside Winnipeg, they are also less likely to have formed youth justice committees. In these communities, the challenge of providing social services through community-based intervention is greatest; these communities are often geographically isolated and constrained by having to negotiate separately with federal and provincial bureaucracies regarding native self-government. Conversely, other communities, often in relatively prosperous rural areas, have a long tradition of community participation, have formed youth justice committees and are challenged by the need to maintain the motivation of their members in the face of very infrequent referrals.

There are also issues and problems related to the actual operation of the committees. Across the province, there is wide divergence on the severity of committee dispositions and no mechanism yet exists for achieving greater consistency between committees. There is also inconsistency between committees in monitoring compliance with their orders. Some committees, for example, are far less concerned about unfulfilled community service orders than others. Committees often find it difficult to identify community service options because some community work, appropriate to the nature of the offence, violates collective agreements with the employees of the town or city and is therefore unavailable for assignment. There are also problems in the referral process. Some committees complain that probation officers withhold alternative measures cases that could legitimately be referred to them, while others complain that they are receiving cases that, in their judgment, should not be handled by alternative measures. As in the corrections system generally, youth justice committees lack reliable information that could guide the selection of the most effective dispositions given the circumstances of a particular case. Instead, committees appear to adopt favourite or habitual approaches to dealing with young offenders and, as noted above, these approaches vary considerably between committees.

DISCUSSION

In our evaluation of Working Together, we were impressed by the high degree of community interest in becoming involved in the juvenile justice system. It may well be that provisions of the *YOA* struck a responsive chord with public sentiment in Manitoba, combining as they do the requirement of greater accountability on the offender's part and the potential for effecting that accountability through citizen participation. There was the sense that if more staff time had been available to foster their emergence, even more youth justice committees would have been formed. We found little evidence of disinterest (except in some reserve communities) or entrenched resistance to the concept.

During the assessment process, we sought to explain the wide staff attention and community interest in the project despite the absence of precise definition of community development and detailed instructions for field operations (Ryant & Heinrich, 1987). The existence of a uniform plan to implement the project is difficult to discern and the actual operational steps vary widely from one region of the province to another.

Part of the explanation for this variation may lie in the rhetorical value attached to the notion of community development (see, for example,

Compton, 1971; Head, 1971; Hill, 1982; Rubin & Rubin, 1986; Stinson, 1982; Wharf, 1979), particularly in a province in which half the population lives in relatively small and highly dispersed settlements under the domination of one major city. Empowerment, a new catchword in human services, becomes more salient. Empirically, the substantial general interest in youth justice committees now, and in western and northwestern Manitoba earlier, may be partly due to the desire to place a particular cast on program delivery that is independent of Winnipeg domination and definition. Centralized control may be more legitimately resisted if, instead of appearing as resistance, it is justified by the regional staff paying attention to the expressed wishes of the communities in their district. The community development approach makes a virtue of this variation.

Of perhaps equal importance are changes occurring with respect to native communities; these changes fit precisely with a community development ideology. In Manitoba, there is increasing political pressure to devolve responsibility for services to either band councils or tribal councils. Some of this has already occurred under time-limited agreements between tribal councils and the two levels of government (the federal government is responsible for registered Indians living on reserve and the provincial government has responsibility for the administration and delivery of both child welfare and young offender services). A number of probation staff, particularly in northern Manitoba, regard the devolution of responsibility both as intrinsically valuable and as a way to improve services through the provision of a full-time local presence. For these reasons, they regard community development as a useful strategy. For obvious reasons, native politicians also support approaches that transfer power to the community.

The fiscal crisis in social services also helps to explain the attractiveness of a conceptually under-defined program such as Working Together. Budgetary restraint in public spending has increased accountability for cost effectiveness. A number of regional managers believe that the use of volunteers and community participation in work otherwise performed by probation officers will save money in the long run.

Curiously, administrative strategies to seek greater cost effectiveness might have been more vigorously resisted were they not given the gloss of the attractive ideology of community development. Justifying the move to increasing community participation in activities that were the former preserve of staff alone on the basis of such community development objectives as locality development, empowerment or the intrinsic goodness of participation itself, may mask such administrative objectives as redefining workload, de-skilling, privatization, and/or contracting out. Elements of all these administrative acts have been noted; staff reactions have been tempered by their interest in the greater good called community development and/or by their preference for the redefinition of their job descriptions made possible by community participation.

CONCLUSION

The Working Together project is highly susceptible to the specific attitudes and beliefs of key actors in the system. There are numerous examples of how project appearance has been flavoured as much by the individual preferences of regional and local participants as by central office managers. For example, victim-offender mediation was hailed as the most appropriate alternative measure by some committees while community service work was the preferred measure of others. This variability is a natural consequence of both the decentralized program management of probation services and an approach that stresses community control.

Despite its avowed intention to involve the community more completely in dealing with young offenders, we believe that organizational change was a major latent intention of Working Together (Rogers, 1983). The ultimate goal of Working Together was to nurture organizational assimilation of the community development philosophy. Strategies included working with youth justice committees, recruiting volunteers and developing community-based alternative measures. Much effort was expended to change attitudes and develop alternatives to traditional approaches. There appear to be two motives for this strategy. First, it is considered to be a more effective way of dealing with many offenders and, second, it is seen as a more cost-effective approach to service delivery. Contracting out certain components of the job, especially to volunteers, should result in cost-savings in the long run. Thus, the organization is drawn, both philosophically and pragmatically, to this approach. Perhaps Working Together was viewed as a way to convince the rest of the organization of the potential merits and benefits of community involvement. The development of a significant number of youth justice committees in Manitoba has been one practical result.

REFERENCES

Bracken, D., & Loewen, L. (1983). *Juvenile court committees in Manitoba*. Winnipeg: Report presented to the Consultation Centre, Ministry of the Solicitor General of Canada, Prairie Region.

Compton, F. (1971). Community development theory and practice. In J. Draper (Ed.), *Citizen participation: Canada* (pp. 382–396). Toronto: New Press.

Head, W. (1971). The ideology and practice of citizen participation. In J. Draper (Ed.), *Citizen participation: Canada* (pp. 14–29). Toronto: New Press.

Hill, K. (1982). Too difficult for ordinary folk? *Perception*, 5(3), 18–19.

Lotz, J. (1969). Community developer: Outsider in the middle. *International Review of Community Development*, 21/22, 261–280.

Manitoba Community Services and Youth Corrections (1985). *A Manitoba proposal for province-wide community involvement in the youth justice system*. Winnipeg: Department of Community Services and Corrections.

Manitoba Community Services and Youth Corrections (1986). *Working Together: Progress report*. Winnipeg: Department of Community Services and Corrections.

Rogers, E. (1983). *Diffusion of innovations*. 3rd Edition. New York: Collier Macmillan.

Rubin, H., & Rubin, I. (1986). *Community organizing and development*. Columbus: Merrill Publishing Company.

Ryant, J., & Heinrich, C. (1987). *Working Together: A community development approach to the Young Offenders Act in Manitoba*. Paper presented at the 3rd Conference on Provincial Social Welfare Policy, Banff, AB.

Stinson, A. (1982). Defining participation. *Perception*, 5(3), 14–15.

Wharf, B. (1979). *Community work in Canada*. Toronto: McClelland and Stewart.

LEGISLATION

Juvenile Delinquents Act, Revised Statutes of Canada 1970, c. J–3.

Young Offenders Act, Statutes of Canada 1980–81–82–83, c. 110.

CHAPTER 8

FACE-TO-FACE
VICTIM-OFFENDER MEDIATION
UNDER THE YOUNG OFFENDERS ACT[1]

Kimberly J. Pate and Dean E. Peachey

Head bowed, voice lowered, eyes avoiding contact, she twists the corner of her jacket nervously. Across from the 15-year-old sits the security officer for the department store. He asks again, why did she try to leave the store without paying for the make-up? The question is asked directly, but not harshly. She hesitates, then shrugs. After a brief silence, a third person, seated between them, speaks. The mediator, a skilled professional, suggests that perhaps they can come back to that question a little later.

* * *

A little stress is showing in each of the faces around the circle. Mother and father are embarrassed and feel betrayed. Their son, hunched on his chair between them, cannot prevent the anxiety from showing through his nonchalant veneer. Seated across from him, the school principal is struggling to understand what prompted one of her best Grade 9 students to break into the school and create a flood in the washrooms. Next to her, the police officer is beginning to feel sympathetic toward the teenager who had been so cocky burping his beer the night he was arrested. Two trained volunteer mediators complete the circle. They exchange glances, wanting to ease the tension as they begin the introductions and start the meeting.

INTRODUCTION

Since the proclamation of the *Young Offenders Act* (1982), there has been a growing interest across Canada in developing opportunities for mediation and reconciliation to occur between young offenders and their victims. There are presently about 30 mediation and reconciliation programs operating in nine provinces and territories. These efforts are aimed at encouraging young persons who have committed offences to take responsibility for their actions and to make amends to the furthest extent possible under the circumstances. Unlike the court process, a mediation session

---

[1] This chapter is based upon information that was available at the time of preparation and does not represent a comprehensive review of programming across Canada.

gives the youth an opportunity to discuss matters with the victim and have a direct impact on the outcome of the case. The youth is encouraged to say what he or she thinks is fair and realistic in the circumstances.

In contrast to court proceedings, mediation and diversion programs also enable the victim to participate and have an impact on the resolution of the matter. Through mediation, the views, concerns and needs of the victim are identified. These may include a desire for peace of mind, an understanding of the offender's motivation, or an interest in receiving monetary compensation. Evaluation of a Saskatchewan diversion project (Fischer & Jeune, 1987) found that most program participants strongly preferred the victim-offender mediation experience over judicial proceedings.

The Victim-Offender Reconciliation Program in Kitchener, Ontario, was initiated by the 1974 "Elmira Case" (Peachey, in press) and is often identified as the prototype and impetus for the flourishing of victim-offender reconciliation programs in Canada (Peachey & Skeen, 1988), the United States, England, New Zealand (Coates & Gehm, 1985) and, most recently, in Australia (Clarke, 1987). The Elmira case involved two youths who had vandalized property belonging to 22 victims. At the suggestion of a probation officer, the judge ordered the two youths to meet with and arrange to compensate each of the victims. The positive reaction of the victims and community to the approach caused it to gain popularity.

The aims and philosophies underlying current victim-offender programming initiatives across the country are diverse. Some programs are rooted in the diversion efforts of the 1960s and 1970s which attempted to prevent offenders from entering the criminal justice system, either in order to streamline the system or avoid the consequences of labelling youth as criminals (Law Reform Commission of Canada, 1975). Other programs have been heavily influenced by the alternative dispute resolution movement, which advocates applying informal mediation to virtually all types of disputes, including minor crimes, small claims cases, and custody disputes in divorce situations (Abel, 1982; Pruitt & Kressel, 1985). Increasing interest in restitution, either as a means of holding the offender accountable for wrong-doing, or meeting the monetary needs of victims, has also contributed to the emergence of victim-offender mediation programs (Hudson & Galaway, 1977; Galaway & Hudson, 1978; Schneider, 1986).

Still other programs have explicitly tried to operationalize Christie's (1977) view that the modern state uses the criminal justice system to "steal" conflicts from the affected parties. This perspective views crime as conflicts or breaks in human relationships rather than as offences against society at large and suggests that conflict resolution should be returned to the individuals and communities most directly affected by those conflicts. This approach aims to eliminate, or at least dramatically alter, the role of the criminal justice system. This view is particularly well received in certain native communities, where the state is often viewed as a foreign entity and memories of informal justice are only a generation or two old.

The goals of diverting selected cases from the legal system, fostering reconciliation and conflict resolution within the community, promoting restitution and dramatically reworking the criminal justice system are both competing and converging forces in the growing popularity of victim-offender reconciliation programs for young offenders. Programs vary widely in terms of the number and training of mediators, the style and "feel" of mediation sessions, and the nature and extent of the involvement of victims, parents of offenders and police. Program characteristics are influenced by program orientation and goals. Regardless of their differences, mediation programming initiatives have shared in the boon occasioned by the proclamation of the *Young Offenders Act* (*YOA*) in 1984. Of the 28 programs currently documented, 16 were established after the *YOA* came into effect (Peachey & Skeen, 1988).

The "Declaration of Principle" outlined in section 3 of the *YOA* provides a legislative framework and contains philosophical elements that are congruent with those of victim-offender mediation. Section 3(1)(a) specifies that young persons who commit offences should "bear responsibility for their contraventions." Section 3(1)(d) stipulates that, "where it is not inconsistent with the protection of society, taking no measures or taking measures other than judicial proceedings should be considered for dealing with young persons who have committed offences." Further, in addition to their rights under the *Canadian Charter of Rights and Freedoms*, youth have the "right to be heard in the course of, and to participate in, the processes that lead to decisions that affect them" (*Young Offenders Act*, section 3(1)(e)).

In addition, one of the primary objectives of the alternative measures provisions of the *YOA* (section 4) is to foster community awareness and promote community involvement in juvenile justice issues by encouraging "participation in alternative measures programs and the placement of greater emphasis on restitution and victim involvement in such programs" (Bala & Lilles, 1982, p. 21).

Instead of advocating that society "cure" the social ills associated with delinquency, the *YOA* encourages a participatory role for the young person. The Act recognizes that young people have special needs and should not always be held accountable in the same manner or suffer the same consequences as adults; nevertheless, the Act clearly identifies that young people must bear responsibility for their behaviour. In this context the *YOA* implies that responsibility has three components: young persons "must, firstly, exercise responsibility towards society, secondly, towards the victims of their crime, by making amends, where possible, and thirdly, towards themselves by actively participating in their own reformation and self-improvement" (Archambault, 1983, p. 4).

These views find particular expression in the alternative measures provisions of the *YOA*. Programs established pursuant to section 4 generally operate as alternatives to formal court proceedings, allowing youths who might be charged with criminal offences to take responsibility and account for their actions without incurring any sort of criminal record. Possible alternative measures include victim-offender mediation, community service work and special educational or guidance activities. If a young person successfully completes the program, the records are destroyed two years from the date a young person enters the alternative measures program.

Alternative measures programs vary according to the policies developed by the various provincial authorities (e.g., Alberta Solicitor General, 1987; British Columbia Ministry of Attorney General, 1985; Manitoba Community Services, 1985; Nova Scotia Department of Social Services, 1986; Northwest Territories Social Services, 1985; Prince Edward Island Department of Justice, 1986; and Saskatchewan Social Services, 1987). Most victim-young offender reconciliation programs operate as pre-trial alternatives to court, even though similar efforts with adult offenders have existed primarily as post-trial sentencing alternatives (Wright & Galaway, in press).

Only a few programs are operated directly by the provincial government departments responsible for their implementation; most are administered by voluntary, non-profit organizations (e.g., program profiles listed by Peachey and Skeen (1988)). Some of the private organizations offering reconciliation programs are multi-service agencies. For example, all three victim-young offender reconciliation programs in Alberta are operated by the John Howard Society. Similarly, several programs in Saskatchewan are operated by the John Howard Society, while the remainder are sponsored by Native Friendship Centres. Meanwhile, Nova Scotia has developed a network of independent agencies, some of which were created for the sole purpose of providing alternative measures services. Peachey and Skeen (1988) developed a directory of such programs; most of the private organizations listed receive at least partial government funding from provincial departments to provide reconciliation services for victims and young offenders.

MEDIATION PROCESS

Eligibility for Referral

Most youth who participate in victim-offender reconciliation programs are first-time offenders who have committed relatively minor offences. Generally, these and other eligibility criteria are established by the provincial authorities responsible for juvenile corrections. In Alberta, for example, the Alberta Solicitor General specifies the offence categories and offender characteristics that determine a young person's eligibility for alternative measures. For instance, a youth with a prior record or any previously recorded referrals to an alternative measures program is ineligible for alternative measures (Alberta Solicitor General, 1985).

In other jurisdictions (British Columbia, Manitoba, Northwest Territories and Saskatchewan, for example), the referring agents or the program administrators have the discretion to allow repeat offenders to enter the program depending upon the nature and severity of the subsequent offence. Most do not accept cases that involve violent or persistent antisocial behaviour patterns on the part of the youth.

Newfoundland, on the other hand, prohibits repeat offenders from re-entering alternative measures programs, but allows each local program, in conjunction with local justice system officials, to establish its own offence categories. Once established, however, the categories must be utilized as the primary criteria for referral. Subjective factors such as attitudes or attributes of the offender are not expected to be given consideration.

In nearly all jurisdictions, referral criteria are based upon either the characteristics of the offender or the offence. All too often, criteria are not developed with a view toward what type of victims or victim-offender relationships are most appropriate for mediation.

Referral Procedures

Under section 4(1) of the *YOA*, the Attorney General of each province has the power to authorize alternative measures programs. The Attorney General may also provide guidelines on the eligibility of cases for alternative measures. The ability to refer specific cases is generally delegated to Crown prosecutors for youth court.

The Crown must ensure that there is sufficient evidence to support a charge against a young person before referring him/her to an alternative measures program. Following the pattern set by pre-existing diversion programs under the *Juvenile Delinquents Act* (1970), however, police officers remain the informal gatekeepers of programs in most jurisdictions. They have the discretion to recommend eligible young persons to alternative measures programs.

In many jurisdictions, Crown prosecutors rarely investigate police recommendations, either because they do not have or do not take the time to do so. Therefore, despite long-standing concerns regarding police discretion, they rely heavily upon police assessments. Once the Crown decides to refer a case, the appropriate department or private agency responsible for the alternative measures program is notified.

Given the variation in program goals, provincial policy and administrative structures, it is not surprising that the actual operations of programs are quite varied. In most victim-offender reconciliation programs, the young person is contacted to determine whether he or she wishes to participate in the program. In some jurisdictions, if the youth does not wish to participate in alternative measures, a charge will be laid and proceedings commenced in youth court. Thus the extent to which a young person's decision to participate in the program may be termed voluntary is questionable at best.

Some programs seek to minimize the anxiety that many young people experience when confronted with the prospect of meeting with their victim, and the reconciliation program staff may devote considerable effort to preparing the youth for the meeting. In Calgary, for instance, this preparation frequently involves the use of role plays or practice sessions for the young person prior to his or her meeting with the victim. However, for other programs, such as those in Nova Scotia, the only contact between the youth and victim prior to the mediation is by mail or telephone.

The victim is also contacted and invited to attend a reconciliation meeting with the young person and in some programs (e.g., Grande Prairie, Alberta and Halifax, Nova Scotia) community volunteers act as surrogate victims. Other programs (e.g., Northwest Territories Community Justice Committees) utilize volunteer panel members to negotiate on behalf of the ultimate victim, the community at large.

In Canada, most cases referred to alternative measures programs involve shoplifting offences (Fischer & Jeune, 1987; Alberta Solicitor General, 1988). Testimonial accounts from programmers and policymakers alike reveal that, in terms of victims, most of the potential participants for victim-offender reconciliation programs across Canada are commercial victims of shoplifting offences. This poses a complex set of issues for a mediation program.

The concept of victim-offender reconciliation presumes that a conflict exists between two parties. Who is the second party when the victim is a corporate entity, particularly if it is part of a corporate chain for which ownership and control may reside thousands of miles from the scene of the crime? Is the department store victim to be represented by the store manager, a retail clerk from the affected department, or the security guard who spotted the shoplifter? In practice, it can be any of these people, depending to a large extent upon whom the store is prepared to release from other duties to participate in the mediation session with the young person.

Regardless of who represents the commercial victim, a negotiating session between a 15-year-old accused of having stolen a cassette tape from a sales bin and an older, formally-dressed, articulate representative of a national or multi-national corporation raises a variety of questions in relation to power balances and fairness in mediation and the extent to which a young person is able to take responsibility and account directly to the victim (assuming, of course, that the victim is even motivated to participate in the mediation process—which often may not be the case). Frequently commercial victims do not view an offence in personal terms. They consequently tend to see little reason to devote their time to meeting with an offender.

Mediators

Most victim-offender mediation programs are coordinated by either a part-time or a full-time paid staff person. For most coordinators, the role combines general administrative and direct service delivery functions. The academic and professional backgrounds of individual program coordinators vary extensively, ranging from lawyers, social workers and criminologists to persons who have received all of their training in an "on-the-job" fashion.

With the exception of some programs in Saskatchewan, most programs also utilize volunteers as mediators. Some programs routinely have two mediators working together in the meeting, while others customarily have one. The role of the mediator is to facilitate the meetings between victim and offender, not by deciding or recommending the outcome, but rather by assisting the parties in their negotiation of a mutually acceptable agreement. The objectives in utilizing volunteers as mediators vary between programs and may include: encouraging community involvement in the juvenile justice system, raising community awareness about the reconciliation process, and reducing program costs.

Training and utilizing community volunteers as mediators can increase community awareness of and involvement in a program, even if this impact is limited to the volunteers and their circle of friends and family members. It is certainly regarded as a rewarding volunteer activity, as evidenced by informal testimonials of volunteers who frequently continue in such roles for several years. However, the use of community volunteers as mediators has been criticized as an example of programming policy which puts the perceived needs of "an inner circle of child-savers...all self-appointed representatives of the community" (Berlin & Allard, 1980, p. 455) ahead of those of both the victim and the offender.

In programs where referral rates and the number of mediated cases are low, training and supervising volunteers could cost additional money, rather than resulting in cost savings (Collins, 1984, p. 21). An example of a program where volunteer usage is clearly not motivated by any cost-saving considerations is the Calgary Victim-Young Offender Reconciliation Program. There, although a volunteer mediator conducts each mediation session, the program coordinator also routinely attends the meetings as an observer. If necessary, the coordinator acts a resource person for the mediator or the negotiating parties.

Other Participants

The tension between encouraging young persons to bear responsibility for their actions and fostering broader community involvement tends to affect the number and the nature of other persons who might also participate in a mediation session. For example, most programs in Saskatchewan and Alberta do not urge the parents of participating young persons to attend the mediation session. The reason for this is to encourage the youth to accept responsibility for their behaviour and to limit the possibility of parents "bailing out" the youth or otherwise unduly influencing the proceedings. In contrast, Nova Scotia programs actively encourage the parents of all participating youth to attend the mediation session because it is thought that parents should be aware of significant events in the lives of their teenagers so that they will be able to support their children both during and after the mediation.

Nova Scotia programs also routinely invite investigating police officers to participate in the reconciliation meetings; this practice generally raises eyebrows in other jurisdictions but serves to solidify police support for the program. It also provides an opportunity for a youth to encounter the police officer in a somewhat supportive role, in contrast to the role of an arresting officer.

Reconciliation Meetings

Reconciliation meetings provide an opportunity for both the victim and the offender to discuss the offence and describe its impact on their lives. In the final stage of mediation, the parties negotiate what the young person will do to resolve the matter with the victim. Reparation is not necessarily intended to represent the actual value of the harm done. Particularly in situations where a loss has been substantial, reparation generally involves the young person making amends in a partial or symbolic way.

Common terms of victim-young person agreements may include one or more of the following: direct monetary compensation or repayment to the victim; personal service work hours or the completion of specified tasks for the victim; service work hours to be completed for a charitable organization in the community; written or personal apologies to the victim; and participation by the youth in specified counselling or educational programs. Predictably, the specific conditions available, particularly for programs officially designated as Alternative Measures Programs, vary both between provinces and between programs. However, apologies and personal or community service work appear to be the most common components of such agreements.

CLIENT FOLLOW-UP AND EVALUATION OF MEDIATION PROGRAMS

Pursuant to section 4(5) of the *YOA*, charges may be laid or proceedings commenced against young persons who do not complete the terms of their mediated alternative measures agreements. Accordingly, all programs monitor the agreements until their terms have been fulfilled. In some programs (Grande Prairie and Halifax, for example) the volunteer mediators follow the case through to its completion. In others, such as the Calgary and Regina programs, the program coordinators perform this function.

Apart from identifying the extent to which agreements are fulfilled, assessing the success of the various programming efforts can be difficult. Critiques of diversion (Bullington et al., 1978; Blomberg, 1983; Kopelman & Moyer, 1983) have highlighted the paucity of empirical research on the success of attempts to reconcile young offenders and their victims. Although many program coordinators would argue that the primary objectives of the programs are to hold young persons accountable for their behaviour and to directly address the needs of the victims, the yardstick more commonly applied by external sources to determine the success of such programs is the recidivism rate of participating young persons.

Regardless of the criteria used, assessments of success or failure are hampered by a lack of accurate comparative data across programs or in relation to judicial proceedings. Evaluations of individual programs, such as those in Grande Prairie (Collins, 1984) and Lethbridge (Collins, 1983), tend to be more descriptive than analytical. Although such studies, along with national program inventories (Solicitor General of Canada, 1979), provide overall descriptions of the vast variety of pre-trial, police screening and community-based models utilized by the respective programs, critics such as Cressey and McDermott (1973), Palmer and Lewis (1980), Berlin and Allard (1980), Ericson and Baranek (1982), and Kopelman and Moyer (1983) call for the use of more rigorous methodology and empirical data collection. With the exception of a recent evaluation by Fischer and Jeune (1987) of a Saskatchewan victim-young offender reconciliation program, there has been little conclusive research in this area.

This fact notwithstanding, Hackler (1974) and to a lesser degree Moyer (1980) support the manner in which most programs are evaluated, namely through the systematic administration of follow-up questionnaires and interviews with program participants and referral sources. Methodology of this sort is generally designed to measure whether programs are meeting the clients' needs.

MEDIATION PROGRAM ISSUES

Clarifying program objectives is a prerequisite to studying process and outcomes. A central question facing the programs described in this chapter is whether they are diversionary alternative measures programs that merely happen to utilize mediation, or mediation and reconciliation efforts that happen to operate under the alternative measures mandate currently offered by the legislative provisions of the YOA. The answer to this question is fundamental to operating a consistent and cohesive program. At present, many programs appear to be a confused combination of two divergent sets of goals and assumptions. Although programs may endorse the value of encouraging and empowering young persons to take responsibility, make choices and negotiate for themselves, in reality the options are often extremely limited for participating youth. The limitations are apparent in the referral process and selection of cases.

In most programs the referral process is relatively coercive because of the manner in which referrals are received. There are potentially serious consequences for youth who prefer not to meet with the victim, but to go to court instead. Young persons rarely consult with legal counsel prior to entering the mediation program (or any other alternative measures activity), despite the fact that they are generally advised of a right to do so. Indeed, the testimonials of programmers from the Atlantic provinces, as well as from Alberta and Saskatchewan indicate a greater concern for ensuring that young persons do what the programmers perceive is best for them and a relative lack of concern for the due process rights and self-expression of the youth. Additionally, although the right to counsel is articulated in section 3 of the YOA, it is unclear whether young persons referred pursuant to section 4 are eligible for legal aid or, for that matter, to counsel.

It is possible, therefore, that the majority of participating youth, parents, victims, program coordinators and mediators, are often unaware of whether there is sufficient evidence to support a charge in relation to the allegations at hand. Inasmuch as the Crown often does not have sufficient time to fully investigate each case prior to making a referral, it is possible that young persons commonly accept responsibility for offences and enter programs when, if their cases had proceeded to court, the matter might have been abandoned or the young person might have been acquitted.

Although the testimonial accounts from both victims and offenders who participate in the programs indicate that they tend to rate the experience very positively, programs in the early stages of development appear to have difficulty receiving cases that are really appropriate to the mediation process. Program staff and participants alike agree that the victim-offender mediation process is best suited to private victims (as compared to commercial or corporate entities), yet such cases are not usually referred.

Many of the cases referred to the programs do not appear to be particularly well suited for mediation. Most represent relatively minor offences, such as shoplifting, where there is often no individual who personifies the victim. There is reluctance in some jurisdictions to encourage the referral of cases involving private victims, such as in break and enter cases. In Calgary, for example, although police statistics reveal that the annual number of reported break and enter offences involving youthful offenders is almost as high as the number of theft under $1,000 offences (which include shoplifting), the Calgary program has dealt with only three housebreaking offences in the last three years.

Clearly, neither the police nor the Crown prosecutors refer cases on the basis of the need for "reconciliation" between victim and offender. On the contrary, if anything, they tend to avoid referring such cases. Some of the cases referred include no identifiable victim; this situation truly stretches the viable application of the mediation concept.

Referral decisions often seem to be based more on eliminating cases that the system prefers not to prosecute than on identifying appropriate cases for mediation. At times, programs actively debate whether to accept cases involving commercial victims, especially shoplifting victims. In Saskatoon, for example, the John Howard Society has chosen to limit the number of shoplifting cases admitted to their mediation program. The Calgary John Howard Society is currently examining the feasibility of taking a similar stance.

The process is also complicated when the victims of vandalism or break-ins have already been compensated by their insurance companies by the time mediation takes place. Some judges have taken the position that in such cases, restitution should be directed to the insurance company (for example, see *Re L.T.*, 1987). This significantly changes the concept of a young person taking responsibility and making amends for his/her actions by meeting the person who has been harmed. It also raises the possibility that such programs could run the risk of becoming debt collection schemes for corporate and commercial entities, as opposed to providing negotiation or mediation opportunities for individual victims and young persons.

Although private individuals who have been victimized usually express some initial reluctance to meet the person accused of the crime (Kopelman & Moyer, 1983; Fischer & Jeune, 1987), they frequently decide to do so. The key to securing their participation is to provide them with an opportunity to meet with a program representative to ask questions and air any concerns they may have about the proposed meeting or the alternative measures process. The Saskatchewan (Fischer & Jeune, 1987) and Calgary experiences suggest that once victims have met with the program coordinator, they are highly unlikely to refuse to meet with the young person—80%–90% agree to meet with the youth after some form of personal communication with the Saskatchewan program, and 90%–95% of the private victims contacted by the Calgary John Howard Society have agreed to participate in victim-young person reconciliation meetings.

Securing the victim's consent to meet with the youth is complicated in some jurisdictions where the victim is approached by another agency. In Calgary, for instance, initial contacts with all victims of young persons referred to alternative measures are made by the city's social services staff, rather than by the organization operating the reconciliation program. Thus, the people who are most knowledgeable of the program and might be most effective at presenting the idea of mediation to the victim, are precluded from doing so.

Given that victim participation is voluntary and many of the victims are corporate victims whose orientation is to apprehend and prosecute shoplifters, low rates of victim involvement are not surprising. It also appears that there is an overall lack of provincial support for reconciliation initiatives despite stated policies to "ensure" opportunities for victim participation in alternative measures programs (Walker, 1984).

However, responsibility for a low level of victim participation does not always rest with provincial policy, victim disinterest or anxiety, or referral sources. Some diversion programs have opted not to encourage victim participation. For example, some participants in a program workshop in Atlantic Canada had been volunteers with a "mediation" program for several years, yet they vigorously resisted the idea of victim involvement in mediation. In their experience, a mediator simply met with the young person who been charged (and perhaps the youth's parents) and together they agreed on an appropriate resolution of the situation. These volunteers were adamant that the victim had no place in mediation.

Victim-offender reconciliation programs for young offenders operate under a wide variety of philosophies and models across Canada and appear to be gaining popularity. Since the implementation of the *YOA*, however, most alternative measures programs have been designed to fit the *YOA*'s conception of diversion programs.

The most common criticism of alternative measures programs, like their ancestral diversion counterparts, is that they facilitate the construction of wider and deeper nets of social control for youth (e.g., Austin & Krisberg, 1981; Bala et al., 1982; Berlin & Allard, 1980; Blomberg, 1983; Caputo, 1987; Clarke, 1987; Coates & Gehm, 1985; Corrado et al., 1983; Dittenhoffer & Ericson, 1983; Lipsey et al., 1981; Sarri & Bradley, 1980; Vinter et al., 1975). Alternative programs are also frequently viewed as bureaucratic means of increasing the pervasiveness of the social control network of the juvenile justice system, based upon the argument that the introduction of a program may result in an increase, as opposed to the generally intended decrease, in the number of young persons subjected to social control.

Fischer and Jeune (1987) and Morton and West (1977) seem to be the only authors who have been able to comment favourably on Canadian programs in this regard. In both studies, it was found that there was not a corresponding net-widening following the introduction of the programs studied. Moreover, Fischer and Jeune (1987) found that the proportionate number of charges laid decreased following the introduction of the Saskatchewan program. They credited these results to the fact that one of the entry requirements for the program was that the crown prosecutor determine that there was sufficient evidence to proceed with a charge prior to referring the case to the program.

It is interesting to note that although other programs, including the Alberta Alternative Measures Program (Alberta Solicitor General, 1987), include similar eligibility criteria guidelines, recent Alberta statistics (Alberta Solicitor General, 1988) indicate that the introduction of alternative measures programs has resulted in a net-widening effect. Although many of the programs have individualized objectives, most programs must adhere to provincially established guidelines or service delivery standards and are accountable to a provincial authority. In Calgary, for example, although the victim-young offender reconciliation program is privately funded and administered, it must operate in accordance with the alternative measures guidelines set out by the Alberta Solicitor General in order to maintain its designated status as an alternative measures program.

Ericson and Baranek (1982, p. 228) point out that there is "a wealth of evidence that diversion programs may not only lead to more cumbersome procedure, but may also increase the number of persons subject to control and even the intensity of control." Moreover they also indicate that most program guidelines, like section 4 of the *YOA*, discuss programming procedures in terms of "referrals to" system-sanctioned alternatives, as opposed to "diversion from" the juvenile justice system entirely. Victim-young offender reconciliation initiatives that fall within the ambit of alternative measures programs risk being viewed as bureaucratic instruments for increasing the social control network of the juvenile justice system.

Finally, lodging programs with local agencies has encouraged variation in how they are operated. In a positive sense, this can promote a program's responsiveness to local needs and circumstances. The negative aspect of such variation is the increased potential for consistency and quality of service to suffer. Furthermore, services operated directly by the government appear to have less difficulty developing solid referral and funding bases (Divorski, 1987).

CONCLUSION

The number of victim-offender reconciliation programs for young offenders is increasing across Canada, largely in response to the *YOA*. The concept of victim-offender mediation is consistent with the principles of the *YOA*.

Victims and offenders who participate in the programs tend to rate the experience very positively. However, of the many cases appropriate for mediation, relatively few are referred to programs that are in the early stages of development.

Many programs are currently struggling with provincial guidelines and referral procedures because they are geared more toward diverting selected youths from court than toward promoting negotiation and mutual understanding between victim and offender. However, contradictions in implementation are not unusual in the first years after legislation is enacted, and need not be cause for despair. The challenge for these programs, the criminal justice system, and government authorities is to develop procedures and practices that will enable programs more fully to realize their potential for victims, offenders, communities, and the criminal justice system.

* * *

The 15-year-old smiles stuffing her carefully-folded agreement into her back pocket as she heads for the door. She still can't believe that the security guard accepted her offer. He had seemed like kind-of-a-jerk the first time they met, but now she is almost looking forward to helping him on Saturday afternoon.

The security guard sips his coffee, slowly shaking his head. The girl had been much more likeable and responsible than he had expected, and had offered to do three times more work to make amends than he ever would have expected. Although he had come to the meeting planning to demand an essay and an apology from the teenager, he likes the idea of her working for him. He wonders what the Saturday afternoon security tagging will be like...

* * *

After three hours, everyone is relieved that the marathon session is over. Mom and Dad realize that their son has been involved in numerous undesirable activities of late. The rest of the group has urged the family to discuss their problems more often and openly. The youth is feeling rather sheepish, but is relieved that everything is finally out in the open. The school principal and police officer are happy that the youth agreed to work at the children's camp during his spring break, but doubt that they have seen the last of his problem behaviour.

REFERENCES

Abel, R.L. (1982). *The politics of informal justice.* New York: Academic Press.

Alberta Solicitor General. (1985). *Alberta young offender program: Alternative measures.* Edmonton: Alberta Solicitor General, Correctional Services Division.

Alberta Solicitor General. (1987). *Toward the community: A statement of purpose, programs and services for young offenders.* Edmonton: Alberta Solicitor General, Young Offenders Branch, Correctional Services Division.

Alberta Solicitor General. (1988). *Alberta correctional services: Young offender profile by program.* Edmonton: Alberta Solicitor General, Policy Research Assistance Plan and Operational Support, Correctional Services Division.

Archambault, O. (1983). *Young Offenders Act*: Philosophy and principles. *Provincial Judges Journal,* 7(2), 1–7, 20.

Austin, J., & Krisberg, B. (1981). Wider, stronger and different nets: The dialectics of criminal justice reform. *Journal of Research in Crime and Delinquency,* 18(1), 165–196.

Bala, N., Lilles, H., & Thomson, J.G. (1982). *Canadian children's law.* Toronto: Butterworths.

Bala, N., & Lilles, H. (1982). *The Young Offenders Act annotated.* Ottawa: Solicitor General of Canada, Policy Branch.

Berlin, M.L., & Allard, H. (1980). Diversion of children from the juvenile courts. *Canadian Journal of Family Law,* 3, 439–460.

Blomberg, T. (1983). Diversions, disparate results and unresolved questions An integrative evaluation perspective. *Journal of Research in Crime and Delinquency,* 20, 24–38.

British Columbia Ministry of Attorney General. (1985). *Manual of operations Youth programs.* Victoria: British Columbia Ministry of Attorney General, Corrections Branch.

Bullington, B., Sprowls, J., Katkin, D., & Phillips, M. (1978). Critique of diversionary juvenile justice. *Crime and Delinquency,* 24, 59–71.

Caputo, T.C. (1987). The *Young Offenders Act*: Children's rights, children's wrongs. *Canadian Public Policy,* 13, 125–143.

Christie, N. (1977). Conflict as property. *British Journal of Criminology,* 17(1), 1–15.

Clarke, P. (1987). *Victim offender reconciliation program* (Draft Proposal). Sydney, Australia: Department of Youth and Community Services, Juvenile Justice Unit.

Coates, R.B., & Gehm, J. (1985). *Victim meets offender: An evaluation of victim/offender reconciliation programs*. Valpraiso, IN: Prisoners and Community Together, Institute of Justice.

Collins, J.P. (1983). *Final evaluation report of the Lethbridge alternate disposition project for young offenders*. Ottawa: Ministry of the Solicitor General of Canada, Consultation Centre (Prairies).

Collins, J.P. (1984). *Evaluation report: Grande Prairie reconciliation report for young offenders* (sic). Ottawa: Ministry of the Solicitor General of Canada, Consultation Centre (Prairies).

Corrado, R.R., LeBlanc, M., & Trépanier, J. (Eds.). (1983). *Current issues in juvenile justice*. Toronto: Butterworths.

Cressey, D.R., & McDermott, R. (1973). *Diversion from the juvenile justice system*. Ann Arbour: University of Michigan, National Assessment of Juvenile Corrections.

Dittenhoffer, T., & Ericson, R.V. (1983). The victim/offender reconciliation program: A message to correctional reformers. *University of Toronto Law Journal*, 33(3), 315–347.

Divorski, S. (1987). Community mediation is too expensive. *Community Justice Report*, 5(2), 5.

Ericson, R.V., & Baranek, P.M. (1982). *The ordering of justice: A study of accused persons as defendants in the criminal process*. Toronto: University of Toronto Press.

Fischer, D.G., & Jeune, R. (1987). Juvenile diversion: A process analysis. *Canadian Psychology*, 28, 60–70.

Galaway, B., & Hudson, J. (Eds.) (1978). National symposium on restitution. *Offender restitution in theory and action*. Lexington, MA: Lexington Books.

Hackler, J.C. (1974). *Why delinquency prevention programs in Canada should not be evaluated*. Edmonton: University of Alberta.

Hudson, J., & Galaway, B. (Eds.) (1977). *Restitution in criminal justice*. Lexington, MA: Lexington Books.

Kopelman, S., & Moyer, S. (1983). *Juvenile prevention and diversion programs in Canada A report to the research division*. Ottawa: Solicitor General of Canada.

Law Reform Commission of Canada. (1975). *Working paper #7: Diversion*. Ottawa: Information Canada.

Lipsey, M., Cordray, D., & Berger, D. (1981). Evaluation of a juvenile diversion program: Using multiple lines of evidence. *Evaluation Review*, 5, 283–286.

Manitoba Community Services. (1985). *Young Offenders Act info line* (Vols. 1–14), Winnipeg: Corrections Branch.

Moore, C. (1986). *The mediation process: Practical strategies for resolving conflict*. San Francisco: Jossey-Bass.

Morton, M.E., & West, W.G. (1977). *The myth of the community in the ideology surrounding diversion*. Paper presented at the conference, Diversion: A Canadian Concept and Practice, Quebec, PQ.

Moyer, S. (1980). *Diversion from the juvenile justice system and its impact on children: A review of the literature.* Ottawa: Solicitor General of Canada, Research Division.

Northwest Territories Social Services. (1985). *Youth worker's manual.* Chapter 2: Alternative Measures. Yellowknife.

Nova Scotia Department of Social Services. (1986). *The young offender community development project training manual.* Halifax.

Palmer, T., & Lewis, R.V. (1980). *An evaluation of juvenile diversion.* Cambridge, MA: Oelgeschlager, Gunn and Hain.

Peachey, D. (in press). Victim/offender reconciliation: Fruition and frustration in Kitchener. In M. Wright & B. Galaway (Eds.), *Mediation and criminal justice.* London, England: Sage.

Peachey, D., & Skeen, C. (Eds.), (1988). *Directory of Canadian dispute resolution programs.* Kitchener: Network for Community Justice and Conflict Resolution.

Prince Edward Island Department of Justice. (1986). *Alternative measures policy and procedures guidelines.* Charlottetown.

Pruitt, D.G., & Kressel, K. (1985). The mediation of social conflict: An introduction. *Journal of Social Issues, 41*(2), 1–10.

Sarri, R., & Bradley, P. (1980). Juvenile aid panels: An alternative to juvenile court processing in South Australia. *Crime and Delinquency, 26,* 42–62.

Saskatchewan Social Services. (1987). *Alternative measures program policy and procedures manual.* Regina: Saskatchewan Social Services, Young Offenders Branch.

Schneider, A.L. (1986). Restitution and recidivism rates of juvenile offenders: Results from four experimental studies. *Criminology, 24,* 533–552.

Solicitor General of Canada. (1979). *National inventory of diversion projects.* Ottawa.

Vinter, R., Downs, G., & Hall, J. (1975). *Juvenile corrections in the States: Residential programs and de-institutionalization.* Ann Arbor: University of Michigan, National Assessment of Juvenile Corrections.

Walker, J. (1984). *Development of Young Offenders Act: Related programming in Canada.* Unpublished manuscript, John Howard Society of Canada, Ottawa.

Wright, M., & Galaway, B. (Eds.), (in press). *Mediation and criminal justice.* London, England: Sage.

LEGISLATION

Canadian Charter of Rights and Freedoms, Part I of the *Constitution Act,* 1982, being Schedule B of the *Canada Act 1982* (U.K.), 1982, c. 11.

Juvenile Delinquents Act, Revised Statutes of Canada 1970, c. J–3.

Young Offenders Act, Statutes of Canada 1980–81–82–83, c. 110.

CASES

Re L.T. (10 November, 1987). Unreported decision. (Provincial Court of Alberta Family and Youth Division, Fitch, J.)

CHAPTER 9

CUSTODIAL DISPOSITIONS AND THE YOUNG OFFENDERS ACT

Tullio Caputo and Denis C. Bracken

INTRODUCTION

Custodial dispositions for young people have long been at the centre of the juvenile justice debate in Canada. The extensive discussions and consultations which preceded the passage of the *Young Offenders Act* in 1982 demonstrated, once again, the fundamentally different philosophical positions which continue to fuel this debate (Caputo 1987; Reid & Reitsma-Street, 1984; Corrado, 1983). These have been characterized as the justice model, which emphasizes law and order and the protection of society and the welfare model, which focuses on the special needs of young people.

In the justice model, punishments such as custodial dispositions represent the "just deserts" of one's criminal activities and are intended to serve as a deterrent both to the individuals involved and to others. In the welfare model, all dispositions, including custody, are intended less as punishment than as an attempt to resocialize and rehabilitate offenders so that they may be successfully re-integrated into the community. Various elements of both models have been incorporated into the *Young Offenders Act* (*YOA*). In this chapter, the impact of these models on custodial dispositions provided for in the Act is assessed. In particular, we will examine how some provinces have adapted existing institutional arrangements or established new custody placements for young people convicted under the *YOA*.

A brief overview of the history of custodial dispositions for young people serves as a starting point for this discussion. This includes an examination of reform efforts during the middle of the 19th century, culminating in the passage of the *Juvenile Delinquents Act* in 1908 and the establishment of a separate justice system for juveniles. Dispositions available under the *Juvenile Delinquents Act* (*JDA*) and developments leading to the replacement of this legislation with the *YOA* will then be considered. Finally, custodial dispositions available under the *YOA* will be discussed. This will include a brief description of the programs that currently exist in various provinces in Canada as well as a consideration of the consequences of these custodial programs for the young people who come in contact with the juvenile justice system.

THE ESTABLISHMENT OF A JUVENILE
JUSTICE SYSTEM IN CANADA

The development of a separate and distinct system of juvenile justice in Canada began with the efforts of several reform minded individuals in the latter half of the 19th century. This effort reflected the establishment of a child-rescue or child-saving movement similar to those in a number of countries including Great Britain and the United States. This movement was based on a growing concern for the large number of abandoned, neglected and delinquent children that were becoming increasingly visible in the urban centres of Europe and North America. These reform efforts were motivated both by a concern for the criminal activities of these young people and by a humanitarian desire to do something for these hapless and destitute children.

The emergence of a childhood ideal began to alter the way that society defined children. Children came to be viewed as pure and innocent beings who were vulnerable and susceptible to the corrupting influences of society and who, therefore, needed to be protected and nurtured. The poverty and misery of the growing numbers of destitute children at this time and their treatment at the hands of the criminal justice system ran contrary to this idealized view. This led to numerous attempts to deal with the problems of children and in particular, the establishment of various institutions, such as houses of refuge and orphanages, designed specifically for them.

The situation in Canada and the United States up to the middle of the 19th century reflected an earlier view of young people. The imprisonment of young people convicted of criminal offences in the same institutions as adults was a common practice at this time. Children convicted of criminal offences in Upper Canada prior to 1859 served prison terms at the provincial penitentiary at Kingston (Jones, 1988). Bowker (1986) notes that "in Canada's oldest penitentiary at Kingston (dating back to 1835), convicts, women, and children were all caged together. Records from 1846 show that 16 children were imprisoned there along with 11 murderers and 10 rapists" (Bowker, 1986, p. 235).

By the 1850s, however, efforts were underway to establish separate correctional institutions and legal procedures for dealing with juveniles:

> Two acts were passed in 1857: *An Act for Establishing Prisons for Young Offenders* and *An Act for the More Speedy Trial and Punishment of Young Offenders.* The first directed the construction of "reformatory prisons," while the second provided for summary trial procedures and increased powers to discharge juveniles in order to "avoid the evils of their long imprisonment previously to trial." (Hagan & Leon, 1977, p. 591)

In 1859, the first boys were transferred to the juvenile reformatory that had been established in unused military barracks in the village of Penetanguishene on Georgian Bay. A similar institution had been opened in Isle aux Noix on the Richelieu river to serve Canada East (Jones, 1988). While the first group at Penetanguishene consisted of only 40 boys, the institution had an inmate population of 193 by 1870 and by 1882 a record 263 boys were confined there (Jones, 1988, p. 279).

According to Hagan and Leon (1977), this represented the first of three periods which preceded the passage of delinquency legislation in Canada. These included:

> an initial period in which lengthy stays in reformatories replaced sentences spent in common gaols; a second period during which treatment-focused industrial schools began to replace reformatories; and a third period when organized probation emerged as a new treatment strategy influential in the development of delinquency legislation. (Hagan & Leon, 1977, p. 591)

Each of these periods is indicative of the sentiments of mid-Victorian reformers who saw child saving (Platt, 1969; Rooke & Schnell, 1983) as an opportunity to express "their profound optimism about the possibilities of reforming children" (Housten, 1978, p. 178) as well as their more general belief in the concept of rehabilitation.

Support for reformatories for children was mixed right from the beginning since differences existed between the justice model and welfare model proponents. While most viewed the reformatories as a vast improvement over the imprisonment of children, there was still a great deal of disagreement as to the most appropriate form of treatment for young people. For example, there were those who felt that lengthy sentences in special institutions were required for the reformation of young people as well as for the benefit (and protection) of society (Leon, 1977). Others, however, saw the reformatories as little more than a "necessary evil." As W. L. Scott, the principal draftsman of Canada's delinquency legislation, reasoned, "What wise parent would place a naughty child with other naughty children in order to make him better?" (quoted in Leon, 1977, p. 591).

In 1874, the situation began to change toward treatment-focused industrial schools. *An Act Respecting Industrial Schools* (1874) was passed in Ontario, and provided for the establishment of residential training schools. These were intended to be less severe than the reformatories and to provide a place to which police magistrates could send a young person under the age of 14 for as long as they deemed it necessary (indeterminate sentences) for proper training, until the youth reached the age of 16. While the purpose of these schools was to confine young persons, the implicit goal of rehabilitation is unmistakable.

The ongoing debate over the incarceration of young people reflected a variety of concerns since it encompassed both the fears of those worried about the criminal activities of juveniles as well as those interested in their "rescue" and rehabilitation. Many reformers of the day believed that intervention was necessary to prevent these children from falling into a life of crime. Their view was that the source of the problem was rooted "firmly in individual character, nevertheless, character before adulthood was pliable" (Housten, 1978, p. 178). It was the family, as the primary socializing agent, that bore the responsibility for the proper upbringing of children. When a wholesome and salutary family life was lacking, society had to act to provide such an experience for young people. In this way, the provision of a good family and home became a cornerstone of the reform movement.

In 1891, a Commission of Inquiry into the Prison and Reformatory System of Ontario was established. The report handed down by this commission had a significant impact on the direction that correctional practices would take. The report characterized the Ontario Reformatory for Boys in Penatanguishene as a "great mistake." It stated that "[t]he new structure [in Penatanguishene] was but a more commodious prison" (Leon, 1977, p. 84). The report contained various recommendations for changes in the treatment of young people. For example, it supported compulsory school attendance, identifying a good education as a principal way of preventing undesirable behaviour in juveniles. It recommended that industrial schools be set up in every city and large town and that boys be removed from the Reformatory School to more suitable locations. A system of cottages was to be established along with earned remissions. The report also called for the creation of an institution for girls as well as the introduction of various after-care programs and facilities.

"Furthermore, several of the recommendations focused specifically on the differential processing of juvenile offenders before, during, and after trial" (Leon, 1977, p. 85). The report suggested that children arrested for a serious offence should be detained separately from adults and that no child under 14 be detained in a common gaol or reformatory until all other corrective measures had been tried. In addition, the report called for the establishment of a special court for children under 14, who, it felt, should not be tried in public on any charge. The report stated further that trivial offenders could be discharged

> with an admonition, particularly when parents or guardians would undertake closer supervision; that a system of suspended sentences under the supervision of police be used except when the home environment was extremely bad; and that certain powers be given to probation officers who could also serve as truant officers. (Leon, 1977, p. 85)

J.J. Kelso, a crusading newspaper reporter, and W.L. Scott, Local Master for the Supreme Court of Ontario and President of the Ottawa Children's Aid Society, were working diligently at that time for the establishment of a separate Children's Court. The federal *Juvenile Delinquents Act* was drafted by Scott and others (Hagan & Leon, 1977) and it was eventually passed in 1908. It served as the basis for the establishment of a separate and distinct system of juvenile justice in Canada. It consolidated various illegal behaviour by young people into a new category called "delinquency" and it provided for special courts and procedures for dealing with "juvenile delinquents."

For over 70 years, the *JDA* formed the basis of the juvenile justice system in Canada and it remained essentially unchanged during this period. However, by the 1960s, proponents of both the justice model and welfare model began to call for changes. The movement for change grew steadily throughout the 1960s and 1970s and eventually resulted in the passage of the *YOA* in 1982. "The new Act was the result of some fifteen years of study, research, consultation, and review directed by the Office of the Solicitor General of Canada" (Bowker, 1986, p. 237). It sought to strike a compromise between welfare and justice model concerns.

CUSTODY AND THE JUVENILE DELINQUENTS ACT

In keeping with the ideal of wide-ranging discretion to be utilized in child welfare proceedings and turn-of-the-century positivist notions about the treatment of young persons who had engaged in anti-social behaviour, the *JDA* provided the courts with the legislative authority for a significant variety of dispositions. These ranged from doing virtually nothing ["suspend final disposition"] to doing almost anything ["impose upon the delinquent such further or other conditions as may be deemed advisable"]. These dispositions are outlined in section 20(1) of the *JDA*. The specific custodial dispositions available to the juvenile court under the *JDA*, as stated in paragraph (i), allowed a judge to "commit the child to an industrial school duly approved by the Lieutenant-Governor in Council."[1] There was no limitation on duration of such committals, beyond the general limitation that the *JDA*'s jurisdiction was to continue until the child reached the age (set by the individual provinces) when *JDA* jurisdiction was to expire. The effect, therefore, was the establishment of a form of indefinite sentences ending only when the maximum age for a given province had been reached. Section 20(3) did allow for the court to

---

[1] The term "industrial school" had been replaced with the term "training school" by the 1960s as most provinces moved to reflect a more rehabilitative philosophy in their correctional terminology.

review any disposition at any time until the offender reached the age of 21. However, release from an industrial school by the court under this provision was subject to the receipt of a report from the school's superintendent recommending such release. The limitation on the use of the custody disposition seems only to be that contained in section 25, which suggested that committal to an industrial school was not to be used on a delinquent under the age of 12 unless all other courses of action had been exhausted.

The *JDA* was silent on the nature and function of an industrial school, beyond saying that an industrial school was whatever a Lieutenant-Governor in Council of a province said it was. More importantly, perhaps, from a consideration of the custodial dispositions of the *JDA*, was the suggestion that once a committal had been made under section 20 (i) [as well as paragraph (h) relating to commitments to the care of a Children's Aid Society] the delinquent was under the control of the province. Section 21(1) directed that, at the discretion of the provincial authorities, the young person was to be treated in all respects as if an order had been lawfully made "in respect of a proceeding instituted under the authority of a statute of the province" and therefore could be transferred, released, etc., as specified in the provincial statute. Clearly, the intention of this section was to allow for the use of provincial child welfare regulations when dealing with young persons in custody by virtue of the *JDA*. Further review by the juvenile court was not necessary, barring future offences, once the young person had been committed and the provincial authority had chosen to use provincial legislation to deal with the young person.

CUSTODY AND THE YOUNG OFFENDERS ACT

The Declaration of Principle in the *YOA* (section 3) reflects both justice model and welfare model concerns. However, the custodial dispositions available under the *YOA* are on balance more of a reflection of the justice model approach of classical criminology than of the welfare model. *YOA* limitations on administrative discretion and the power of the court to specify certain types of dispositions clearly differentiates the *YOA* philosophy from that of the *JDA*. Furthermore, the *YOA* guarantees a young person rights of due process prior to imposition of a custodial disposition; this provision is in keeping with the principles outlined in the American *Gault* decision of 1967. For example, specific forms of custody are differentiated, lengths for custodial dispositions are enunciated, and periodic reviews of the custodial dispositions are required. Perhaps the three most important areas related to custody dispositions under the *YOA* are those specifying the nature of the custodial institution, the length of sentence, and the conditions for release. These three areas, as well as other aspects of custody covered in the *YOA*, are written in terms designed to limit the discretion given to youth court judges and custodial authorities or to spell out more clearly the application of discretionary powers.

The two types of custodial dispositions available under the *YOA* are open custody and secure custody. These reflect the idea that a custodial setting could range from the relative freedom of a group home setting (presumably based on the welfare model approach) or wilderness camp, to the restrictions of a very secure prison-like institution. Importantly, the level of custody is determined by the youth court judge at the time a disposition is handed down. This differs from the *JDA* approach, which left the decision on the best type of custodial setting up to provincial authorities. One could argue that the nature of custodial dispositions can no longer be seen as the result of some presumably rational, child welfare-oriented determination of what constitutes "the best interests" of the young person. Rather, the youth court judge is to make the decision, guided only by the *YOA*'s Declaration of Principle, which calls for some balance between society's and the young person's rights, taking into account the seriousness of the offence.

The indeterminate disposition (indeterminate that is until the age of majority) was the hallmark of the *JDA*, which was influenced by the positivist (welfare-oriented) school of criminology. The indeterminate disposition is virtually non-existent in the *YOA*. The justice model approach to crime and delinquency is evident in the specification of custodial disposition length of two or three years, depending on the presumed seriousness of the offence. Originally, the combined maximum length of a custodial (or for that matter other) disposition under the *YOA* when more than one offence was involved, was three years. However, amendments to the Act in 1986 allowed for consecutive sentencing, resulting in total custodial dispositions of over three years when an offence was committed while serving the disposition for a previous offence.

Under the *JDA*, provincial authorities were allowed discretion with respect to release based on the use of provincial statutory (usually child welfare) authority; such discretion has been curtailed under the *YOA*. Regular youth court reviews of custodial dispositions are mandatory under the *YOA* if the disposition length is greater than one year. They may also be requested by the young person, the youth's family, or by provincial authorities. Such reviews may result in a reduction in the length of disposition, or in a change in the type of disposition. Although transfer from more to less restrictive forms of custody (i.e. from secure to open) is not difficult (written permission from a youth court is required), the reverse is, at least in theory, more difficult to accomplish. A judicial review is required in any case where transfer is deemed to be necessary. For example, a transfer from open to secure custody may be required due to failure to remain in an open custody setting. The youth court could then, following a review at which the youth is present, order a more onerous disposition such as secure custody. Some discretion was left to provincial authorities to move a young person from open to secure custody when some violation of regulations had occurred. This was to last for a maximum of 15 days and seemed designed to provide provincial authorities with some type of weapon for use when open custody inmates were perceived to be getting out of hand. Section 24(9) of the YOA suggests that repeated attempts at escape from open custody (presumably a relatively easy thing to do) or "serious misconduct" are grounds for a temporary transfer. The 1986 amendments (Bill C–106, section 24.2(9)) changed the wording in this part of the YOA to give clearer direction on the use of temporary transfer. The behaviour of the young offender for whom such transfer is contemplated must be such that the safety of the young person or others at the open custody facility is considered in jeopardy.

SOME PROVINCIAL EXAMPLES OF CUSTODY UNDER THE YOA

The way in which the provinces have chosen to interpret the custodial dispositions available to youth courts in their jurisdiction may shed some light on the way in which the YOA has been generally implemented across the country. The proclamation of the YOA required the provinces to (a) review the institutions that had been established to fulfill the custody provisions of the JDA and (b) determine the utility of such institutions for the future. In addition, the introduction of open custody as a disposition under the YOA required provinces to designate some facilities as open custody. In the remainder of this section, the ways in which various provinces deal with custodial dispositions under the YOA are examined. Though not exhaustive, the provinces considered in this review include examples from western, central and eastern Canada and highlight some of the salient similarities and differences in custodial dispositions for young people across the country.

British Columbia

In British Columbia, all facilities are operated by the Corrections Branch of the provincial government. By the fall of 1986, British Columbia had designated seven open custody facilities and four secure custody facilities for a total of 336 spaces (186 secure and 150 open). In British Columbia, there appears to have been some utilization of existing facilities, including those set up originally as places of temporary detention. Two of the three urban open custody facilities co-exist with adult correctional facilities on the same grounds, while all open custody spaces outside urban areas are in forestry camps. It should be noted that camps are mentioned specifically in the YOA as possible open custody facilities. The secure custody places are mostly in detention centres, although one forestry camp is designated as a place of secure custody. There is apparently some consideration as to which secure or open custody placement is most appropriate for particular young offenders. For example, those with perceived "special needs" are unlikely to be sent to a camp where they would be further from whatever programs or resources might be necessary. Instead, they would be more likely to stay in an urban setting. British Columbia appears to have concentrated its resources in larger, institutional-type settings for both open and secure custody offenders.

Manitoba

Manitoba addressed the issue of custody under the YOA by designating the Manitoba Youth Centre (MYC), originally designed as a short-term holding centre in Winnipeg, as a place of both open and secure custody, as defined by section 24 of the Act. In addition, the Agassiz Centre for Youth in Portage la Prairie, which was actually the old Manitoba Industrial School and had been used as a custody facility under the JDA, was also designated as a place of both open and secure custody as defined by section 24 of the YOA. These institutions are both divided into "cottages" within secure settings, and certain cottages within each are designated as open custody while others are secure. Expansion to other types of open custody placement settings since 1985 has resulted in 10 privately operated open custody homes in Winnipeg providing up to 22 spaces in total, and seven privately operated homes outside Winnipeg, including three in Thompson to serve northern Manitoba. Open custody cases are first sent to MYC (open custody section) for assessment. Eventually, a youth is placed either in Agassiz (open custody) or in a private, single-family open custody home. These homes are designated as open custody placements under the YOA, and normally have space for a maximum of four young offenders. In addition, an open custody support unit was established to ensure that these homes adhered to specified standards and to provide support to the operators. Secure custody settings continue to exist at Agassiz in Portage la Prairie and at the MYC in Winnipeg. Agassiz is the major secure custody institution for the province. It operates using positive peer culture as its major treatment approach. No expansion of secure custody facilities in Manitoba is currently contemplated.

New Brunswick

Two secure custody facilities are operated by the Solicitor General's department in New Brunswick. The New Brunswick Training School in Fredericton has 60 secure custody beds (48 for males and 12 for females) and the Madawaska Regional Corrections Centre has 66 secure custody beds, which can be used for males or females. These are both multi-purpose facilities that can be used for secure custody, temporary detention and remand.

There are 90 open custody beds spread throughout New Brunswick. These are exclusively in group homes and specialized foster homes. Group homes are operated by the volunteer sector with government funding and can be found in almost all municipalities in the province. There are about six beds per group home. A Community Resource Centre is operated directly by the government and provides open custody beds for older youth.

Nova Scotia

Nova Scotia is the only province besides Ontario that administers the *YOA* under a split jurisdiction. In Nova Scotia, the Department of Community Services is responsible for young people 12 to 15 years old while the Solicitor General (formerly the Attorney General of Nova Scotia) is responsible for 16- and 17-year-olds. Since the number of 16- and 17-year-old females is very small (two or three) the Solicitor General retains legal responsibility for them but contracts for services with the provincial Department of Community Services which already operates appropriate facilities for these clients.

The Department of Community Services operates the Shelbourne Youth Centre in Shelbourne. This is a large multi-purpose institution designated to provide open and secure custody and temporary detention facilities. It has a capacity for 100 residents and handles cases from throughout the province. The Department of Community Services also contracts the Salvation Army in Sydney to operate the Cape Breton Youth Resources Centre. This centre has 10 beds for males and is designed as an open custody, temporary detention facility. Temporary detention in this case is for the purposes of obtaining an outpatient assessment. Two proctor homes are also operated to provide services for female clients. These proctor homes have the same designation as the Cape Breton Youth Resources Centre and their clients have access to the facilities and programs of the Centre.

Secure custody facilities in Nova Scotia for 16- and 17-year-olds are under the jurisdiction of the Attorney General. At the present time, a new facility, the Nova Scotia Youth Centre is being built and is scheduled to open in August 1988. This facility is located in Waterville (approximately 100 km from Halifax in King's County) and it has 120 places. It will provide both open and secure custody beds. Currently, secure custody beds are located in four interim facilities that were formerly adult institutions. These include: the Lunenberg Correctional Centre, which has 28 spaces;

the Queens Correctional Centre, which has 11 spaces; the Antigonish Correctional Centre, which has 17 spaces; and the Shelbourne Youth Centre where 40 spaces are provided for open custody clients 16 and 17 years of age. Various services are shared at the Shelbourne facilities, however, each Ministry utilizes its own staff. These 40 open custody beds will be transferred to the Nova Scotia Youth Centre once that facility is operational. An additional six secure custody beds are currently available in adult facilities if needed.

The Ministry of the Solicitor General also has plans to build an open custody facility for 16- and 17-year-olds in Glace Bay. This will have space for 15 males and females and is expected to be completed in the summer of 1989.

Ontario

Responsibility for custodial dispositions under the YOA in Ontario falls under the jurisdiction of both the Ministry of Community and Social Services and the Ministry of Correctional Services. Young people from 12 to 15 years of age who are dealt with under the YOA are classified as Phase One cases and fall under the jurisdiction of the Ministry of Community and Social Services. Phase Two cases consist of young people 16 and 17 years of age who are dealt with under the YOA; these cases fall under the jurisdiction of the Ministry of Correctional Services. A range of open and secure custody facilities is available for both Phase One and Phase Two clients.

There are approximately 470 secure custody spaces (420 for males and 50 for females) available in Ontario. Many of these are located in Young Offenders Units of regional correctional centres. The Young Offenders Unit of the Maplehurst Correctional Centre in Milton is the largest secure custody facility with space for approximately 100 males. The Bluewater Centre for Young Offenders in Goderich is the other large facility in the province; it houses 72 males. There are four facilities that house between 30 and 50 young offenders: the Young Offenders Unit at the Thunder Bay Correctional Centre with 25 male and five female spaces; the Young Offenders Unit of the Hamilton-Wentworth Detention Centre with space for 40 males and six females; the Young Offenders Unit of the Metropolitan Toronto East Detention Centre with space for 30 males; and the Young Offenders Unit of the Monteith Correctional Centre with 25 spaces for males and five spaces for females. The remainder of the facilities have approximately 20 spaces each although some, like the Windsor Jail, are quite small with space for only five males and three females.

There are approximately 490 open custody spaces available at the present time for Phase Two clients. This includes 50 special spaces, of which 30 are family assisted and 20 are band assisted places for young people mainly from the north. A total of 617 open custody spaces are planned to be in place by April of 1989. These open custody spaces are located in approximately 61 privately-operated, government-sponsored residences. These residences have from four to 15 spaces available with 10 spaces being the average size. The Portage residence in Elora is the largest of the Phase Two open custody facilities with 42 beds. Portage is unique in offering a variety of specialized programs such as drug and alcohol abuse treatment.

At the present time, the Ministry of Community and Social Services is in the process of developing facilities for Phase One clients. This Ministry had been responsible for young people up to the age of 16 years under the *JDA* and operated large training schools for this purpose. With the passage of the *YOA*, these facilities were turned over to the Ministry of Correctional Services. However, approximately 70 beds in these facilities are still being utilized by the Ministry of Community and Social Services on an interim basis for Phase One clients serving secure custody dispositions. For example, about 40 beds in the Cecil Facer Youth Centre in Sudbury are available to the Ministry of Community and Social Services for Phase One clients serving secure custody dispositions. The other two institutions in this category are the Brookside facility in Cobourg and the Sprucedale facility in Simcoe, each of which has approximately 10 to 15 secure custody beds available for Phase One clients.

A network of 17 smaller facilities, spread across the province, is in the process of being established. When completed, the system will have approximately 300 secure custody beds for Phase One clients. The goals of this system are to establish smaller facilities so that young people can be kept closer to their own communities and to provide services in smaller, less impersonal settings. Currently, the Central Region is the most developed, with three secure custody facilities. These include the Syl Apps Centre in Oakville and the York Centre and St. John's Centre in Toronto. Each of these facilities has approximately 40 Phase One secure custody beds. Facilities in the other regions of the province are somewhat less developed at the present time but each region does have access to secure custody facilities either within their own boundaries or in other regions of the province. In December 1987 the average daily number of Phase One secure custody beds in Ontario was 185.

The Ministry of Community and Social Services also contracts with approximately 200 privately-run, government supported group homes across the province which offer open custody facilities for Phase One clients. These group homes average five to 10 beds but some are larger and may hold as many as 25 residents. The Ministry is able to contract for these services as demand warrants. In December 1987 the average daily number of Phase One open custody beds in Ontario was 252.

There is some concern in Ontario over the split jurisdiction for cases under the *YOA*. Under the *JDA*, the responsibility for young people who were 16 years old or younger and in trouble with the law, lay solely with the Ministry of Community and Social Services. Programs were based on the welfare philosophy of the *JDA* and emphasized rehabilitation. Young adult offenders (over the age of 16) were dealt with by the Ministry of Correctional Services in adult facilities.

With the passage of the *YOA*, the Ministry of Community and Social Services retained its responsibility for young people up to 15 years of age while the Ministry of Correctional Services became responsible for young people 16 and 17 years of age. The difference for the Ministry of Correctional Services was that it was now providing services and programming under the *YOA* and the juvenile justice system for 16- and 17-year-old clients and not under the auspices of the adult justice and correctional systems. This constitutes a fundamentally different orientation, philosophy and treatment strategy and reflects the differences between the juvenile and the adult systems.

Some of the questions that have emerged over the split jurisdiction in Ontario focus on issues such as continuity of service, especially in the case of young people who are passing from one jurisdiction to another and the type of service being provided by the different ministries. Since one ministry has a rehabilitative orientation and the other a corrections orientation, there is some question about how this affects the programs offered by the two. It seems to have resulted in a two-tier system of juvenile justice, one for younger and one for older juveniles. Many questions exist as to whether a single act can be effectively and fairly implemented under such an arrangement.

Quebec

The situation in the Province of Quebec differs somewhat from that of other provinces because of the province's *Youth Protection Act* (1977). A series of Rehabilitation Centres (Centres D'Accueil) were established in the Province of Quebec in the late 1970s to administer the *Youth Protection Act* (*YPA*), which required close cooperation between the child welfare and criminal justice systems. With the passage of the *YOA*, various modifications have been made to the system in Quebec to bring it into line with the requirements of the new legislation. Nevertheless, the close contact between the child welfare and the juvenile justice system has been maintained. A number of institutions throughout the province serve various functions under the *YPA* and the *YOA*.

There are 42 facilities spread among 11 socio-economic regions throughout the province of Quebec. Twenty of these facilities operate under a special mandate that allows them to designate some of their space as secure custody. Sixteen of these facilities are able to serve as temporary detention centres as well. Some facilities (mainly in Montreal and Quebec City) have what is referred to as "triple designation" since they can serve as open, secure and temporary custody facilities. This represents an effort to provide young people with a full range of services and programs within a single institution. The institutions maintain a high degree of flexibility in being able to tailor programs and treatment strategies for individual clients. This orientation is important since YPA and YOA programs are often housed in the same facility.

In Quebec, there are five large institutions that are used almost exclusively for young people sentenced under the YOA. Three of these facilities are in Montreal, one is located south of Montreal and one is in Quebec City. These institutions provide the bulk of the secure custody spaces for the province. Because of the flexibility in the system for providing secure custody spaces, there is no specific number of spaces exclusively designated as secure custody. However, the number of spaces utilized for this purpose ranges from 200 to 300 spaces and may reach as high as 450 spaces at certain times.

Approximately 4,300 open custody spaces (1800 for females and 2500 for males) are available in the Province of Quebec for young people under both the YPA and the YOA. Of these, approximately 1,200 are in government-run group homes. Group homes average from five to eight residents. Other open custody facilities include supervised apartments where young people can participate in independent living under adult supervision. Additional programs are available through various group homes and Rehabilitation Centres and offer a range of employment and educational opportunities including work in forestry camps.

Regional Rehabilitation Centres play an important role in both the juvenile justice and child welfare systems in the Province of Quebec. These centres can serve as emergency shelters under the YPA or as temporary detention facilities under the YOA. They provide a place for young people until the appropriate authorities determine what action is to be taken. Some centres offer a wide range of programs and can accommodate both open and secure custody clients. Others are designed as essentially open custody facilities. In general, the system in Quebec appears to offer a more integrated approach to dealing with young people, with a combination of child welfare and juvenile justice programs.

Saskatchewan

All young offender programs in Saskatchewan are based on the concept of the "youth model," which is derived from the principles articulated in the preamble to the YOA. The youth model assumes that young people are responsible for their actions and should be held accountable but in ways different from adults and that the least level of intervention into the young person's life should be used. Programming, under this model, is designed to utilize group therapy to foster positive and appropriate behaviour. Wherever possible, regular community services such as educational programs, vocational training, recreation and work are utilized.

Saskatchewan currently provides a variety of facilities for open and secure custody dispositions including both government and non-government run group homes, camps and institutions. Secure custody is provided at three locations: the Paul Dojack Youth Centre in Regina, which has 88 spaces for 12- to 17-year-olds inclusive (12 for females and 76 for males); the North Battleford Youth Centre which has 44 spaces for males 15 to 17 years old; and Kilburn Hall in Saskatoon which has 32 spaces for 12- to 17-year-olds (6 for females and 26 for males). As of May 1987, youth were no longer held in adult facilities in the province. Prior to that time, some secure custody places were located in the Youth Unit at the Saskatoon Provincial Correctional Centre and the Youth Unit at the Prince Albert Centre (phased out in April of 1987). The average daily secure custody population for Saskatchewan for 1987 was 104 youths.

Open custody dispositions are available in a variety of facilities in the province. Four group homes are currently in operation in Saskatchewan, three of which are operated by non-governmental agencies. Group homes have a capacity for eight to ten residents and are designed for youth in the 12- to 15-year-old age group. Community Youth Residences are another form of open custody. These are designed to accommodate up to 12 male residents, 16 years of age or over and are located in or near an urban centre to provide easy access to specialized services such as counselling for mental health problems or substance abuse, employment and educational opportunities. At the present time there are four such facilities operating: Saskatoon Community Youth Residence; Creighton Community Youth Residence; Battleford Youth Cottage; and the Salvation Army Residence in Regina.

In addition, there are two Youth Camps in Saskatchewan: the Kenosee Youth Camp, and the Prince Albert Youth Camp. These camps are designed for 14 males, 16 years of age or older and are located in park areas. Youths in these programs do community work in and around the park and are involved in activities such as trail clearing, campsite development and clean-up, wood splitting and snow removal.

Finally, there are two Youth Centres in the province, the Dales House in Regina, which shares some facilities with Family Services, and Kilburn Hall. These Youth Centres are relatively large facilities that have internal programming in addition to utilizing the resources available in the surrounding communities. In 1987, the average open custody population in Saskatchewan was 120 youths.

PROGRAMMING FOR YOUTH IN CUSTODY

The wide variety of programs available to young people in custody in Canada precludes a detailed description of specific programs. However, it is possible to outline some of the general principles and parameters used in the conceptualization and implementation of many of these programs.

The concept of open custody is premised on the notion that a person receiving such a disposition requires somewhat more structure and supervision than is available through alternative measures, community service orders, probation or other less onerous dispositions. A residential setting is used to provide a positive peer culture wherein the young person is supposed to learn how to interact with others and behave in a responsible manner. An integral part of such a program is the utilization of existing community services such as schools, employment opportunities or specialized counselling facilities for such things as alcohol or drug abuse problems, or psychiatric care. This is accomplished through regular short-term releases from the facility and supervised outings. In addition to participation in community programs, some lifeskills and behaviour training is usually available on site. In the case of camps, appropriate behaviour and positive values are inculcated through the experience of working together in a group, in a setting that is removed from the normal pressures of an urban environment.

Secure custody dispositions are usually served in larger institutional settings that incorporate a variety of programs. In most cases, these larger institutions are divided into smaller units of 10 to 15 young people who are exposed to various aspects of custody, treatment, and case management in their daily routines. This may include a work assignment, either in the institution or in the community, pre-vocational training or participation in an academic program. Recreational programs are also usually available in these institutions and constitute an important part of the inmates' regular routine. In addition, young people in a secure custody facility are normally provided with individual and/or group counselling. In many institutions, part of the programming is designed to prepare the young person for eventual release into the community. This may consist of periodic home visits, supervised outings into the community and temporary passes. In short, the overall intent is to provide a comprehensive treatment regimen for the young person, including: (a) counselling to foster an understanding of the reasons behind his/her detention; (b) participation in vocational, educational and recreational activities; (c) a supervised peer environment designed to aid in the development of appropriate behaviour and positive attitudes; and (d) an opportunity to become a productive member of society.

SUMMARY

Custodial dispositions for young people have long been at the centre of the juvenile justice debate in Canada. With the passage of the *YOA*, a new dimension has been added to this debate. As an attempt to strike a compromise between justice model and welfare model approaches, the Act provides for both open and secure custody dispositions. Based on a philosophy of the least interference consistent with the protection of society, secure custody dispositions are to be used only as a last resort. In spite of the admonitions contained in the Act's Declaration of Principle (section 3), however, serious questions about custodial dispositions under this legislation remain.

To begin with, there is a great deal of variability in what actually constitutes open custody. This is partly based on whether the term "open" or "custody" is emphasized. Thus, as in the case of Manitoba, a facility within the boundaries of a secure institution can be designated as an open custody facility. At the other extreme, a regular family home or a group home with few restrictions on residents' movements can be designated as an open custody facility. A group home may also be designated an open custody facility even when it imposes almost as many restrictions on the movements of residents as do some secure facilities. In the Manitoba situation, a cottage within the grounds of the Manitoba Youth Centre (which had been designated as a secure custody setting) was designated as an open custody setting. In *Re F and the Queen et al.* (1984), an appeal of an open custody disposition resulted initially in that designation being overturned by a Queen's Bench judge. Subsequently, however, the Court of Appeal (following some re-designation by the province so that portions of the MYC were considered secure and others considered open) suggested that the Lieutenant-Governor in Council has the authority to define what constitutes open or secure custody (*C.F. v. R.*, 1984). Commenting on the case, Robinson (1985) points out that the Court of Appeal in Manitoba, at least as far as this case is concerned, accepted

> the de jure designation of the Lieutenant Governor in Council or his delegate, without examining the de facto openness or security of the custody arrangements, as long as the designation falls within one of the generic descriptions which are found in para. 24(1)(a) [of the *YOA*]. (p. 7513)

The implications of this decision are that the vagueness of the "generic descriptions" in the Act may allow provincial administrators to make their own determination as to what is and is not an open or secure facility. A "child care institution" could be a place characterized by a high level of security, yet might also qualify as a place of open custody under section 24.1(1)(a) of the *YOA*.

The characteristics of places currently designated as open custody facilities are quite variable. As a result, the custodial sentence received by a young person may vary by location (urban centres are more likely to have open custody facilities) and by the availability of both governmental and non-governmental resources in a particular community. Thus, the treatment young offenders receive from the juvenile justice system may depend more on where they live than on the offence for which they have been convicted. Moreover, the "openness" of many custodial dispositions is variable, which may result in far greater use of this disposition than was originally intended by those drafting the *YOA*. In the final analysis, it must be remembered that whether it is open or not, custody restricts a person's freedom.

In the case of secure custody dispositions, more homogeneity may exist in programs available across the country. One of the questions raised with respect to secure custody dispositions, however, deals with the apparent increase in the numbers of young people given custodial dispositions and the length of time that these young people are spending in custody. The limited information available suggests that more young people are being incarcerated and for longer periods of time under the *YOA* than had previously been the case under the *JDA* (Leschied & Jaffe, 1985; Caputo, 1987). The 1986 amendments to section 24(1) of the Act (Bill C–106, 1986) have required judges to consider certain factors before imposing a custodial sentence. (The original Act had specified this procedure only prior to imposition of a secure custody disposition.) If this increase in custodial dispositions is actually occurring, it suggests that the justice model may have taken precedence over the welfare model in the implementation of the *YOA*. One can only speculate in what manner the section 24 requirements and the Declaration of Principle are being applied prior to the imposition of a custodial sentence.

A final concern has to do with who decides what type of custody is suitable for a particular young offender. Under the *JDA*, this responsibility fell to the Lieutenant-Governor in Council, which effectively gave control over these matters to the provincial authorities in charge of juvenile justice administration. Under the *YOA*, the designation of facilities as open or secure still rests with the Lieutenant-Governor in Council while the decision about level of custody is to be made by the judge on the basis of information available in court. This represents a subtle but important change. There has been some discussion about the practicality of this process for the actual administration of the *YOA*. Some suggestions for returning this power to the provincial authorities have also emerged ("Open or Secure…," 1987). What seems to occur now is that although the

Youth Court judge determines the level of custody (open or secure), exactly which placement within each category is left to the provincial administrators. As pointed out by Robinson (1985):

> the judge may commit a youth to open custody in the expectation that it would be served in a wilderness camp close to the young offender's home in a remote area of the province, but the provincial director may decide to send the youth to a group home in a large metropolitan city which is a foreign environment to the youth and which is hundreds of miles away from his family. If the youth court judge could have anticipated such a decision by the provincial director, the judge may not have opted for any form of custody. (p. 7514.)

This raises several questions including: Who should be making these choices? What criteria should be used in making these decisions? What impact will giving these powers back to the provincial authorities have on custodial dispositions? The problem may be that those most familiar with young people and the various programs available are not the ones deciding which program should be utilized. On the other hand, the YOA was designed specifically to control the discretion exercised in decisions affecting the lives of young people in the juvenile justice system. If changes are made to the existing procedures, will they include safeguards for the rights of young offenders?

These questions highlight only a few of the important issues that have emerged as a result of the implementation of the YOA. The legislation is relatively new and there is a lack of evidence available by which to judge its performance. Nevertheless, certain trends and tendencies have already been established and these indicate a particular flavour of juvenile justice administration in Canada. In the case of custodial dispositions, the evidence presented above suggests that we have moved away from the less formal, rehabilitative approach of the welfare model, which characterized the juvenile justice system under the JDA, to a more formal and more punitive justice model approach under the YOA. The use of custodial dispositions has increased as has the length of custodial sentence. The variability in the definition of open custody results in the differential treatment of young people convicted of similar offences in different parts of the country. This variability may also account for some of the increase in the use of custodial dispositions since it is not entirely clear how "open" these dispositions actually are. Also unknown is the perception of youth court judges of the custodial options provided for in the Act. For example, do judges consider custody to be a rehabilitative option, a punishment for wrongful behaviour, or both? The seriousness of custodial dispositions and the extent to which they impinge on the freedom of young offenders was well recognized by those who drafted the YOA but less so by those charged with its implementation.

It may be easier, more expedient and more desirable on the part of youth court judges to err on the side of community protection in opting for custodial dispositions as opposed to other sentencing alternatives, especially if these are "open" custody dispositions. The same may be said regarding the provision of sentencing alternatives by provincial authorities. Custodial dispositions have a long history in Canadian criminal justice, both generally, and in juvenile justice, and existing ideas and practices are easily adapted to fit the demands of the current legislation. However, the outcome of these practices may not be what was intended when the YOA was designed, passed and implemented. The resulting practices have serious implications for young people convicted of crimes. Thus, it seems that the current experience with custodial dispositions has done little to resolve the debate and controversy over the desired nature of juvenile justice in Canada and serious questions about the use of custodial dispositions remain unanswered.

REFERENCES

Bowker, M.M. (1986). Juvenile court in retrospective: Seven decades of history. In Alberta (1913–1984). *Alberta Law Review*, 24(2), 234–274.

Caputo, T.C. (1987). The *Young Offenders Act*: Children's rights, children's wrongs." *Canadian Public Policy—Analyse de Politiques*, 23(2), 125–143.

Corrado, R. (1983). Introduction. In R.R. Corrado, M. LeBlanc & J. Trépanier (Eds.), *Current issues in juvenile justice* (pp. 1–27). Toronto: Butterworths.

Hagan, J., & Leon, J. (1977). Rediscovering delinquency: Social history, political ideology and the sociology of law. *American Sociological Review*, 42, 587–598.

Housten, S. (1978). The Victorian origins of juvenile delinquency. In W.K. Greenaway & S. Brickey (Eds.), *Law and social control in Canada* (pp. 168–190). Toronto: Prentice-Hall.

Jones, A. (1988). Closing Penetanguishene Reformatory: An attempt to deinstitutionalize treatment of young offenders in early twentieth century Ontario. In R.C. Macleod (Ed.), *Lawful authority: Readings in the history of criminal justice in Canada* (pp. 277–292). Toronto: Copp Clark Pitman.

Leon, J.S. (1977). The development of Canadian juvenile justice: A background for reform. *Osgoode Hall Law Journal*, 15(1), 71–106.

Leschied, A.W., & Jaffe, P. (1985). *Implications of the Young Offenders Act in modifying the juvenile justice system: Some early trends.* Unpublished manuscript, London, ON: Family Court Clinic.

Open or secure custody? *Perception*, 11(1), 4.

Platt, A. (1969). *The child savers*. Chicago, IL: University of Chicago Press.

Reid, S.A., & Reitsma-Street, M. (1984). Assumptions and implications of the new Canadian legislation for young offenders. *Canadian Criminology Forum, 7*, 1–19.

Robinson, L. (1985). Open custody: Some questions about definition, designation and escape therefrom. In N. Bala & H. Lilles (Eds.), *Young offenders service. Volume 2*. Toronto: Butterworth & Co.

Rooke, P.T., & Schnell, R.L. (1983). *Discarding the asylum: From child rescue to the welfare state in English-Canada (1800–1950)*. Lantham, MD: University Press of America.

LEGISLATION

An Act for Establishing Prisons for Young Offenders, for the Better Government of Public Asylums, Hospitals and Prisons, and for the Better Construction of Common Gaols, Statutes of Canada 1857, c. 28.

An Act for the More Speedy Trial and Punishment of Young Offenders, Statutes of Canada 1857, c. 29.

An Act Respecting Industrial Schools, Statutes of Ontario 1874, c. 29.

An Act to Amend the Young Offenders Act, the Criminal Code, the Penitentiary Act and the Prisons and Reformatories Act (Bill C–106), Statutes of Canada 1984–85–86, c. 32.

Juvenile Delinquents Act, Revised Statutes of Canada 1970, c. J–3.

Young Offenders Act, Statutes of Canada 1980–81–82–83, c. 110.

Youth Protection Act, Statutes of Quebec 1977, c. 20.

CASES

C.F. v. R. (1984), 2 Western Weekly Reports 379 (Man. C.A.).

Re F and the Queen et al. (1984), 14 Canadian Criminal Cases (3d) 161 (Man. Q.B.).

In re Gault, 1967 387 U.S. 1, 18L. Ed. 2d 527, 87 S.Ct. 1428.

CHAPTER 10

THE VOLUNTARY SECTOR RESPONSE TO THE YOUNG OFFENDERS ACT

Richard Weiler and Brian Ward[1]

INTRODUCTION

This chapter examines the role of national voluntary organizations in a number of key activities involving young offenders. An examination of the past and present work of these organizations illustrates the changing role of the voluntary sector in response to the *Young Offenders Act* (1982). Under each heading, examples of the contributions made by voluntary groups are provided.[2]

THE CONTEXT OF VOLUNTARY SECTOR INVOLVEMENT IN JUVENILE JUSTICE

The voluntary sector concerned with juvenile justice issues is represented by a diverse group of organizations. Comprised of national, provincial and local organizations, these groups provide a wide range of services on behalf of young offenders, including direct services, advocacy, research, public education and community development.

Historically, the voluntary sector provided for neglected young people on a charitable basis, usually through religious organizations. This work continues today under the *Young Offenders Act* (*YOA*). However, the range of activities has expanded and the ability of the voluntary sector to carry out its activities is now often enhanced by government funding.

Although it is possible to discuss the roles undertaken by the voluntary sector, it is important to note that there is no unified coordinated entity by that name. Most of the groups act independently and often focus on one type of activity, such as service provision. However, networking and information exchange amongst the volunteer groups contribute to a

---

[1] The authors would like to acknowledge the work of Patricia File and Phyllis Drennan-Searson for their ideas and assistance in writing this chapter.

[2] A list of groups is provided in Appendix A for readers who wish more extensive information on the specific activities outlined or want information on other groups involved in similar activities.

collective wisdom and often result in a common consensus as to the problems and the need for different approaches in dealing with young offenders. In addition, most of the national voluntary organizations are associations of many local organizations, such as the Elizabeth Fry or John Howard Societies. Their ability to provide an overview of activities across the country gives them valuable insight into and motivation for developing policy alternatives. These national groups are often involved in a full range of activities regarding the *YOA*. Many of the national organizations have also worked together at various times on issues of common concern regarding young offenders.

THE ROLE OF THE VOLUNTARY SECTOR IN DEVELOPING THE YOUNG OFFENDERS ACT

In the 1960s and 1970s, the voluntary sector played a key role in lobbying for specific changes to the former *Juvenile Delinquents Act* (1970). Development of the *YOA* involved a number of public processes over the last 25 years. Voluntary groups met with and presented briefs to the Justice Committee on Juvenile Delinquency, which was formed in November 1961. They also criticized the Committee's 1965 report. Bill C–192, *An Act Respecting Young Offenders and to Repeal the Juvenile Delinquents Act*, was tabled in the House of Commons in November 1970. However, it was withdrawn in November 1971 partly because of public criticism by voluntary organizations. A subsequent committee produced a report entitled *Young Persons in Conflict with the Law*, again with major contributions from the voluntary sector (Solicitor General Canada, 1975).

From 1975 to 1983, the voluntary sector continued to meet with and present briefs to various committees involved in drafting the proposed legislation (Bill C–61) and dealing with the *YOA* in Parliament. Since 1984, when the Act was proclaimed in force, the voluntary sector has continued to urge amendments to the *YOA*.

Most voluntary groups urged a shift in juvenile justice philosophy and endorsed the new set of principles adopted in the Act. They rejected the *parens patriae* model of the juvenile court. They also insisted that there be a clear definition of the young offender and that a higher minimum age be set for prosecuting a young person in conflict with the law. In particular, they urged alternatives to incarceration and emphasized the need for the community to be more involved in juvenile justice. They also requested more coordination and cooperation among those responsible for dealing with young people through the judicial and social welfare systems.

THE ROLE OF THE VOLUNTARY SECTOR IN IMPLEMENTING THE YOUNG OFFENDERS ACT

The voluntary sector plays a number of key roles in the implementation of the *YOA*, including direct service provision, public education, networking, research, community development, action monitoring and law reform work. Each of these areas is discussed below.

Services

In 1983, the Canadian Council on Social Development (CCSD) and the Canadian Council on Children and Youth (CCCY) conducted a survey of over 300 selected national, regional and local voluntary organizations concerned with young offenders. The survey focused on *YOA*-related activities and plans of the organizations. Since then, the survey has been expanded and conducted on an annual basis by CCCY. Information from these surveys is compiled in a computerized database and is available to the public on a user-fee basis.

The most recent survey of programs in the voluntary sector noted a total of 208 service programs in 1987–88 (Canadian Council on Children and Youth, 1988). Some of these programs (95) consisted of direct service provision only, while others provided a combination of direct and educational services. The status of these service programs has shifted over the last three years from demonstration projects to ongoing projects. Though many of the ongoing projects are still dependent on annual contracts with provincial governments, they are considered ongoing by the operating agency. The scope of the programs has expanded beyond the local community to include responsibility for services in regions and in some instances, provinces. However, support for programs with a national focus has diminished (Canadian Council on Children and Youth, 1988).

Table 1 summarizes changes in the activities and number of service programs from 1986 to 1988. All of the activities under alternative programs have increased over the last three years, with community service orders (CSOs) and victim-offender reconciliation programs (VORPs) being the most common programs. Of note in the court-related programs is the doubling in the number of assessment programs over the last year and an increase in the number of counselling programs. Sentencing options grew the most over the last three years, with community service orders, fine options, and attendance centres accounting for most of the growth. The fact that two secure custody programs entered the Inventory indicates that voluntary organizations are beginning to provide this type of service. Programs dealing with treatment orders remained at seven, down from 11 in the first year. Other programs, which peaked at 21 the previous year,

TABLE 1
NUMBER OF ACTIVITIES BY SERVICE
DELIVERY PROGRAMS

Programs[1] Activities	Programs/Number of Activities		
	1986	1987	1988
Alternative Programs	70	91	97
Activities:			
Victim-Offender Reconciliation	34	40	45
Community Service Order	46	59	58
Restitution through Service	28	38	39
Financial Restitution	22	31	33
Apology	20	29	30
Counselling	31	39	41
Other	25	21	17
Court Programs	46	57	56
Activities:			
Counselling	31	32	37
Court Work	16	23	19
Attendance Centre	4	8	8
Assessment	6	5	10
Judicial Interim Release	8	7	7
Bail Supervision	12	14	15
Chaplaincy	8	10	10
Other	8	7	10
Sentencing Options Programs	101	121	134
Activities:			
Victim-Offender Reconciliation	16	27	30
Community Service Order	57	62	68
Restitution through Service	12	17	18
Financial Restitution	12	19	20
Apology	4	11	12
Probation Supervision	11	14	19
Fine Option	3	7	15
Counselling	32	45	45
Treatment Orders	11	7	7
Attendance Centre	4	13	18
Open Custody	22	25	27
Secure Custody	–	–	2
Other	10	21	1
Institutional Programs	15	20	28
Activities:			
Chaplaincy	7	10	15
Volunteer Programs	8	13	19
Other	–	8	11

[1]Note: Many programs had more than one focus area and many activities.

SOURCE: Canadian Council on Children and Youth (1988). *Young Offenders Act, Third annual survey of programs in the voluntary sector, 1987–88*. (Appendix D.) Unpublished manuscript, Ottawa, ON.

dropped off sharply to only one program in 1988. The number of institutional settings using volunteers increased again from 1987 to 1988.

The survey also noted an increase in the number of programs dealing with young persons with special needs. The number of programs dealing specifically with learning disabled youth increased from 19 programs in 1987 to 24 programs in 1988. The number of programs serving a distinct cultural group increased from 18 to 29 programs over the same period. These programs are often aimed at native youth. There has also been substantial increase in the number of drug and alcohol abuse programs in the past few years; the number increased from 55 programs in 1986–87 to 64 programs 1987–88 (Canadian Council on Children and Youth, 1988, p.5).

Most major voluntary organizations assume significant service provision responsibilities, often with different program orientations. For example, the Salvation Army provides a wide range of court-related programs, sentence alternatives, custody options and rehabilitation services across Canada. In contrast, the YMCA has developed its juvenile justice programs with an emphasis on providing a positive group experience to youth in conflict with the law. For example, programs at the Montreal YMCA include juvenile diversion clubs, group opportunities to provide retribution to the community for wrongdoing, and alternative schools.

Public Education

Education programs developed by the voluntary sector have been primarily directed towards the public, persons interested in juvenile justice, youth, and professionals within the juvenile justice system. Public education programs are a major activity of volunteer organizations and, next to service delivery programs, they constitute the second major theme in the CCCY Survey/Inventory database (Canadian Council on Children and Youth, 1988). There were 141 public education programs in 1987–88 out of a total of 236 programs offered by voluntary organizations. The survey showed that the most common education activities were lectures, the production of written materials, workshops and guest speakers. While referral to YOA programs experienced the most significant growth in 1986–87, this activity declined by more than half in 1987–88. In 1987–88, more programs were directed toward students; in the previous year, the emphasis was on professional audiences. The types of material produced paralleled the increased emphasis on students and youth. For example, more information was made available on the legal rights and responsibilities of young offenders and general information on the youth justice system (Canadian Council on Children and Youth, 1988).

Much of the public education is achieved through the circulation of newsletters and journals to the memberships of the voluntary organizations. In addition to informing people of the programs available in their community under the *YOA*, these articles also highlight problems, provide analysis and stimulate action in the juvenile justice area. For example, *Youth Policy Today* is a quarterly publication of the Canadian Youth Foundation, a policy and research institute for young people, which reviews a wide range of issues relevant to youth. Most of the articles give a concise and pertinent analysis of proposed government initiatives and their projected impact on youth and most volumes contain a piece on the *YOA*. For example, a recent article surveyed government proposals to amend the dispositional sections of the *YOA* (Clarke, 1987).

One area of particular relevance to young offenders is that of learning disabilities. The Learning Disabilities Association of Canada has developed a Legal Resources Handbook (Stutt, 1986) and an education package, including a video, for judges, lawyers, probation officers and other judicial personnel (Bourgeau, 1987). Since 1985, the organization has held workshops in nine provinces, involving a total of 185 judges. The workshops focused on the relationship between learning disabilities and the behaviour of young offenders. They use a range of resource materials, in addition to discussion with parents, fellow professionals, and experts. A video of a simulated disposition hearing for a young offender allows judges to prepare a disposition in light of their new insights into this problem and then discuss it with fellow judges. The materials also examine other stages of the *YOA* process in which learning disabilities may require special consideration. The critical significance of these issues for judges and lawyers is illustrated throughout the program. For example, difficulty in understanding written and oral instructions may limit a young person's understanding of the standard police warning regarding their rights to "retain and instruct counsel."

Networking

The national voluntary organizations network within their own groups through meetings and various information-sharing activities such as newsletters. Conferences are another vehicle for networking and information exchange. In each of its national biennial congresses, the Canadian Criminal Justice Association provides a major forum for discussion of issues affecting young offenders, particularly those pertaining to the *YOA*. CCSD also held a National Workshop on Crime Prevention Through Social Development in February 1987.

One of the most significant, ongoing vehicles for networking is the National *YOA* Table. It is a coalition of 12 national voluntary organizations concerned with the welfare of young offenders. It has met on a regular basis since January 1985 and has facilitated a fairly sophisticated response by the voluntary sector to the implementation of the *YOA*. The *YOA* Table meetings have encouraged sharing of information about young offender activities, discussion of ways to improve services for young offenders, exploration of ways to monitor the implementation of the *YOA*, discussion of government policy and program initiatives, and provision of support to front-line workers in this field. Various initiatives are discussed at the Table and one or more of the groups is encouraged to undertake a specific activity. The CCSD and CCCY survey to produce the Inventory of Programs Provided by the Voluntary Sector, discussed above, is an example of such work.

Research

The voluntary sector has been actively involved in a number of *YOA* research areas including: determining the patterns of voluntary sector involvement under the *YOA*; assessing the effectiveness of the system in adopting the principles of the Act; and research on specific matters of concern.

The CCCY Survey/Inventory outlined above showed a total of 236 programs operated by the voluntary sector in response to the *YOA* during the 1987–88 year. This was up 5.3% over the previous year, and up from 206 programs in 1985–86. While there were 34 new programs during 1987–88, 21 programs from previous years were cancelled. There were also only 11 proposed programs, all of which were from organizations already involved in *YOA* programs. Thus, the survey concluded there is a trend towards stability and limited expansion in programs and in the *YOA* program community (Canadian Council on Children and Youth, 1988).

In early March 1985, CCSD and CCCY surveyed 100 community organizations and 100 individuals working with the juvenile justice system across Canada. Essentially, the survey provided a snapshot view of the perceptions of people involved in the implementation of the *YOA* (Weiler & Ward, 1985). The survey results demonstrate a number of emerging strengths and weaknesses of the Act. With the exception of Quebec, where many of the Act's provisions were already in place, most provinces were only in minimal compliance with the Act. The intent of the Act to provide an appropriate and authentic youth justice system appeared to be in difficulty. There was variation across the country in implementation of the Act, suggesting that some provinces were emphasizing alternative measures, while others were focusing on open and secure custody. The relationship between child welfare legislation and associated programs and the *YOA* legislation and programs was problematic. There were no consistent patterns regarding the availability of assessment services, alternative dispositional options, treatment options, or open and secure custody options. In particular, most provinces that had to increase the age limit for criminal responsibility to 18 had few services to deal with 16- and 17-year olds.

The researchers conducting the survey were disturbed by the extent of incarceration of youth. This was particularly noted in the length of pre-trial detention, which ranged from four to 40 days, often because of delays in obtaining legal counsel. They were also struck by the late and haphazard planning of some provinces for implementation of the YOA and the lack of awareness of some provinces about successful programs elsewhere, such as in Quebec. While it appeared that considerable progress had been made to ensure access to legal services by young offenders, the survey noted that young people were not aware of their rights to retain counsel, legal services were not available in rural areas of some provinces, legal aid officials in some areas did not understand or, perhaps, wish to comply with the YOA by giving full legal services to young people, and some crown prosecutors and defence lawyers did not seem to understand the full import of the Act.

Research by the voluntary sector provides more than information. It can be more blunt, more public, more accessible, less partisan and more truthful in its observations than either bureaucratic or ministerial surveys. It can also serve as a networking vehicle, bringing information on various groups' activities to the attention of other groups, revealing common problems and encouraging common action.

The truth-telling role of the voluntary sector in researching and revealing problems with the YOA is especially significant in the case of contentious observations. This type of research can also identify policy and program needs and be a catalyst in fulfilling those needs. An example of this type of research is the work on the female young offender done by the Canadian Association of Elizabeth Fry Societies (1987). They conducted a survey in the summer of 1987 to discover what programs and services were available through voluntary agencies in Canada under the YOA, particularly for young women in conflict with the law. They also wanted to assess program needs for women. The survey showed that despite an increase in the numbers of young women being arrested and sentenced under the YOA and an average of about 20% of the client population being young women, there was an almost total lack of specific programs designed to meet the special needs of young women in conflict with the law. Agencies were asked to list the needs of the young women who came to them for help and then to list the programs that they provided. The five most frequently listed needs were basic life skills, development of self-confidence and autonomy, upgrading education, having time away from a problematic surrounding and addiction counselling. However, the five most frequently listed programs offered were community service orders, victim-offender reconciliation programs, compensation, improvement of social skills and individual counselling. Though shoplifting was the most common offence committed by young women in contact with the agencies, shoplifting programs ranked 14th on the list of programs provided. The numbers of young mothers in conflict with the law highlighted the need for programs which took into consideration needs for daycare and other support programs for these women. The survey showed that while agencies were able to identify the needs of young women, they were not providing the programs.

Community Development

Many groups in the voluntary sector do community development work. Such work is often focused on generating community awareness about the problem of juvenile crime, how we are dealing with it, and how we could better be dealing with it. Most voluntary groups believe that for the YOA to realize its full potential, communities must respond to needs generated by the Act, such as provision for constructive alternative measures.

Recently, the Church Council on Justice and Corrections developed a manual entitled *Watching Youth in Court-An Invitation to Community Involvement under the Young Offenders Act* (Macdonald & Bala, 1987). It contains an extensive description of the Act and encourages the community to get involved in a number of ways, emphasizing courtwatching as a program activity.

Another example is a major project of the John Howard Society of Canada entitled *Development of Community Participation in the Implementation and Operation of the Young Offender Act*. It completed two phases of its work by December 1986. The objectives of this program were to assist member societies in developing community-based YOA programs, to establish a communication network, and to establish a John Howard Society of Canada national clearinghouse for their YOA activities. In aid of this project, speakers were sent to public meetings, inter-agency meetings and to meetings of society staff, board and volunteers to talk about the YOA and to give specific information such as program criteria for development of community-based YOA programs. As a clearinghouse for YOA information, the John Howard Society is a community resource for interested members of the public, students, other voluntary associations, and professionals.

Action Monitoring

The voluntary sector has been playing an increasing role in monitoring both general implementation of the YOA and specific activities such as courtwatching. Courtwatching focuses on individual cases, ensuring that the YOA is being administered fairly. Courtworker programs for natives and female offenders often perform this role in addition to providing advice to offenders. The Church Council's publication *Watching Youth in Court* (Macdonald & Bala, 1987), described above, is an example of work designed for action monitoring. The manual encourages its readers to monitor the *YOA* in court in the hopes that their very attention may cause those who work in the youth justice system to perform their duties more conscientiously. The manual has a list of questions for courtwatchers to consider and provides a courtwatching form to facilitate notetaking. It also encourages individuals to get involved in cases and become a friend to a young person in trouble with the law.

Law Reform

Much of the impetus for law reform in the field of juvenile justice has come from the voluntary sector. Groups like the Canadian Criminal Justice Association, which bring together various criminal justice professionals such as police officers, lawyers, judges, probation, parole and other correctional workers and laypersons interested in criminal justice issues, have participated throughout the development of the *YOA*. Their Legislation Committee has provided comments and recommendations to various government departments and agencies and to the general public. Most of the other national voluntary organizations have been and continue to be involved in these activities. Much of this work is now being facilitated by the National *YOA* Table. In response to requests from the *YOA* Directorate of the federal government, the Table has given its views on proposed amendments to the Act and the development of a self-evaluation guide intended for the use of staff in community-based alternative programs. Department officials have attended meetings of the *YOA* Table and received information on problems arising from the implementation of the Act. Much of this information has come from the surveys referred to above.

FUTURE CHALLENGES

The foregoing discussion illustrates the significant role of the voluntary sector in the development, implementation and evaluation of the *YOA*. Through their work with young offenders, the public, and professionals within the system, voluntary organizations are trying to ensure that programs live up to the spirit of the Act. They are the main providers of alternative programs under the Act and education programs about the Act. Their work in this regard, will likely increase over the next few years. In addition, their commitment to community-based justice will likely result in more emphasis being placed on community development. A number of issues will affect the role of the voluntary sector in response to the *YOA* and these are discussed below. The voluntary sector must address a number of challenges if it is to fulfill vital responsibilities regarding the *YOA*.

Prevention

Although the *YOA* introduced a fairer process than previous legislation, it also focuses more on controlling young offenders than it does on caring for young offenders. It does little to address the basic social and economic causes of crime, such as poverty and unemployment. Canada's voluntary sector has become increasingly active in encouraging government to deal with the factors associated with chronic criminal behaviour. However, social development initiatives are needed to deal with concerns in the fields of health, social services, housing, education and employment. Such initiatives receive little attention in the shaping of Canadian crime prevention strategies. The major challenge for the voluntary sector will be to persuade governments to develop the necessary programs rather than expending all of their own resources in providing stop-gap measures such as drop-in centres and shelters for runaway youth. By emphasizing these measures, government has failed to deal with the real problems underlying juvenile delinquency.

Government Funding

National organizations are often largely dependent on federal government financial support. Major initiatives of these organizations are usually supported through short-term project grants. However, such funding is becoming limited. The federal government has also become increasingly conscious about ensuring that activities funded by federal funds are sensitive to, and have the support of, provincial governments. Moreover, many organizations at community and regional levels depend on provincial government financial support. This means that the types of initiatives developed by the voluntary sector are affected by funding cutbacks, pressure to be involved in privatization of direct services or pressure to carry out specific government agendas. The independence of the voluntary sector is also important to its ability to provide non-direct services, including advocacy and providing critiques of government actions.

Participation in Policy and Program Development

The federal government is currently undertaking a comprehensive review of the role of the national voluntary sector and its relationship with the Departments of Justice and the Solicitor General. The voluntary organizations, through the National *YOA* Table and other means, are attempting to develop processes whereby they can play a greater role in policy and program development. Because these issues are increasingly being dealt with through federal-provincial negotiations, commitment from both levels of government is needed in order to develop a meaningful and timely consultation process and to provide sufficient resources and time for voluntary sector participation.

REFERENCES

Bourgeau, J. (1987). Learning disabilities and the young offender. *Just Cause*, 4(4).

Canadian Association of Elizabeth Fry Societies. (1987). *Inventory of programs and services for young women in conflict with the law*. Unpublished manuscript, Ottawa.

Canadian Council on Children and Youth. (1988). *Young Offenders Act, Third annual survey of programs in the voluntary sector, 1987–88*. Unpublished manuscript, Ottawa.

Clarke, M. (1987). The Canadian Youth Foundation. *Youth Policy Today*, 2(5), 1.

John Howard Society of Canada. (1986). *Report on YOA development activities, phase II, 1985–1986*. Unpublished manuscript, Ottawa.

Justice Committee on Juvenile Delinquency. (1965). *Juvenile delinquency in Canada: The report of the Department of Justice Committee on Juvenile Delinquency*. Ottawa: Queen's Printer.

Macdonald, R., & Bala, N. (1987). *Watching youth in court: An invitation to community involvement under the Young Offenders Act*. Ottawa: Church Council on Justice and Corrections.

Solicitor General Canada. (1975). *Young persons in conflict with the law*. A report of the Solicitor General's committee on proposals for new legislation to replace the *Juvenile Delinquents Act*. Ottawa: Author.

Stutt, H. (1986). *Learning disabilities and the young offender: Arrest to disposition*. Ottawa: Learning Disabilities Association of Canada (formerly known as the Canadian Association for Children and Adults with Learning Disabilities).

Weiler, R., & Ward, B. (1985). A national overview of the implementation of YOA: One year later. *Perception*, 8(5), 7–13.

LEGISLATION

An Act to Amend the Young Offenders Act, the Criminal Code, The Penitentiary Act and the Prisons and Reformatories Act (Bill C–106), Statutes of Canada 1984–85–86, c.32.

Bill C–192, *An Act Respecting Young Offenders and to Repeal the Juvenile Delinquents Act*, 3d Sess., 28th Parl., 1970–71–72.

Juvenile Delinquents Act, Revised Statutes of Canada 1970, c. J–3.

Young Offenders Act (Bill C–61), Statutes of Canada 1980–81–82–83, c.110.

APPENDIX A

National Voluntary Organizations Involved with the National YOA Table

Canadian Association of Elizabeth Fry Societies
251 Bank Street, Suite 600, Ottawa, ON K2P 1X3
(613) 238–2422

Canadian Child Welfare Association
2211 Riverside Drive, Suite 401, Ottawa, ON K1H 7X5
(613) 738–0697

Canadian Council on Children and Youth (CCCY)
2211 Riverside Drive, Suite 11, Ottawa, ON K1H 7X5
(613) 738–0200

Canadian Council on Social Development (CCSD)
55 Parkdale Avenue, P.O. Box 3505, Stn C, Ottawa, ON K1Y 4G1
(613) 728–1865

Canadian Criminal Justice Association
55 Parkdale Avenue, Ottawa, ON K1Y 1E5
(613) 725–3715

Canadian Law Information Council
600 Eglinton Avenue East, Suite 205, Toronto, ON M4P 1P3
(416) 483–3802

Church Council on Justice and Corrections
507 Bank Street, Ottawa, ON K2P 1Z5
(613) 563–1688

John Howard Society of Canada
55 Parkdale Avenue, Ottawa, ON K1Y 1E5
(613) 728–1865

Learning Disabilities Association of Canada
323 Chapel, Suite 200, Ottawa, ON K1N 7Z2
(613) 238–5721

National Youth in Care Network
2211 Riverside Drive, Suite 401, Ottawa, ON K1H 7X5
(613) 738–0915

St. Leonard's Society of Canada
575 Windsor Avenue, Suite 104, Windsor, ON N9A 1J4
(519) 254–9430

The Salvation Army of Canada (Brampton)
c/o 44 Nelson Street West, Brampton, ON L6X 1C1

YMCA of Montreal
1441 Drummond Street, Montreal, PQ H3G 1W3
(514) 849–8393

CHAPTER 11

THE YOUNG OFFENDERS ACT AND ABORIGINAL YOUTH

Carol Pitcher LaPrairie

This chapter has three objectives. First, to identify the issue of aboriginal youth in conflict with the law by examining crime incidence; second, to examine some dimensions of aboriginal life in Canadian society; finally, to discuss the implications of this life situation for the impact of the *Young Offenders Act* (1982) on the lives of aboriginal young offenders.

ABORIGINAL YOUTH AND CRIME

Prior to 1981, there was almost no empirical research dealing with aboriginal delinquency in Canada. This was largely due to difficulties in undertaking research on the topic. In addition, aboriginal delinquency has not been a major priority of either government or aboriginal agencies. As a result there is a lack of systematic, comprehensive information on aboriginal delinquency rates over different time periods. The available data are sketchy and offer only a preliminary basis for assessing the scope and magnitude of comparative delinquency involvement.

Although there are no complete or comprehensive national data available on the nature and extent of crime among aboriginal youth, there are some isolated references from various locales across the country. One of the first empirical studies on the incidence of aboriginal delinquency was conducted by LaPrairie and Griffiths (1982) in a northern primary resource community. These authors reported that while there did not appear to be any significant difference in the kinds of offences committed by aboriginal and non-aboriginal youth, aboriginal youth were significantly over-represented in the juvenile justice system relative to their numbers in the general population. Furthermore, there were major structural differences between the two groups with regard to income, education levels and family situation.

In examining characteristics of adult aboriginal inmates in Ontario, a study by the Ontario Native Council on Justice (1981) revealed that 37% of inmates interviewed had been involved in the juvenile justice system as children. Furthermore, the same study reported that Indian children in Ontario's child welfare system (which might be considered the other side of the juvenile justice coin) constituted 10% of the total; this represents 10 times the rate of involvement for the general population (Ontario Native Council on Justice, 1981).

Jolly (1983) provides some additional data on aboriginal young offenders. His *Fact Sheet on the Indian Young People in the Juvenile Justice and Child Welfare Systems of Ontario* revealed that in 1981–82, status Indians under the age of 20 made up only 0.7% of the total population of Ontario but in comparison to non-Indian young people, they were: (a) two-and-a-half times more likely to be placed on probation; (b) four times more likely to be committed to training school, and; (c) four times more likely to be admitted to a Children's Aid Society facility.

In addition, as of March 31, 1982, status Indian youth were three times more likely to be on probation, two-and-a-half times more likely to be a training school ward and three times more likely to be placed in an observation and detention facility (Jolly, 1983). These figures pertain to the status Indian population only and do not include non-status and métis youth.

These data tell us several things. First, they make an argument for the systematic collection of valid and reliable data to better inform the issue of aboriginal delinquency from a number of perspectives: (a) the nature and scope of the problem in a variety of geographic locations; (b) the charging, prosecution and sentencing of aboriginal youth; and (c) the relationship between the justice system and the child welfare system. Although there is a dearth of good national data, the available evidence points to a bleak future for many aboriginal youth in this country. How has this situation come about and what are its implications for the fair and equitable application of the *Young Offenders Act* (*YOA*)?

SOCIO-ECONOMIC CONTEXT OF ABORIGINAL DELINQUENCY

The social, economic and political context in which aboriginal delinquency occurs is directly related to the situation of aboriginal people within the dominant non-aboriginal Canadian society. The dual processes of colonization and under-development have created a welfare ghetto and a status of social, political and economic marginality for the majority of aboriginal people (LaPrairie, 1987). This status is exhibited by high rates of unemployment, suicide, alcohol abuse and illness among aboriginal people. Dependency upon welfare and government is reflected in the erosion of traditional lifestyles and economies. The generally disorganized state of many communities is seen in family violence, sexual abuse, and in the breakdown of traditional gender roles and social relations. Much of modern aboriginal life is characterized by feelings of hopelessness, despair, inferiority and dependency.

Whether on reserves or living in rural, semi-urban or urban areas, life for most aboriginal youth is bleak. This situation provides the context for understanding the high rates of involvement of aboriginal youth in both the juvenile justice and child welfare systems. Many aboriginal youth face a host of difficulties in everyday living; difficulties not normally encountered by the majority of non-aboriginal youth. The decline in aboriginal culture and community cohesion has meant that for this group, life is often confusing and dislocating, with little hope or expectation for change. Research on aboriginal delinquency has pointed to culture conflict, boredom, loss of parental discipline and feelings of hopelessness on the part of aboriginal youth as the primary causes of delinquency (Kueneman et al., 1986; Bouchard & Pelletier, 1986; Bissonnette, 1985).

Aboriginal youth appear to experience conflict with the law at younger ages than do non-aboriginal youth (LaPrairie & Griffiths, 1982). The propensity of some aboriginal youth to get into trouble at an early age may reflect the loss of traditional activities in the social life of the community and meaningful work and recreational opportunities. This loss may play a major role in generating feelings of alienation and poor self-image. For youth residing near or attached to a predominantly non-aboriginal community, there may not be a sense of belonging either to a supportive aboriginal community, where role relationships are traditionally defined, or to the life of the dominant community. Furthermore, culture conflict is not restricted to these settings. Even in communities that are predominantly aboriginal, the intrusion of non-aboriginal values and western ideology through modernization have served to culturally dislocate youth. For many, culture conflict is compounded by the lack of opportunities widely available to the majority of Canadian youth. Aboriginal youth are frequently excluded from these opportunities due to various circumstances of geography, poor education, employment histories and overt discrimination.

Incidents of violence, alcohol abuse and suicide are common in many contemporary aboriginal communities, as is the general lethargy that accompanies widespread and prolonged unemployment, and the lack of recreation and other activities. Clearly one must be careful about making broad generalizations of this nature, particularly in light of the cultural regeneration that has occurred over the past two decades and the fact that in some communities, tradition and culture have prevailed. The effects of years of colonization and underdevelopment, however, are not easily or quickly dispelled, and for many communities the effects have been, and continue to be, devastating.

The effects of the loss of traditional activities and the general exclusion of aboriginal people from mainstream economy and society is compounded by the geographic isolation of many aboriginal communities.

Communities are often either: (a) too isolated to become economically self-sufficient in the modern sense, attached to hinterland primary-resource towns where the values of hard living and hard drinking spill over and/or reinforce activities in the aboriginal community; or (b) ghettos within urban cores. The very nature of much of economically deprived and marginal community life suggests the potential to adopt deviant or delinquent values.

Finally, within the context of aboriginal delinquency it is useful to consider briefly the impact of the now-extinct residential school system on the lives of many aboriginal people. This continues to be a relevant issue; the forced attendance of many of the parents during their formative years have implications for today's aboriginal youth.

MacLean (1978), Kellough (1980) and Cardinal (1969) have described the effects of residential school life on aboriginal people. Kellough (1980, p. 349) notes that the belief that "...all the Indian's problems would vanish if only they could be made to adopt white values and beliefs..." was at the root of the residential school system. Schools were seen as a way of accelerating the assimilation process by taking Indian youth away from their homes and communities in order to re-socialize them more quickly. Thus, contact with parents was minimized and youth were enrolled in the schools at very young ages (MacLean, 1978). Children experienced severe alienation because the schools:

> ...alienated the child from his family, they alienated him from his own way of life without in any way preparing him for a different society; they alienated the child from his own religion and turned his head resolutely against the conforming substitute the missionaries offered. (Cardinal, 1969, p. 54)

Perhaps the most critical feature of this process was that children growing up in these schools were inhibited in learning parenting skills because: (a) they were kept away from their own parents who could have served as role models; and (b) they did not experience being parented. While no empirical research exists to support this claim, it should be considered, nevertheless, in understanding the context of contemporary aboriginal delinquency.

The general situation in which Canadian aboriginal youth find themselves may best be summarized in the following description of a typical aboriginal youth offender as provided by McCaskill in 1970 (p.26):

> It would appear that a profile of the typical native youth offender would include: a community of origin which is economically impoverished, an unstable family background, a high degree of contact with social service agencies (particularly white foster homes), limited knowledge and participation in Indian affairs, a low degree of Indian culture and a great sense of alienation from mainstream society.

The situation for aboriginal youth is not very different in 1988. It is with this in mind that we turn to a discussion of the implications of the *YOA* for aboriginal youth and aboriginal communities.

FACTORS AFFECTING THE IMPACT OF THE YOUNG OFFENDERS ACT ON ABORIGINAL YOUTH

Lacking empirical data we are left to infer the application and effect of the *YOA* on aboriginal youth. This requires taking into account the environmental factors of geographic isolation, socio-economic marginality and what has generally come to be regarded as the socially disorganized state of many aboriginal communities.

Geograpaphic Isolation

The potential for geographic isolation to affect the fair and equitable treatment of aboriginal juveniles has been identified by several researchers (Kueneman et al., 1986; Bouchard & Pelletier, 1986; Miller, 1984). Living in areas of geographic isolation is, in some respects, tantamount to being aboriginal in Canada. Many aboriginal people live primarily in the vast reaches north of 60 and in the expanses of mid-belt, hinterland territory. For the administration of criminal justice, geographic isolation often means that aboriginal people have only limited access to justice services. Attempts to redress the difficulties caused by geographic isolation with circuit courts and courtworker services have been only partially successful. Kueneman et al. (1986) examined northern and rural juvenile courts in Manitoba and found a strong correlation between the remoteness of communities and the quality and availability of service. Some of the major problems they identified were: (a) lack of criminal justice and social services; (b) lack of experienced local legal counsel; (c) lack of local detention facilities; (d) too much work and too little time for court officials to handle cases most effectively; (e) lack of knowledge on the part of youth about the criminal justice system and/or youths' rights. In comparing aboriginal and non-aboriginal northern and rural communities the authors concluded that in general "Native communities have high needs and lower levels of resources" (Kueneman et al., 1986, p. 154).

In commenting on the implications of the *YOA* for the right to counsel in the Northwest Territories, Miller touches on the effect of regional disparity when he states that: "In the northern justice system, the major problem will be lack of availability of counsel in that the only opportunity within the present circuit system for consultation will be when counsel arrives at the community on circuit" (Miller, 1984, p. 4).

Miller (1984) points out that the adequacy of legal counsel is particularly critical to aboriginal youth because of: (a) the greater emphasis on legal rights in the Act; (b) possible cultural and linguistic differences among aboriginal youth that must be interpreted for the courts; (c) the formality of the justice system under the *YOA*; (d) the need to raise all legal defences on behalf of the youth; and (e) the need to ensure that the disposition involves the least possible interference with the young person's freedom. Miller (1984) notes, however, that fulfilling those desired criteria will be particularly difficult for court circuit counsel due to time constraints, inadequate understanding of native culture, inability to interview clients and difficulties often related to the geographic isolation of many northern communities. Further evidence of the effects of geographic isolation for aboriginal youth in conflict with the law is available from Bissonnette's (1985) work in Quebec. Bissonnette (1985) notes the infrequency of court circuits, ignorance of the provisions of the *YOA* and a lack of available services and resources at the community level.

Socio-Economic Marginality

The available research clearly shows that in relation to mainstream society, aboriginal society has been relegated to a status of socio-economic marginality. Aboriginal communities commonly have weak or non-existent economies, large numbers of dependent children and single parents, few employment opportunities, limited recreational and social services and high rates of alcohol and solvent abuse (Kueneman et al., 1986).

The effects of socio-economic marginality may be most critical with respect to those sections of the *YOA* that rely on a determination of community or parental suitability for supervision upon release. For example, the way in which aboriginal parents may be perceived by probation officers and/or judges with respect to those sections of the Act (i.e. sections 7 and 8 on judicial interim release) where judges have the discretion to place the young person in the care of a responsible adult as an alternative to detention (LaPrairie, 1983). This may well mean that more aboriginal youth receive detention. Responsibility would likely be decided on the basis of parental employment, perceived stability of family and community surroundings and a number of other environmental factors. It may be difficult for many aboriginal parents to pass the responsibility "test" given their socio-economic circumstances and the state of many of their communities.

The marginal status of communities and the lack of community facilities to enable youth to attain acceptable education and/or employment levels are no doubt reflected in predisposition reports that exist to make judges aware of the wider context within which crimes occur. The very nature of the information collected and presented in pre-sentence reports may adversely affect the chances of a youth receiving probation rather than detention. Judges are concerned with the offender's potential for rehabilitation. Therefore, personal and socio-economic characteristics such as family background, education, employment history, and drug and alcohol use, are an integral part of judicial decision making in considering sentencing options. It would seem reasonable to conclude that if nothing else, the kind of background information that is presented on the majority of aboriginal youth, and the severe lack of community resources, greatly reduces the ability of judges to adopt many of the available sentencing options. Even with respect to custodial reviews (section 28) there is probably less likelihood that the circumstances of aboriginal youth have changed in a way that could facilitate release.

Social Disorganization

It is in the area of community alternatives to incarceration where the socially disorganized status of many aboriginal communities create the greatest potential for inaction. The development and use of community alternatives to incarceration may be most affected by the social disorganization of aboriginal communities. Non-custodial dispositions assume the availability of support services and resources, which are generally absent in these kinds of communities.

Kueneman et al. (1986) noted that in many of the aboriginal communities they studied there were major deficiencies in the ability of the communities to develop alternatives to incarceration. For example, the youth court committees are difficult to establish when apathy and general social disorganization inhibit organized social action. There was often no key criminal justice group in the community to facilitate or initiate the development of resources such as youth committees. It would appear that those communities most in need of resources and services are the least able to develop or sustain them.

The situation of many contemporary aboriginal communities is probably best explained in terms of underdevelopment theory. The basic premise of underdevelopment in relation to aboriginal people in Canada has been the lack of development that would create economic independence for communities. Not only does a lack of development exist but most reserves are situated on land generally unsuitable for a durable economic infrastructure. The erosion of traditional economic activities and the exclusion from modern ones has considerably altered social structures and social relations in aboriginal communities, and has put many of them into a political, social and economic "no-man's land."

CONCLUSION

The impact of environmental factors such as geographic isolation, socio-economic marginality and community erosion illustrate that aboriginal youth may be more vulnerable than non-aboriginal youth to justice processing and, as a result, to the harsher effects of certain *YOA* provisions.

A fundamental problem that the criminal justice system alone cannot resolve is the structural inequality that creates systematic discrimination of the kind discussed in this paper. The wheels of the system can be "greased" by implementing more sophisticated and careful legislation, by developing more sensitive policies and procedures and by trying to ensure that rights and responsibilities are recognized and enforced. Structural equality will not, however, be generated through the workings of the justice system, no matter how smoothly it functions.

This seems to leave juvenile justice matters affecting aboriginal people at the level of redressing the structural imbalance as far as possible by facilitating community efforts to assume more control over criminal justice matters. Adopting this strategy should enable the youth justice system to better reflect the community context from which delinquency originates and within which it can be best resolved. Always removing individual offenders from the community to be externally processed increases the potential for environmental factors to negatively influence decision making.

Youth courts and youth justice committees provided for by the *YOA* may be vehicles for communities to exercise greater authority and control in juvenile matters. For example, aboriginal justices-of-the-peace could preside over youth courts in aboriginal communities, sitting individually or as a council (similar to a council of elders), where they could deal with all youth matters. The value of having more than one individual making case decisions is that it would decrease pressure on a single individual and would also incorporate the experience and knowledge of several individuals.

At a recent Human Rights conference in Iqualuit, Northwest Territories, one participant described the potential role and function of youth justice committees in the following way:

> What can Youth Justice Committees do? By acting as a kind of informal court in the community, they protect the rights of young people and help to keep them out of the formal court system. They can ask young people to make amends by doing service for the people they have hurt. Youth Justice Committees know what resources there are in the community to help deal with a young person's needs. They can provide attention for the young person, try to understand why a young person did something wrong, and help

that person to see why he shouldn't do it again. They can exert discipline from the community or from the extended family.

Youth Justice Committees can also develop programmes, both for individual youth or for young people, in the community as a whole. They can form recreation committees, on-the-land programmes with help from Hunters and Trappers Associations, and other measures. They can use community resources to resolve some of the problems that encourage young people to get into trouble. (Report of the Baffin Human Rights Conference, 1987, p. 31)

From a cultural perspective, council of elders or aboriginal justices of the peace presiding in youth courts and youth justice committees have the potential to incorporate traditional customs, values and practices. From a community perspective, existing resources can be mobilized to meet offender needs or, perhaps as importantly, to identify and champion the need for resources to enable the community to deal with offenders. Finally, alternatives such as youth committees may assist crime prevention by keeping other youth from offending in the first place.

The need to create or amplify resources at the community level is not restricted to the predominantly non-urban communities. Research to date has focused on communities in isolated, rural or semi-urban locations as being most in need of local control and expanded resources, but it is becoming abundantly clear that urban settings require attention with respect to both adult and juvenile aboriginal justice matters; this attention has been notably absent to date.

Perhaps all of this means that in order to reduce the impact of environmental factors on justice processing and decision making affecting aboriginal youth, it is necessary to begin thinking about how to redress, in part, the imbalances created through structural inequalities. Strategies such as augmenting existing services and developing new ones come most readily to mind. It will be necessary, however, to be more committed and creative in these undertakings if the pressing issue of aboriginal youth in conflict with the law is to be better addressed.

REFERENCES

Bissonnette, A. (1985). *Native juveniles and criminal law: Preliminary study of needs and services in some native communities of Quebec.* Ottawa: Department of Justice.

Bouchard, S., & Pelletier, C. (1986). *Justice in question.* Quebec: Department of Justice.

Cardinal, H. (1969). *The unjust society.* Edmonton: M.G. Hurtig Ltd.

Jolly, S. (1983, February). *The kids are hurting: Fact sheet on the disproportionate involvement of Indian young people in the juvenile justice and child welfare systems of Ontario.* (Available from Ontario Native Council on Justice, Toronto.)

Kellough, G. (1980). From colonialism to economic imperialism: The experience of the Canadian Indian. In J. Harp & J. Hofley (Eds.), *Structured inequality in Canada* (pp. 343–377). Toronto: Prentice-Hall.

Kueneman, R., Linden, R., & Kosmick, R. (1986). *A study of Manitoba's northern and rural juvenile courts (User Report No. 1986–29)*. Ottawa: Ministry of the Solicitor General.

LaPrairie, C. (1983). Native juveniles in court: Some preliminary observations. In T. Fleming & L. Visano (Eds.), *Deviant designations* (pp. 337–350). Toronto: Butterworths.

LaPrairie, C. (1987). Native women and crime in Canada: A theoretical model. In E. Adelberg & C. Currie (Eds.), *Too few to count*. Vancouver: Press Gang Publishers.

LaPrairie, C.P., & Griffiths, C.T. (1982). Native Indian delinquency: A review of recent findings. *Native people and justice in Canada*, Special Issue, Part I, *Canadian Legal Aid Bulletin*, 5(1), 39–46.

McCaskill, D. (1970). *Needs and resources related to offenders of native origin in Manitoba*. Correctional Planning Branch, Correctional Services of Canada.

McCaskill, D. (1974). *Patterns of native criminality—Part II*. Unpublished manuscript, Trent University.

MacLean, H. (1978). *The hidden agenda: Methodist attitudes to the Ojibway and the development of Indian schooling in Upper Canada 1821–1860*. Unpublished master's thesis, University of Toronto.

Miller, D. (1984, March). *Implications of the Young Offenders Act/ordinance with respect to the right to counsel in the N.W.T.* Paper prepared for the Northern Conference, Yellowknife, NT.

Ontario Native Council on Justice. (1981). *Justice-related children and family services for native people in Ontario*. Discussion paper, Toronto.

Report of the Baffin Human Rights Conference. (1987, May). Sponsored by Malisanik Tukisiniakuik Legal Services, Iqualuit, NT.

LEGISLATION

Young Offenders Act, Statutes of Canada 1980–81–82–83, c.110.

CHAPTER 12

SUMMARY AND FUTURE DIRECTIONS

*Joseph P. Hornick, Barbara A. Burrows, Joe Hudson,
and Howard Sapers*

The general aims of the *Young Offenders Act* (1982) are to hold young persons who break the law responsible for their actions, protect society from illegal behaviour and at the same time, protect the legal rights of young offenders. The chapters in this book have described specific characteristics of the *Young Offenders Act* (*YOA*) and identified issues arising from its design, implementation and operation. The purpose of this chapter is to: summarize briefly the general characteristics of the Act; summarize the key issues and concerns identified by the authors; and, propose an agenda to guide future research efforts.

GENERAL CHARACTERISTICS OF THE ACT

By placing the state *in loco parentis*, the *parens patriae* doctrine of the *Juvenile Delinquents Act* (1970) emphasized the needs of young persons for "parental" guidance and help. This has often occurred at the expense of regard for due process and the young person's rights. In contrast, the *YOA* guarantees youths the same fundamental rights as adults. Thus, the *YOA* grants young offenders the right to legal counsel at all stages of proceedings, the right to an open and fair trial, the right of access to bail, the right to remain silent and the right to have a parent or other adult of their choice present during pre-trial detention and court proceedings. All young offenders must be fully informed of these rights. The increased attention to due process under the *YOA* also includes the right to appeal; this stands in contrast to the limited recourse available under the *Juvenile Delinquents Act* (*JDA*) (Wardell, 1982). The youth court differs from adult court in that preliminary hearings and jury trials are not possible (Bala, 1986); however, this reflects a desire to make the youth court less formal than the adult court and to expedite the court process as much as possible, rather than disregard for due process.

Reform initiatives in the 1960s led to the development of diversion programs under the *JDA*. These were subsequently incorporated into the *YOA* in the form of alternative measures. Section 4 of the *YOA* provides legislative sanction for steering youth away from the court process in certain circumstances. Alternative measures are intended to reduce the caseloads of juvenile courts and correctional facilities, and to prevent as much as possible the stigma associated with being labelled a troublesome youth. Alternative measures are intended to provide a constructive alternative to court, and may be used for a first offender if the following conditions are met: (a) there is enough evidence to prosecute; (b) the person considering whether to use such measures (usually the police or crown prosecutor) considers alternative measures to be appropriate in a particular case; (c) the youth accepts responsibility for the offence; and, (d) the youth freely and fully agrees to participate in an alternative measures program. The program itself may involve an apology, community service, counselling, restitution or some combination of these and other actions.

If the youth declines to participate in the program, then formal court proceedings commence. Upon successful completion of the program, charges against the youth are dropped and the youth will have no criminal record. If, however, the youth fails to complete the program satisfactorily, the case may be dealt with in youth court.

In marked contrast to the *JDA*, which was characterized by highly variable, ill-defined and open-ended dispositions, dispositions under the *YOA* are explicitly specified. Under the *YOA*, they also tend to be less severe than adult criminal dispositions, reflecting the concept of limited accountability for youth. The dispositions available to the judge are (a) absolute discharge; (b) fine up to $1,000; (c) compensation order; (d) restitution; (e) personal service to the victim; (f) community service; (g) prohibition, seizure or forfeiture order; (h) treatment by consent; (i) probation; and (j) custody.

The *YOA* rejects the use of indeterminacy and the notion of administrative discretion as governing principles of sentencing. The Act requires that the length of the disposition be specified when an order is made. For example, the Act specifies that probation may not exceed two years, custody may not exceed three years, and personal and community service orders may not exceed 240 hours.

Committal to custody is the most serious penalty for a young offender, short of transfer to adult court, which can only be imposed for indictable offences. Custody may be either open (e.g., in a community group home or wilderness camp) or secure (i.e., in a locked facility), but in either case may not exceed three years. Before any custody order can be made (section 24(2)), a predisposition report based on interviews with the offender, the offender's parents and the victim, if possible, must be considered by the judge. The report also contains other factual information, such as the offender's attitudes towards the crime and improving his or her behaviour and the history of previous offences.

The Act stipulates that young offenders are subject to the jurisdiction of the youth court throughout their disposition. Thus, in contrast to the JDA, the YOA does not permit corrections administrators unilaterally to alter the youth court's decision on the disposition given. Only the court can change the young offender's custody level, approve a transfer to an adult facility or approve early release to the community. Administering agencies, rather than the courts, are empowered to move offenders between institutions and programs within a given custody level.

ISSUES AND CONCERNS

Protection of children's rights is undeniably a major element of the YOA. Bala contends in Chapter 2 that the YOA seems to have achieved due process objectives, especially in protecting the rights of young persons and recognizing society's right to protection. Despite these achievements, however, the YOA has created new concerns that must be addressed if an equitable juvenile justice system is to be attained in Canada. Attaining equality is difficult in this country because it is characterized by an ongoing struggle for control between local and central authorities. Many of the issues and concerns raised in this book are discussed below, and this struggle between national and regional control is a common underlying theme.

Consent to Treatment

In Chapter 5, Leschied and Jaffe dispute whether the YOA should grant young persons the right to veto a treatment recommendation. Among the reasons for raising this question is their judgment that the youth's developmental stage may be too low to permit a reasoned decision; the youth's psychopathology may be a factor in refusing treatment; other legislation (e.g., mental health legislation) does not grant that power to minors; and such a provision ignores the potential benefits of treatment.

There are also several arguments for youth having the right to refuse services. These include the view that coerced participation in correctional programs has not been shown to be effective in reducing crime and that voluntary participation is likely to prove more productive than coerced participation. Another argument is that programs catering to willing participants may be of higher, more consistent quality than those serving only non-voluntary participants.

The use of coerced participation also raises questions about the infringement of young offenders' rights of privacy, personal dignity and autonomy. Clearly, granting young offenders the right to refuse services is based on the assumption that they are competent to determine whether they should participate. Sanford Fox argues that "far from being presumptively incompetent," juveniles "are bordering on the acquisition of full rights of citizenship so that the presumption should be the other way—that they do know best—better than any others, save perhaps their own parents, what is good for them" (Fox, 1973, p. 5). Similarly, Shireman and Reamer have argued for providing noncoercive program opportunities to young offenders on the grounds that; "...the possible loss of freedom, the invasion of privacy, the danger of psychological or other harm, and the possible debasement of treatment programs is too high a price to pay for the often dubious benefits of enforced therapy"   (1986, p. 147).

In Chapter 2, Bala confirms that few treatment orders (under section 13), which would allow placement of the youth in a treatment facility, have been made. In Chapter 5, Leschied and Jaffe indicate that in Southwestern Ontario, there was an absence of orders for treatment. Leschied and Jaffe advocate removal of the consent to treatment provision, because they maintain that few youths needing treatment are willing to consent to it and other safeguards exist in the YOA to protect youth from inappropriate treatment. Bala, on the other hand, points out that some therapy and counselling is available at most custodial facilities and that the insanity provisions of the *Criminal Code* and mental health legislation may be used to commit a youth to a mental health facility. The implication is that the YOA should not be used as mental health legislation, because other laws exist for that purpose.

Transfer to Adult Court

Another major issue identified in this book is the transfer of youth to adult court. The YOA calls upon judges to order transfer only for youths over 14 charged with a serious indictable offence, and only after careful consideration of the "interest of society...having regard to the needs of the young person." Bala states in Chapter 2 that interpretation of this standard has varied. For example, in Manitoba, society's needs have been given priority, leading to a relatively high transfer rate. In other jurisdictions, however, judges have used the transfer provision less often; Bala suggests that one reason for not using the transfer provision is the judge's perception that a youth may be amenable to rehabilitation and that in the long term, the interests of the youth and society would be better served by rehabilitation than by punishment in the adult justice system.

Thus, it appears that youths charged with similar offences may be treated differently, depending on the "interpretive mood" of the jurisdiction in which they reside. Of course, persons favouring local autonomy might see this as a positive feature of the YOA, because it allows for the expression of local community values.

Two-tier Court System

The use of the two-tier court system is considered to be a threat to due process by a number of authors in this book. Bala (Chapter 2), Leschied and Jaffe (Chapter 5) and Caputo and Bracken (Chapter 9) discuss the issue of a two-tier court system or split jurisdiction for young offenders in Ontario and Nova Scotia. In both Ontario and Nova Scotia, 12- to 15-year-olds and 16- and 17-year-olds are handled by different government departments and different courts—12- to 15-year-olds are dealt with in the Youth Court division of Family Court, while 16- and 17-year olds are dealt with in an adult court temporarily designated as a youth court, but with adult court personnel. The two-tier system in these provinces seems to be rooted in a resistance to raising the maximum age to 18. The two-tier court system raises questions about the equity with which 16- and 17-year-olds are treated from one province to another and the relative importance of local autonomy versus central control.

Access to Legal Services

Inequities in access to legal services imposed by geographic isolation and small populations is considered a major problem by many authors. As pointed out by Laprairie in Chapter 11, there are disparities between rural and urban areas in terms of the YOA's due process achievements. Laprairie points out that the geographic isolation of communities, especially native ones, results in only limited access to justice services. For example, there is a lack of both experienced local legal counsel and detention facilities. Laprairie points to one study that suggests remote aboriginal communities are even worse off than other rural communities. Circuit courts and courtworker services have only partially addressed the problems associated with geographic isolation.

Referral to Alternative Measures

Berlin and Allard (1980) indicate that diverting a child from the court process threatens due process, in that there is potential for alternative measures to be used in cases for which there is insufficient evidence to support court prosecution. This problem is echoed by LeBlanc and Beaumont in their discussion of Quebec practices under the 1977 *Youth Protection Act* (Chapter 6). Further, there is concern about police having the authority to recommend the appropriateness of diversion in a given case. According to Berlin and Allard (1980), the problem with police discretion is that "...such practices appear inconsistent with the ideal of equality of justice under the law" (Berlin & Allard, 1980, p. 445).

Voluntary Participation in Alternative Measures

There has been general concern that although the *YOA* tries to protect the young offender from being coerced into participating in an alternative measures program, diversion may not be "voluntary" when the only alternative is formal court proceedings, an intimidating prospect for many young offenders. O'Brien (1984, p. 218) suggests that the "admission of responsibility for an offence prior to legal proof of such is inherently coercive."

Widening the Net of Control

Another issue that has emerged is that alternative measures may "widen the net" of social control exercised by the state over individuals. Net-widening can occur when the creation of a program or set of services leads to the expansion of control over the lives of youth who otherwise would have been ignored or handled less intrusively. As Pate and Peachey point out in Chapter 8, there is evidence that net-widening has occurred. It may be regarded as a prominent, unintended and expensive by-product of alternative measures services. Some professionals see this as a positive development and argue that net-widening has increased the likelihood that youth in need of services will have access to them. Critics argue, however, that the benefits of diversion services have yet to be proven and that until they are, the broadening of juvenile justice may take the dangerous form of the benevolent state gone haywire (Austin & Krisberg, 1981). Youths who in earlier times might have been released with a warning are now referred to a "diversion" program and their behaviour is monitored. Failure—in whatever form—in the diversion scheme may well be grounds for more severe sanctions, and a kind of pyramid of escalating pathology ensues (Trépanier, 1981).

Effectiveness of Alternative Measures

The effectiveness of alternative measures is another concern. In Chapter 2, Bala points out that there is debate over the relative efficacy of alternative measures as compared with the court process in terms of reducing offence recidivism. In Chapter 8, Pate and Peachey indicate that evaluation of alternative measures programs is scarce, and that studies to date have been more descriptive than analytical.

Provincial Authorization of Alternative Measures

A common criticism levelled at the *YOA* is that while the Act sanctions alternative measures, it does not prescribe a particular model and allows provincial jurisdictions the freedom to develop programs to suit their particular circumstances. Thus, implementation decisions concerning alternative measures have been left to the individual provinces. This has led to court challenge in Ontario, where alternative measures were not available until a recent Court of Appeal decision. As expressed by a judge, with respect to the lack of alternate measures in Ontario: "Can it not be argued that an essential element contemplated by the law has been denied any young person appearing before the court?" (Bennett, 1985, p. 17). On the other hand, Leschied and Jaffe point out in Chapter 5 that reasons for Ontario's position include the perception that alternative measures may threaten due process and young persons' rights and may widen the net of social control over young persons. A key question with regard to alternative measures is where does healthy local variation end and fairness and equity begin?

There is substantial variation between provinces in the extent to which alternative measures have been adopted. This has been partly dependent on the extent of provincial support for such programs. In Chapter 8, Pate and Peachey maintain that there is an overall lack of provincial support for reconciliation initiatives.

As demonstrated by Ryant and Heinrich in Chapter 7, development of alternative measures programs also depends on the willingness and extent of community involvement. These authors demonstrate that adoption of alternative measures in Manitoba was greatly facilitated by historical precedents in that province, namely "intrinsic local interest in citizen participation and professional commitment to community development within the probation service."

Local Variation in Adopting Alternative Measures

Community interest and commitment are also necessary at the local level to ensure the availability of alternative measures. Even in Manitoba where, according to Ryant and Heinrich (Chapter 7), alternative measures are promoted, there is substantial variation between communities in the availability of alternative measures. In general, one might expect large centres to be more able to support a broad range of services, and small communities to be more limited in this regard. For example, as pointed out by LaPrairie in Chapter 11, geographically isolated native communities lacking in community organization are particularly disadvantaged in their ability to provide such services to their young people. In the absence of suitable community alternatives, Wardell holds that a more punitive reaction often results: "Without sufficient resources the punishment aspect may be resorted to by courts by default of having few palatable alternatives" (Wardell, 1982, p. 388).

Besides the availability of alternative measures generally at the local level, there are also local concerns about the type of services available. For example, as Weiler and Ward state in Chapter 10, the most common offence committed by young women in contact with the agencies surveyed was shoplifting, yet there was a paucity of programs to serve this client group. There was also a lack of related services, such as daycare. Thus, equitable treatment may be compromised by the lack of certain kinds of services.

Use of Treatment

In Chapter 5, Leschied and Jaffe criticize the lack of attention to rehabilitation and treatment under the Act. It has been pointed out by other authors that becoming engrossed with procedural issues can be dangerous because "...the usually much more complex issue of what is to be done with [a youth] once he has been found [guilty] is barely considered" (Shireman & Reamer, 1986, p. 37). Thus, while it is important to ensure that youths' rights are protected, some would argue that this should not be done at the expense of their needs, and does not by itself signify or guarantee that justice has been effected. As summarized by Shireman and Reamer (1986, p. 38), "It is in the ultimate disposition and treatment of the child that the fundamental issues of the substance and purpose of the juvenile court and the associated elements of the justice system lie." Concern has been raised that belief in the ineffectiveness of rehabilitating efforts have produced a juvenile justice system in which "treatment options do not seem to be pursued" (Leschied & Jaffe, 1987, p. 427).

In Chapter 4, Mason explains that when the Alberta Solicitor General's department took over responsibility for young offenders upon implementation of the YOA, some professionals feared that the department would emphasize custody at the expense of treatment. Mason discounts this concern by pointing to the department's "long history developing non-custodial programs for adult offenders." He also indicates that because the Solicitor General took over many of the staff and programs from the provincial Social Services department, which had lengthy experience dealing with young offenders, it was in a good position to respond to youths' treatment needs.

In Chapter 5, Leschied and Jaffe suggest the following key question: To what extent should legislation such as the YOA facilitate intervention, and to what extent should it emphasize family autonomy and protection of civil rights?

Severity of Dispositions

Another major issue of national scope is the severity of dispositions under the YOA. Some have complained that the maximum sentence of three years is far too lenient for certain offences and in 1985, petitions were forwarded to the Minister of Justice requesting that young offenders charged with violent crimes be treated in the adult justice system ("Two mothers," 1985, p. A7). Others, however, have complained that dispositions are too harsh, and have charged that judges emphasize the more punitive aspects of the YOA. Bala (Chapter 2) Leschied and Jaffe (Chapter 5), and Caputo and Bracken (Chapter 9) report an increased use in custody under the YOA.

In a study of youth courts in nine southern Ontario counties during the first eight months after the YOA was implemented, Leschied and Jaffe (1985) found that the level of charges remained about the same even though the police no longer charged persons seven to eleven years of age under the YOA. Further, the authors reported the following trends: custodial dispositions increased significantly; periods of pre-trial and predisposition detention increased; and the authors identified a 30% increase in requests for social histories, which they suggest are made in anticipation of an order for custody. In contrast to these trends, a 50% decrease in requests for clinical assessments occurred. On the basis of their study, Leschied and Jaffe (1985, p. 5) concluded that the YOA "reflect[s] a major shift away from the *parens patriae*, rehabilitative emphasis of the *JDA*."

Thus, it appears that more young people have been incarcerated since the YOA came into effect and that they are being held in custody for longer periods of time. The results of investigative reporting presented in the mass media have documented similar findings. An article in the Toronto Star indicates that:

> Average sentences for young law-breakers in Ontario have more than doubled under Canada's *Young Offenders Act*... In Ontario, the average sentence for offenders aged 12 to 15 has increased 135 percent for those being sent to training schools—called closed custody—and 210 percent for those sentenced to group homes—open custody. ("Young Offenders," 1985, p. A9)

Another article states:

> Despite all the talk about the special needs of youngsters, and using custody as a last resort, the federal government by its very approval of the Act has called on judges to lay down a firm hand. The Act in itself is a process by which to lock up youngsters. Therefore, a kid with a lengthy list of crimes is out of luck regardless of the reasons for his behaviour. ("Courts getting blame," 1986, p. A6)

Variation in Definition of Custody

In Chapter 9, Caputo and Bracken state that the definition of what constitutes an open custody facility varies from one province to another. The Act only defines open and secure custody in a generic way, leaving provincial administrators the leeway to determine what constitutes an open or secure facility. There is considerable variation in what constitutes open custody, with obvious potential for inequitable treatment of youth. Again, proponents of local autonomy view this as a positive characteristic because it allows for expression of local community values, in light of local circumstances. The danger, however, lies in basing definitional differences on convenience rather than community uniqueness.

Caputo and Bracken suggest that there may be more homogeneity in secure custody programs across the country, but that the apparent increase in the number of young people receiving such dispositions, along with an increase in the length of secure custody sentences, is cause for concern.

Equity in dispositions is a problem at the local level too. As pointed out by Caputo and Bracken in Chapter 9, larger centres are more likely than smaller centres to have open custody facilities. Further, the range of government and community resources varies from one community to another. Thus, as concluded in Chapter 9, the treatment received by a young person may depend more on where he/she lives than on the offence committed.

Minimum Age

Police have complained that they are unable to charge children under the age of 12, even if they pose a threat to society (Vienneau, 1985; White, 1985). The Toronto Chief of Police has called for amendments to allow officers to charge children under 12 with certain types of offences. Concern has also been expressed about the possibility that the immunity of the under-12s will lead older offenders or adults to recruit children to commit break-and-enters or drug-related offences (White, 1985). Children under 12 are supposed to be dealt with under provincial child welfare legislation.

Female Offenders

Adelberg and Currie (1987) have documented the special problem of dealing with female offenders in general. However, very little information is available concerning young female offenders. In Chapter 9, Caputo and Bracken refer to the comparatively few custodial spaces allocated to young female offenders. The lack of programs and services available for young female offenders is also well documented in Chapter 10 by Weiler and Ward. For example, "the numbers of young mothers in conflict with the law highlighted the need for daycare and other support programs for these women," yet such programs are in short supply.

Non-federal Offences

The *JDA* could be applied in violations against federal or provincial statutes, municipal by-laws, or ordinances. In contrast the *YOA* only applies to criminal offences against federal law such as the *Criminal Code*

(1970), the *Narcotic Control Act* (1970) and the *Food and Drugs Act* (1970). Provinces are left to deal with status offences and infractions against provincial law.

It was also common under the *JDA* for youths to be charged for offences such as truancy and sexual immorality, which would not be considered criminal offences if committed by adults. These so-called "status offences" have been eliminated under the *YOA* on the grounds that acts such as running away from home and truancy are problems that should best be dealt with by social service agencies rather than the juvenile justice system, and therefore should not be classified as offences. Proponents of dropping status offences from the reach of juvenile justice claimed two major benefits: First, that the volume of cases handled in the justice system would be substantially reduced, thus allowing more time for handling more serious cases; second, that providing services to youth under the auspices of social service agencies rather than the juvenile court would diminish the potential for young people to be stigmatized by labels and experiences often thought to be associated with being processed by juvenile justice agencies.

Bala (1986) confirms that the provincial governments have largely adopted the *YOA* model for handling violations against provincial statutes. Some provinces, however, have retained offences such as truancy.

RESEARCH NEEDS

As summarized in the preceding section of this chapter, the case studies in this book illustrate that there are several complex issues and concerns associated with the implementation of the *YOA*. Unfortunately, as many of the authors have indicated, there is a lack of information on both the nature of the issues and how to deal with them.

Research to Date

Despite the fact that the *YOA* came into force over four years ago, very little systematic information has been collected through the use of information systems established for administrative purposes and/or empirical research. As Coflin points out in Chapter 3, the federal government allocated more than $12 million for the design and implementation of automated information systems to create the young offenders record registry provided for in section 42 of the Act. However, Coflin states that most of these funds were used to create, modify or enhance provincial information systems. The resulting systems do not facilitate easy access to information by the numerous organizations that use the information.

The federal government also attempted to provide some baseline data for a later evaluation of the *YOA* by initiating the *National Study of the Functioning of the Juvenile Courts* in the late 1970s. Additional limited funding has been provided for research conducted by specific organizations. For example, the federal government contributed toward the cost of establishing and evaluating the Working Together program discussed in Chapter 7. However, as pointed out by Coflin in Chapter 3, the primary focus of the federal government has been on the information systems mentioned above, as opposed to empirical research.

Overall, a review of the information system and research to date suggests that there is little information available. Examples of research conducted are the voluntary sector service program surveys conducted by the Canadian Council on Children and Youth (CCCY) discussed by Weiler and Ward in Chapter 10; the work of Leschied and Jaffe discussed in Chapter 5; and the evaluation of specific programs mentioned in Chapter 8 by Pate and Peachey.

Research Agenda

Identification of the extent to which the *YOA* has been implemented in various jurisdictions and recommendations for the future development of *YOA* components are contingent on understanding both the intended and unintended impacts to date. Thus, below we suggest a general research strategy for obtaining essential information regarding the Act. This strategy focuses on four general research objectives, which are to: (a) Describe the characteristics of youth affected by the *YOA*, and their offences; (b) Identify and describe the decision-making processes and procedures of various jurisdictions and assess whether they are consistent with the *YOA*; (c) Identify the availability and test the effectiveness of the resources and programs established for implementing various components of the *YOA*; and (d) Identify other systems that deal with youth in difficulty and describe how they relate to the justice system.

Characteristics of Young Offenders and Offences

The first type of information that should be collected and analyzed deals with the identification of the number and characteristics of persons moving into, through, and out of the young offender systems across the country. Trend information by provinces and programs under the Act, such as admission rate, lengths of confinement, expenditures, conditions of confinement and supervision, is very much needed. This information could be provided through a large-scale analysis of information systems data from the various jurisdictions involved.

Decision-making Process and Procedures

A second type of data needed is information on critical decisions made by officials at different points in the young offender system, especially decisions pertaining to the use of alternative measures, detention, dispositions, placement and review. We need information on who makes decisions and on what basis. What is the process followed for making decisions, what procedures are used and what safeguards are in place to ensure appropriate decision making? Who is responsible for making decisions about young people and what criteria are being used for these decisions? Are the policies, procedures and decision-making processes consistent with the Act? These are important questions on which adequate information is not currently available.

Analysis of the general decision-making processes could be based on the provincial information systems. Such an analysis, however, would have to be supplemented by a review of regional policy manuals used by police and crown attorneys as well as an in-depth review of files and tracking of active cases.

Program Resources and Effectiveness

Third, information is needed to clarify the types of programs established under the *YOA* and evaluate these programs. Too often, program labels or descriptions are used as substitutes for detailed information on programs. Unfortunately, program titles provide little information about the specific services actually provided in a particular program and the causal relationships or theory that underlie program approaches. Instead of relying on program labels, effort should be directed to describing and defining specific programs that have been implemented. What are the causal assumptions that underlie program activities? How are program objectives supposed to be obtained? What theory do program staff hold about what they do in order to accomplish the results they want? What is the effectiveness of the program? Is the program cost effective?

The specific strategy for studying these research questions would involve at least two major study stages. A typology of service programs should be identified through a survey and/or interview technique. This typology should be based on the actual activities of the various programs and the specific needs of clients served by the program. The second study component would involve a detailed evaluation of specific types of programs from various jurisdictions. This analysis would focus on identifying independent variables (i.e., program activities) expected to have an effect on program outcomes, as well as identifying the success of programs in achieving these objectives.

Justice System and Other Systems

An inaccurate and distorted view of the young offender system is possible if we fail to consider that other systems, such as child welfare or mental health, also deal with young people in difficulty, particularly those under 12 years of age. Lerman (1982), for example, was one of the first to point out in a systematic way that one develops a narrow-minded view of the impact of juvenile justice policies by focusing solely on the juvenile justice system. Lerman suggests that policy gains made in the justice system might well be offset by corresponding strain on the child welfare or mental health systems within a particular jurisdiction. In short, we must expand our frame of reference by adopting the framework of a youth-serving system consisting of interacting sub-systems of child welfare and juvenile justice. A tracking study of children under 12 who commit criminal offences would shed light on the impact of justice system changes on other systems that deal with youth in difficulty.

REFERENCES

Adelberg, E., & Currie, C. (Eds.) (1987). Too few to count: Canadian women in conflict with the law. Vancouver: Press Gang Publishers.

Austin, J., & Krisberg, B. (1981). Wider, stronger, and different nets: The dialectics of criminal justice reform. Journal of Research in Crime and Delinquency, 18, 165–196.

Bala, N. (1986). The Young Offenders Act: A new era in juvenile justice? In B. Landau (Ed.), Children's rights in the practice of family law (pp. 238–254). Toronto: Carswell.

Bennett, J.F. (1985). Concerns about the Young Offenders Act. Provincial Judges Journal, 8(4), 17–18.

Berlin, M.L., & Allard, H.A. (1980). Diversion of children from the juvenile courts. Canadian Journal of Family Law, 3(4), 439–460.

Courts getting blame for young offender tangles. (1986, July 26). Calgary Herald, p. A6.

Fox, S. (1973). The reform of juvenile justice: The child's right to punishment. Juvenile Justice, 25(2), 5.

Lerman, P. (1982). Deinstitutionalization and the welfare state. New Brunswick, NJ: Rutgers University Press.

Leschied, A.W., & Jaffe, P.G. (1985). Implications of the Young Offenders Act in modifying the juvenile justice system: Some early trends. London, ON: London Family Court Clinic.

Leschied, A.W., & Jaffe, P.G. (1987). Impact of the Young Offenders Act on court dispositions: A comparative analysis. Canadian Journal of Criminology, 29(4), 421–430.

O'Brien, D. (1984). Juvenile diversion: An issues perspective from the Atlantic provinces. Canadian Journal of Criminology, 26(2), 217–230.

Shireman, C.H., & Reamer, F.G. (1986). *Rehabilitating juvenile justice.* New York: Columbia University Press.

Trépanier, J. (1981). La déjudiciarisation des mineurs délinquants au Canada et les projets législatifs du gouvernement fédéral. *Canadian Journal of Criminology,* 23(3), 279–289.

Two mothers urge tightening of new youth law. (1985, May 30). *Toronto Star,* p. A7.

Vienneau, D. (1985, May 30). Metro chief urges changes to *Young Offenders Act. Toronto Star,* p. A7.

Wardell, W. (1982). Legislative note—The *Young Offenders Act. Saskatchewan Law Review,* 47(2), 381–387.

White, C.A. (1985). Growing pains for new law. *Canada & the World,* 51(4), 26–27.

Young offenders jailed longer under new law Ontario official says. (1985, August 6). *Toronto Star,* p. A9.

LEGISLATION

Criminal Code, Revised Statutes of Canada 1970, c. C–34.

Food and Drugs Act, Revised Statutes of Canada 1970, c. F–27.

Juvenile Delinquents Act, Revised Statutes of Canada 1970, c. J–3.

Narcotic Control Act, Revised Statutes of Canada 1970, c. N–1.

Young Offenders Act, Statutes of Canada 1980–81–82–83, c. 110.

Youth Protection Act, Statutes of Quebec 1977, c. 20.

INDEX